Strategic Systems Planning
for
Financial Institutions

Using Automated Solutions and Technology for Competitive Advantages

Geoffrey H. Wold
Robert F. Shriver

PROBUS PUBLISHING COMPANY
BANKERS PUBLISHING COMPANY
Chicago, Illinois
Cambridge, England

A Bankline Publication

CONTENTS

FIGURES

PREFACE

The need for a strategic, comprehensive information systems resources plan in financial institutions is more evident today than ever before. Improved management information has become more vital in effectively and efficiently managing bank operations. Increased internal and external reporting requirements have expanded the need for more comprehensive management information. Many of these information needs can be satisfied in a cost-effective manner through increased utilization of automation and technology.

Financial institutions depend heavily on automated systems and procedures. The systems environment has been subject to rapid change due to the technological advances associated with the industry. The strategic planning process is especially important in view of the variety of functions and operations within a financial institution and the many diverse automated and manual systems in place. Because the information systems resources are limited, a plan to optimize data processing expenditures is required.

This book describes a methodology for developing a strategic information systems plan that can guide the effective management of information resources. The process can identify new technologies that can help financial institutions achieve both short-term and long-range objectives in a cost-effective manner. The approach is based on a proven technique that results in documented and informed strategies and decisions. Several forms, charts, and diagrams are included to make it easier to complete the process in a logical and efficient manner.

We appreciate the contribution of our support staff: Ms. Tina Vick, who provided extraordinary effort in text formatting and document preparation; Ms. Jacalyn Ragan, who provided desktop publishing assistance; and Ms. Mary Krummel, who assisted with the various figures.

Geoffrey H. Wold, CPA, CMA, CSP, CDP, CISA, CMC
and
Robert F. Shriver, CMC, CDP, CSP, CISA
Partners
McGladrey & Pullen

1 INTRODUCTION

BACKGROUND

Strategic information systems planning has undergone a number of name changes in the last two decades, including long-range EDP planning, business systems planning, information technology (IT) planning, and strategic information technology planning, just to name a few. According to Webster, *planning* is "the establishment of goals, policies and procedures for a social or economic unit." Several other definitions that have applicability to this subject include:

Strategic	"of great importance within an integrated whole"
Information	"the communication or acceptance of knowledge or intelligence"
Systems	"sets or arrangements of things so related as to form a whole; a regular orderly way of doing things"
Planning	"making an outline, structure or map; having in mind a purpose or objective"

Other definitions that may add substance to the thought of planning include:

Long-range	"taking the future into consideration"
Technology	"a scientific method of achieving a practical purpose"

From these definitions, it is clear that many words exist that can express the ideas associated with strategic information systems planning. But it is also clear that a plan can be expressed or represented in a variety of ways--each with its own special characteristics.

A plan can be represented as a diagram or a map, containing paths to a goal or an end objective. It can also be represented mathematically as a detailed formulation of activities, such as economic results or growth in a business environment. A plan should provide "order" to previously unarranged components that, in combination, help meet some original design objectives. A plan can be presented in narrative form; in a schematic format; as a series of mathematical formulae; or any combination of these presentation methods.

When these definitions are applied to business planning, the following dimensions are added:

- The business plan is a "road map," which focuses available resources toward a common end.
- The plan's goals, strategies, and objectives often relate to market share, profitability, growth--all quantifiable measurements of performance.
- The plan provides order to the business environment, reducing the number of real unknowns to a handful of manageable variables through techniques of assumption, presumption, supposition, and premise.

For the purposes of this publication, Strategic Information Systems Planning is defined as:

the process of establishing goals and objectives, defining strategies and policies to achieve these objectives, and developing detailed plans to ensure that the strategies are implemented.

This process should result in a three- to five-year strategic plan that enables information systems and technology to effectively achieve the financial institution's goals and objectives, as identified in its strategic business plan. The plan should be viewed as a dynamic tool that is revised and updated as conditions and requirements change within the financial institution. The methodology employed in the development of the initial plan should be used in the future to update the plan at least once each year.

In this way, the strategic information systems plan will be a vehicle to continuously guide the activities of the MIS function. If planning is not an ongoing process, certain objectives may not be realized because the objective itself may change as the financial institution and its environment change. Plans will change and strategic alternatives should be considered at that time.

The information systems plan establishes the overall framework for maintenance and development of required systems in a well-structured and controlled manner. This includes projected systems and technology expenditures for personnel, equipment, software, and other costs to assist management with decisions regarding the allocation of future resources.

More specifically to financial institutions, the strategic information systems plan serves many useful purposes, including:

- It provides a formal method for communicating the financial institution's future growth and automation plans.
- It provides a basis for current decision making and involves department heads directly in the decision making process.
- It provides an opportunity for all management levels to review, discuss, and integrate their objectives for information systems needs into a common medium.
- It creates an understanding of proposed plans and priorities and serves as a motivational tool to provide management with an overall picture of what is to be accomplished and why.
- It promotes the usefulness of information by ensuring its consistency, completeness, and accessibility.

Broadly speaking, planning should offer an organization a look into the future based on the best possible information available at the time. A plan has a number of characteristics that differentiate it from other concepts, such as:

- Using a continuous process.

  The planning process is continuous. Once the initial structure of the plan is defined, it should be adaptable from period to period and year to year. The values and parameters that form the basis of the plan should be adjusted to fit the current business climate and organization capacity. The plan is a working document, which implies that it should be as voluminous as necessary to summarize and communicate the results of the process that creates it, but be simple enough in its presentation to ensure that it is workable and manageable as changes occur.

- Considering the current situation of the organization and the business climate surrounding the financial institution.

Although some goals and strategies may remain constant over time, others must change to reflect real-world results and situations. The organization that plans for 15 percent growth per year will double in 5 years. Yet, this may not realistically portray growth rates during a recession or a severe inflationary period. If the last two years have provided the organization with only a 3 percent average annual growth, a 15 percent growth is highly unlikely, regardless of the outside economic climate. Internal factors, if unrecognized and unchanged, may severely restrict the attainment of the simplest of goals.

- Providing a means for management to monitor performance and make informed decisions about future directions.

A good plan should provide a summary of "key factors" that can be used to monitor success in achieving the goals and objectives of the plan. It should provide the means for management to evaluate decisions and judge the impact, both short-term and long-term, of various alternatives in reaching the desired objectives.

1.   Strategic Information Systems Planning--a Derivative of Business Planning

Strategic information systems planning shares many of the characteristics of business planning, but is typically focused on the achievement of business strategies through the use of information technology (IT). This should strongly suggest that an information technology plan cannot be satisfactorily or successfully developed without a clearly defined strategic business plan. It also suggests that the presence of a strategic business plan does not ensure that the foundation will be present for a good IT plan. Certain elements are necessary in a business plan to provide the basis for a good IT plan.

What if no strategic business plan exists? Or what if its form is not conducive to beginning the IT planning process? The answer is simple, although the solution to this dilemma may not be: Strategies must be defined.

The first step in IT planning is to review the business strategies, goals and objectives developed during the business planning process. If the business plan exists in the proper form, the IT planning process can begin. If not, some time is required for these key items to be developed and understood.

2.   **Symptoms Indicating the Need for Strategic Information Systems Planning**

Financial institutions are often faced with the following questions:

- Are computing resources lacking?
- Is information marginally useful because it is inaccurate or not timely?
- Are data processing costs unreasonably high?
- Do individual departments in the financial institution appear to be moving independently with computer acquisitions and utilization of systems?
- Is the financial institution spending its automation dollars unwisely?

If the answer to any of these questions is yes, the financial institution should consider developing a strategic information systems plan. Other potential symptoms indicating that strategic information systems planning is necessary include the following:

- Lack of flexibility in existing systems to meet competitive and/or regulatory changes.
- Excessive manual manipulation of data to obtain desired management and operational reports.
- Current systems not meeting business needs or not staying current in the competitive business environment.
- Changes in current systems requiring significant resource commitments.
- An increased need for improved information systems support.
- Current systems emphasis on operational reporting rather than on information necessary for management decision making.
- Multiple hardware platforms in use throughout the financial institution.
- Difficulty in obtaining ongoing technical support internally and/or externally.

- Obsolete systems in which technical architecture no longer supports add-on applications without significant change.
- Excessive dependence on specific vendor support for technical assistance, custom programming, user assistance, and other support matters.
- Paper-intensive systems with little or no exception reporting.
- Limited hardware capacities and growth capability.
- Limited technical personnel resources to implement desired changes.
- Difficulty in assimilating mergers/acquisitions into current systems.
- Need for immediate relief of workloads in specific departmental or functional areas.
- Data processing expenditures exceeding industry averages.
- Increased costs in maintaining current systems.
- Lack of availability of current resources.
- Lack of credibility and confidence in the MIS function in solving problems and affecting changes in current systems.
- Poor systems application and user documentation.
- Limited use of strategic development tools, such as CASE (computer-aided software engineering) tools to improve programmer productivity.

REGULATORY CONSIDERATIONS

Regulatory agencies are extremely interested in strategic information systems planning within financial institutions. The Federal Financial Institution Examination Council (FFIEC) issued an interagency regulation regarding strategic information systems planning. The FFIEC includes the following organizations:

- Board of Governors of the Federal Reserve System
- Federal Deposit Insurance Corporation
- Office of Thrift Supervision
- Office of the Comptroller of the Currency

This regulation states:

> "Information is a valuable corporate asset which is vital to the success of all financial institutions. The ability to remain competitive, introduce new products and services, and attain desired corporate goals often depends on the effective management of information systems technology.
>
> Corporate level strategic planning is important in all financial institutions to effectively utilize available resources and achieve the long-term goals and objectives of the organization. Strategic information systems planning is integral to the overall corporate strategic planning process and must support individual business strategies throughout the institution. The information systems strategic plan should address technology risks affecting all areas of operation, including contingency planning and disaster recovery, information security, systems and programming, computer operations, and end-user computing."

It recommends that:

> "Financial institutions should develop and implement a written strategic information systems plan commensurate with the complexity and sophistication of the institution. The plan should be integrated into overall corporate goals and should include in-house, end-user, and service bureau processing, as applicable."

Benefits

The benefits of strategic information systems planning include:

- Achievement of information needs.
- Realization of expected results.
- Optimization of data processing expenditures.
- Increased user satisfaction.
- Responsive and effective information systems.
- Efficient operations.
- Effective management decisions.
- Clear direction for the future.

Although the development of a strategic information systems plan represents a significant undertaking in terms of the commitment required by management, the benefits derived from implementing the plan are equally significant.

PLANNING APPROACHES

A number of approaches to strategic information systems planning have been published and attempted with varying degrees of success. Some better-known planning methodologies include:

*   IBM's BSP (Business Systems Planning)
*   Method/1 information planning methodology
*   BICS (Business Information Control Study) methodology
*   SAM (Stage Assessment Methodology)
*   CNA (Critical Needs Assessment)

One planning methodology suggests that a model of the organization be created using business functions as the basis for the model. Information feeding each business function produces resulting information which, in turn, becomes the input to another major business function--and the process continues *ad infinitum*. While this approach can certainly lead the planners to a different view of systems within the organizational entity, the approach is quite time-consuming and may break down in building information strategies and tactical plans that conform to the organization's business strategies.

Another difficulty with this approach is that it assumes that the major functions within the organization are "important" functions. However, some may be important in satisfying business objectives while others may be present only because of the organization's culture and tradition.

Culture and tradition are two characteristics that can have a profound effect on the direction and ultimate success of the IT planning process. Participants in the planning process should make every effort to understand and control cultural and traditional values of the organization. These characteristics can significantly limit the analysis of data collected during the planning process and impact the alternatives investigated in attempting to achieve organizational goals and objectives. Use of outside experts in facilitating the planning process can help identify and manage these elements, so that their effect is minimized.

Not every organization attempting to perform business and/or strategic information systems planning is successful. Sometimes the plans are destined to fail because they are too aggressive and do not consider the time and costs to implement technological change. In other cases, the planning process itself becomes a detriment to the completion of the plan. Following are some risks and pitfalls that can undermine the planning process and potentially produce an ineffective plan:

- Lack of commitment by top management.

   Commitment by top management in the strategic information systems planning process is essential to its success. As with most projects that potentially impact all organizational entities, the planning project requires significant resource commitment. Even if outside consultants are used to facilitate or supplement the planning process, significant time will be invested by organization personnel in discussions, meetings, and data-collection activities. If the financial institution has already completed a strategic business plan, then executive management should be aware of the time commitments of key departmental personnel. The lack of continued commitment by management could significantly undermine the planning effort.

- Unrealistic expectations for delivery.

   Simple solutions rarely result from complex problems with many variables. This is certainly true of the systems planning process. Unrealistic expectations by management or user department personnel in the delivery of information systems and the time frame for completion of the planning process can also negatively impact the success of the project. Participants in the planning process should set realistic goals and time frames for delivering the plan and implementing its strategies.

- Lack of focus on key strategies.

   Often, one or two departments can potentially misdirect the planning effort by overemphasizing their problems or unduly influencing the priority-setting process. The planning group should maintain its focus on the key business strategies that will help the organization achieve its desired goals and objectives. The information systems plan should represent a single, but important, component in addressing the organization's business needs.

•   Lack of participation by management, users, and technical resources.

Commitment by top management is important, but participation may be more important. Top management and key user department personnel must take "ownership" of the project. The ultimate success of the project is a direct result of the participation and "buy-in" of top management and the various operational departments. Technical personnel also must be a part of the process, but their role should be one of support rather than leadership in the initial stages of the planning process.

•   Overemphasis on technology for plan delivery.

While technology is important in delivering and implementing the various components of the information systems plan, technology should not be overemphasized. Technology is not the solution to business problems, but rather one of the tools in solving problems. Over a three- to five-year period, business strategies and goals will have mild adjustments, but technology will change at a much faster rate. To base the business plan and the information systems plan entirely on specific technologies will only lead to disappointment and frustration as new technologies become available.

•   Improper evaluation of alternatives.

Investigating a broad base of alternatives will yield the best results during the planning process. Focusing on a narrow group of alternatives, whether they are vendor-specific or platform-specific, could potentially lead the planning group to overlook viable and cost-effective alternatives. Likewise, improper evaluation of alternatives could lead to similar problems. The group should be open to a variety of alternatives and delivery systems. Biased evaluations yield biased results--which could mean short-term results that may soon have to be replaced.

- Improper identification of planning constraints.

  During the planning process, a number of planning assumptions should be developed. Some assumptions may relate to the competitive environment, some to the organization structure, and some to the physical requirements of the facilities considered within the scope of the plan. Constraints also exist that need to be recognized by the Planning Team. These constraints may be regulatory in nature, or they may be associated with growth, profit, size, or other factors. Identification of planning constraints will help define the scope of the project and potential limitations in achieving full implementation of desired strategies and goals.

- Failing to recognize ongoing resource requirements.

  The planning process is an ongoing process. The resulting plan is a working document that should change over time and be re-addressed at least on an annual basis. Once the basic structure and content of the plan is developed, the update process should not be nearly as time-consuming as the original planning process, but sufficient time and effort should be dedicated by key organizational personnel to the update process. The control segment of the plan should address ongoing resource requirements. Regular management review of the implementation process and the control plan should help ensure that sufficient resources are involved in the process.

The potential pitfalls and shortcomings in the planning process can be minimized through the use of a structured methodology. The methodology presented in this book provides the necessary structure to successfully complete the strategic information planning process. It offers a practical combination of the advantages of several of the above-mentioned planning approaches because the methodology described in this book:

- Focuses on key business strategies as the starting point of the planning process.
- Requires participation by executives, departmental personnel, and technical resource personnel within the financial institution.
- Uses the current system and technology as a stepping-stone to achieve the planning objectives.
- Identifies and considers organizational and environmental constraints when planners are developing key goals and strategies.

- Helps ensure that technology is a tool in obtaining the desired solution, not the solution itself.
- Recognizes that the financial institution will have ongoing resource requirements throughout the period encompassed by the systems plan.

Because this planning approach is practical and not overburdened by detail, it can be used by both larger and smaller financial institutions in developing and implementing long-term strategies. This planning approach offers a cost-effective and time-efficient method for implementing current technology in today's banking environment. Figure 2.1 in chapter 2 contains a diagram of the strategic information systems planning process described in this book.

BENEFITS OF PLANNING

Those organizations that have successfully performed strategic information technology planning insist that the benefits far outweigh the costs and effort involved in the process. The planning process often produces some immediate benefits through the implementation of high-profile, low-effort changes that have high payback to the organization and can form the foundation for the continued successful implementation of information technology strategies contained within the plan.

Some potential benefits of the strategic information systems planning process include:

- More likely attainment of desired information systems results within the organization.

  Following a structured methodology during and after the planning effort will assist the organization in attaining the desired results of the planning process. Management and planning team members will find that the process helps lead the organization toward the implementation of information systems that are compatible with the financial institution's business plan.

- Improved focus on the Management Information Systems (MIS) department as a service organization offering tools for implementation of organization strategy.

  The MIS department or division should be viewed by the organization as a service entity that provides basic services to all users within the financial institution. Ownership of the planning process should be at the management level, while ownership of information is normally at the department level. The MIS department is the service and support organization that helps each operating entity achieve its business goals.

- Improved effectiveness of current information technology expenditures.

  The strategic information systems plan will provide direction to the organization through the priority-setting process. Estimates of hardware, software, personnel, and other costs are an integral part of the planning process. These estimates will help ensure that information technology expenditures are most effectively applied toward development and implementation of key business systems.

- Better relationships with users of information technology.

  Through the planning process, information technology users provide significant input regarding their needs and requirements. This process tends to build stronger relationships among user department personnel and with the Management Information Systems (MIS) function of the organization.

- Increased user satisfaction with the MIS function and automated systems.

  When users' needs are addressed in a timely manner, user satisfaction with automated systems and the MIS function will certainly improve. User participation in the planning process is the key element in increasing the user's level of knowledge relating to the time, effort, and cost of improving information systems and delivering new automated solutions to the organization.

- More responsive and effective automated systems.

  By designing an information architecture that delivers needed information to the end user, the effectiveness of automated systems will be enhanced. Likewise, the ability of automated systems to respond quickly to changing critical parameters and the reporting of those changes to key decision makers will be a key requirement of any new architectural design.

- More efficient MIS and user operations.

  Ultimately, the MIS function will benefit from a better understanding of organization goals. The plan will provide staffing and budgeting information that will help focus the group on the high-priority applications and tasks. User operations will also benefit through improved efficiencies realized with additional automation.

- Improved sense of direction for employees participating in the process.

  Too often, user department personnel are dissatisfied with the lack of available resources--typically, personnel--in the MIS function to address more immediate needs. This frustration is also evident within the MIS function when they realize that, despite long hours and tedious effort, they are unable to deliver their service at an acceptable rate. The information systems plan provides a sense of direction to all participants in the planning process. It helps set expectations and identifies milestones against which performance can be measured.

- Greater awareness of the effort and time required to implement technical solutions.

  By identifying high-priority application areas and through estimating various resource requirements to deliver and implement these systems, management and user department personnel have a greater appreciation for the complexity of the technical environment. This awareness should lead to more realistic expectations in the future as new systems are designed or purchased and implemented.

•   Better use of existing technology in solving business problems.

When an organization performs a self-evaluation, especially in assessing its current use of available technology, improvements can often be identified that will ultimately lead to more efficient operations. Often, an organization will not have to perform drastic systems replacements to obtain the desired information or result, but can enhance, extract, build upon, or supplement existing systems to provide this information in a more usable form.

•   Improved accountability for systems implementation.

As part of the planning process, deliverables and milestones are identified. Each deliverable has estimated target dates associated with the various stages of its development and/or implementation. Through this process, management will be able to place responsibility on and establish accountability for the implementation of strategic systems.

•   Better utilization of personnel resources.

The staffing component of the plan will provide an overview of the personnel requirements in delivering the technology plan. Ultimately, this leads to better utilization of existing personnel resources and improved use of additional personnel as they are added to the organization.

•   More effective management decisions.

The strategic information systems plan represents the tool for allowing management to meet its business objectives. Identification of key business strategies and providing measurement criteria that can be regularly monitored should lead to more effective business decisions.

- Better integration of systems, especially across multiple platforms and operating environments.

  Information may reside on a variety of platforms within the organization. Specific departmental systems may address more immediate departmental needs, but these systems may lead to redundancy of information, which ultimately could affect data integrity if not properly controlled. Integration of systems, across multiple platforms and using different operating environments, will be an ongoing challenge to systems planners. Once the basic architecture has been designed and implemented, which will allow these systems to communicate with one another, then future systems acquisitions and implementation will require less time and effort. Through this process, user departments can select systems that best fit their requirements, and the systems can be fully integrated with other departmental and distributed systems.

- Potential stimulus for cultural change within the organization.

  Planning offers a chance for changing the culture of an organization. Following a procedure because "it has always been done that way" can be challenged and changed. The self-evaluation process provides information relating to identification of internal and external constraints. Once identified, the organization can step back and determine whether these constraints are actually cultural in nature and, therefore, self-imposed. If they are self-imposed, then they can be changed or eliminated.

- Potential for a more effective response to unexpected business changes.

  A good information systems plan will provide the flexibility to address technology changes and unexpected changes in the business environment. The core information systems identified during the planning process will allow management to more effectively respond to short-term, cyclical, and longer-term changes in the business climate.

BENEFITS OF USING OUTSIDE CONSULTANTS

Financial institutions may also benefit considerably from using outside consulting personnel to perform certain activities within the planning project. Some potential benefits include:

•   Structured approach.

         Most reputable consulting firms use planning methodologies that offer a structured approach in performing information systems planning. This structured approach helps to ensure that appropriate data is collected and analyzed during the initial stages of the project and that alternatives are considered that take advantage of current technologies.

•   An independent evaluation of alternatives.

         Consulting firms typically offer knowledge, experience, and exposure to current technology. They can provide an objective and independent assessment of needs and should be influenced only by vendor capabilities in meeting the requirements identified during the planning project. The financial institution should work only with consulting firms that are independent of vendor solutions and that receive no remuneration from equipment manufacturers and/or software developers.

•   Industry expertise.

         The consulting team should consist of highly specialized individuals with data processing, accounting, and organizational skills. They should have extensive experience in providing consulting services to the financial industry--not only in systems planning, but also in the evaluation and selection of technology solutions. A good consulting firm should be able to assist in implementing the plan once it is developed.

- Hardware expertise.

  Consultants can help bridge the gap between previous systems architectures and current technologies. The selected consulting firm should have knowledge of the financial institution's current hardware platform as well as other midrange and mainframe hardware platforms from the present vendor and from other vendors. Consultants who only recommend one vendor's solutions will potentially limit the choices of alternatives for the organization. Some vendors, which offer high-quality niche products and services, may not be considered unless the consulting team has the necessary exposure and experience with alternative platforms.

- Software expertise.

  Many different turnkey systems are available to financial institutions today for a variety of applications. Some offer a broad base of installed users while others may be relatively new in the marketplace. The consulting team should be experienced in identifying the key factors in selecting software solutions. In some cases, the software solution may dictate the hardware platform for the financial institution. In other cases, the software solution may be compatible with multiple platforms--large and small. The consulting firm should understand these implications and should be open to consider new platforms and technology.

- Involvement of financial institution personnel.

  A project philosophy based on experience and knowledge of financial institution personnel increases the opportunity for successful implementation of recommendations. Involvement of financial institution personnel during the project will help ensure that the final products meet the organization's specific needs.

- Nationally available consulting staff.

  The consulting firm should have an ongoing interest in the project outcome and should be able to provide continued service through a national information technology consulting practice for financial institutions. The consulting firm should not be content simply to provide recommendations, but should have continued interest in ensuring that the results are actually accomplished.

ORGANIZATION OF THE BOOK

This book is organized into chapters that correlate with various activities related to the strategic information systems planning process. Chapters 2 through 6 describe specific activities related to the overall planning methodology, and Chapters 7 through 10 explain additional activities and considerations that may be performed during and/or after the initial plan is developed.

Certain financial institutions may decide to reduce their planning scope and the related level of effort based on their resources and needs. In that case, this book can be especially useful in understanding the most important aspects of technology planning.

2 THE PLANNING PROCESS

OVERVIEW

Information technology planning consists of a combination of activities that allow the financial institution to establish goals and objectives, define strategies and policies to help achieve these objectives, and develop detailed plans to ensure that the strategies are properly implemented. The process results in a three- to five-year "strategic" plan that enables information systems to effectively support the overall goals and objectives of the organization.

The need for strategic, comprehensive information systems planning is more evident today than ever before. Improved management information has become critical in effectively and efficiently managing the operations of every financial institution. Increased external and internal reporting requirements have increased the need for more comprehensive management information. Many of these information needs can be satisfied in a cost-effective manner through increased utilization of current information systems resources and by the addition of supplemental resources that support the requirements of executive information systems. Because information systems resources are limited, a plan to optimize information technology (IT) expenditures is often necessary.

Long-range or strategic planning projects are relatively common in most organizations, although they often vary in scope, approach, and formality. Regardless of scope, they frequently identify the need for additional management information that can best be provided through automated systems. Short-term planning projects may focus on local or wide-area networks, intelligent workstations, platform systems, and/or microcomputers to fit a particular need.

Longer-term projects may focus on establishing a systems architecture that can be used as the foundation of core and ancillary systems throughout the financial institution. This may involve the complete replacement and selection of mainframe hardware and application software as well as peripheral systems, such as the teller equipment, item capture equipment, and other hardware. Or the process may involve supplemental systems, which can be added to the current in-house platform(s) or service center, to meet specific departmental requirements. The current state of information systems and the needs of the financial institution should dictate the direction followed during the IT planning process. In this way, future needs and requirements can be properly developed and implemented to support the goals and objectives of the organization.

Because the IT planning process can apply to all levels of computing within the organization, i.e., PCs, networked systems, midrange computers, and mainframe systems, many similarities exist in the activities appropriate for evaluating the requirements for departmental and organization-wide systems. The process described in this chapter is presented as a guideline for IT planning. The approach does not require complex models or a high level of technical expertise. It attempts to focus on developing a practical plan versus a theoretical or idealistic plan, which typically cannot be easily formulated or implemented. The financial institution should alter its approach accordingly, based on its unique organization, culture, marketplace, budgets, and other situational factors.

The IT planning process normally involves several successive series of activities, with various checkpoints for management decision making regarding automation. The general activities that constitute strategic information systems planning are identified and described below. Figure 2.1 contains a diagram of the Strategic Information Systems Planning Process.

Phase I: Organization Assessment

In the first phase of strategic information systems planning, the initial concentration of effort is to align the information systems plan with the overall objectives of the organization. During this step, it is necessary to:

- Analyze existing organizational goals, plans, and strategies.
- Assess existing Management Information Systems (MIS) department structure, policies, procedures, objectives, and strategies.

In many cases, an organization-wide strategic plan may not have been developed, but through research and discussion with the planning group, it is possible to ascertain the key strategies and goals to which the information systems plan should be aligned. If the information systems plan does not complement and agree with the strategic direction of the financial institution, it will be difficult to obtain the support of the organization, which is critical for success during the implementation phase.

During Phase I the following major activities should be accomplished:

1.   Analyze organization goals and objectives.

2.   Structure the planning team.

3.   Develop the MIS mission statement.

4.   Evaluate the MIS function.

Phase II: Information Requirements

The second phase involves an analysis of the financial institution's information requirements. During this phase, planning focuses on assessing the current and future information needs to support the organization. At this point, an overall information architecture and systems plan for the financial institution should be defined. This phase requires an analysis of the present applications being processed, equipment requirements, file sizes and storage requirements, computer usage by application, and the programs involved in operating the systems. Once the presently automated applications are analyzed, areas should be reviewed that are manually processed to determine:

- Potential for automation.
- Estimated costs.
- Anticipated benefits (quantified where possible).
- Alternative processing methods.

To further define the information architecture, each individual department's needs should be analyzed to better determine their functional objectives and requirements. As part of this process, it is important to identify the processing mode for the potential application (e.g., batch, on-line, or real-time).

During Phase II, the following activities should be accomplished:

1.   Perform information needs assessment.

2.   Classify needs.

3.   Determine priorities.

4.   Develop the systems plan.

Phase III: Resource Determination

The third phase of strategic information systems planning includes research and analysis of the service center, internal hardware, software, data communications, personnel and costs necessary to implement the requirements prioritized in the systems plan.

During Phase III, the following activities should be accomplished:

1.   Perform research.

2.   Develop the hardware plan.

3.   Develop the communications plan.

4.   Develop the software plan.

5.   Develop the staffing plan.

6.   Develop the education plan.

The hardware, communications, software, staffing, and education elements of the plan are usually developed simultaneously. The applications to be processed, along with anticipated trends in hardware and software development, permit the building of the hardware and communications segments of the plan. Hardware and communication requirements can be estimated, and present equipment can be evaluated in an effort to predict replacement or upgrading of key components.

Phase IV: The Implementation Process

The fourth phase consists of the development of policies and procedures for controlling the plan's direction and monitoring actual performance against the plan. During this phase of the information systems planning project, costs associated with each element of the plan are assembled in budget or expense format to comprise the final element of the plan. Budgeted costs should include projected expenditures for personnel, equipment, software, supplies, and other data processing costs. Also, a detailed implementation schedule should be developed that identifies:

- Activity description
- Responsible party(s)
- Target start date
- Target completion date
- Estimated hours

Chapters 3, 4, 5 and 6 further describe the various activities necessary to complete the information systems planning process. Figure 2.2 contains a sample outline of a strategic information systems plan.

PLANNING TEAM

Experts agree that the most critical factor in successfully developing and implementing an IT plan is management's commitment to the process. Management's active involvement and participation in each major activity is critical to the successful completion of the project. Many assumptions and decisions will be made during the project, not to mention interpretation of the major components of the organization's strategic plan. To provide clear direction and minimize the potential for unnecessary work, IT planning team members and the team leader should have a good understanding of the objectives and scope of their assignment, and they should ensure that a clear reporting relationship with management exists before undertaking this responsibility.

Another critical component of the planning process is selection of an IT planning team. Management should designate a group of personnel as the IT planning team or committee and assign them the responsibility of overseeing the IT planning process. Figure 2.3 contains a description of the IT planning team, including objectives, composition, responsibilities, specific functions, and general operation of the team.

Many organizations use a team approach to accomplish the objectives of the project. This ensures that it is staffed with the level of specialization needed for the situation. The proper mix of project personnel helps ensure that the necessary application, operational, and technical knowledge are present during the project. This will contribute to the economic and efficient completion of the various tasks associated with the project. Also, when expertise is needed in areas other than data processing, the team can be expanded to include these specialized skills.

One individual should be assigned responsibility for project leadership and for coordinating the project with management and departmental personnel. This individual should have the following minimal knowledge and skills:

- Knowledge of the financial industry.
- Knowledge of the organization.
- A background in similar projects.
- General understanding of information technology concepts.

The individual should report directly to executive management and should have sufficient authority to carry out the assigned responsibilities. The individual will likely have operational experience in one or more departments, but it is important that the individual maintain the appearance of independence as data is collected, systems prioritized, and systems selected. Obviously, a project of this magnitude requires an adequate commitment of time by the project manager and involved departmental personnel. In some cases, this will be a full-time project for several months.

Preparing the Project Schedule

A project schedule should be developed at the outset of the planning project. The schedule should identify major activities, assigned responsibilities, and target completion dates. The project schedule should be used as a turnaround document between planning team participants and organization management and should provide the information necessary to measure project status and completion. Figure 2.4 contains a sample project schedule for the strategic information systems planning project.

Management Reporting

The planning team should provide management with periodic progress or status reports to keep them informed of team activities and accomplishments on an ongoing basis. A sample project status report is contained in Figure 2.5.

SCOPE

Prior to beginning the IT planning project, the planning team should have a clear understanding of the current IT operating environment as well as management's objectives in desiring or initiating the IT planning process. To better understand the current situation, the following questions should be answered:

- What does management perceive the problem(s) to be?
- What systems (i.e., hardware and software) are presently installed in each department?
- What is the current MIS budget by major category (i.e., hardware, software, personnel, communications, etc.)?
- What preliminary work has been performed relating to the enhancement and/or replacement of existing systems?
- What turnkey vendors, if any, have been considered thus far?
- What assistance in the planning process can be obtained from interested third parties (i.e., independent consultants and vendors)?
- What alternatives does management want to pursue and consider (i.e., in-house systems, service centers, facilities management, software replacement, etc.)?
- Are management's expectations reasonable (i.e., time frame, costs, benefits, etc.)?

Ideally, the planning team should attempt to develop initial time estimates and a project schedule for performing the systems planning project, especially on a project that could require several man-months of effort. The time estimates and schedule will help guide team members throughout the project and should assist in setting expectations regarding the length of time involved in the planning process. It may also help to identify "missing" activities, once reviewed by the management team.

The strategic information systems planning project may require approximately six months elapsed time, assuming a high degree of dedication by internal personnel to the planning process. This time frame could be longer if activities are performed on a part-time basis. The project scope should determine the length of the project. A project addressing selected functional areas will require considerably less time than an organization-wide project.

To properly estimate the scope of work to be performed during the project, the planning team will need to discuss a number of subjects with the management team and appropriate department heads. The answers to these questions will assist the team in estimating hours and preparing the project schedule:

- Will management consider the use of outside consulting personnel to assist in the project?
- Will departmental personnel be involved in data collection and other activities?
- How soon does management want the planning process completed? What implementation time frame is anticipated?
- Is a cost/benefit analysis necessary? What methodology will be used for developing this information?
- Does management hope to justify system changes based on direct labor savings or some other measurable criteria? How will this information be gathered? How long will it take?

The following questions will provide the planning team with a general understanding of the level of equipment needed (i.e., PC, midrange computer, mainframe computer, etc.):

- What applications need to be automated?
- What are the general transaction volumes of the applications to be automated?
- How many terminals and printers will be required by departmental personnel?
- Where will terminals and printers be located--inside and outside the primary facility?
- How many remote locations will be on-line?
- Are there presently MIS personnel in the organization that can assist in the technical evaluation?
- Will management consider the addition of MIS or technical support personnel?

Once these basic questions are addressed, the planning team should have enough information to estimate the resource commitment and time frame for the project, and the assessment process can begin.

Figure 2.1

**Strategic Information
Systems Planning Process**

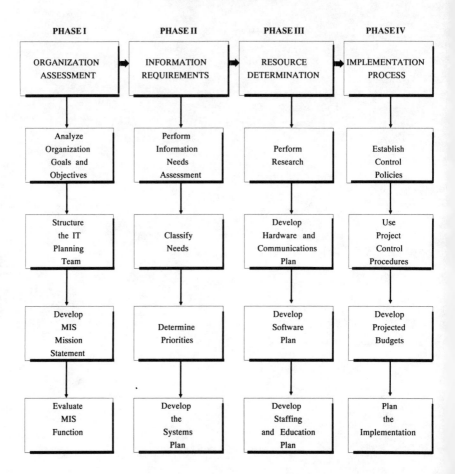

Figure 2.2
Strategic Information Systems Plan
Sample Outline

I.   SYSTEMS PLAN

   A.   Introduction
   B.   Planning factors
   C.   Systems plan assumptions
   D.   Systems plan alternatives
   E.   Description of current
      applications
   F.   Current MIS projects
   G.   Descriptions of planned
      applications
   H.   Implementation priorities
   I.   Anticipated implementation
      schedules

II. HARDWARE PLAN

   A.   Hardware plan assumptions
   B.   Current hardware inventory
      analysis
   C.   Hardware usage analysis
   D.   Anticipated computer requirements
   E.   Current & anticipated hardware
      costs
   F.   Hardware alternatives

III. COMMUNICATIONS PLAN

   A.   Communications plan assumptions
   B.   Current equipment inventory
   C.   Communications usage analysis
   D.   Anticipated communications
      requirements
   E.   Current & anticipated
      communications costs
   F.   Communications alternatives

IV. SOFTWARE PLAN

   A.   Software plan assumptions
   B.   Current software requirements
   C.   Anticipated software
      requirements
   D.   Current & anticipated costs of
      software
   E.   Technical standards plan
   F.   Documentation standards plan
   G.   Software alternatives

V.   STAFFING PLAN

   A.   Staff plan assumptions
   B.   Staffing requirements plan
   C.   Staff education plan
   D.   Job descriptions
   E.   Performance standards

VI. IMPLEMENTATION PLAN

   A.   Organization charts
   B.   Control policies
   C.   Project control procedures
   D.   Implementation schedule
   E.   Projected budgets

Figure 2.3
Sample Description of the IT Planning Team

Objectives of the Team

The objectives of the Information Technology (IT) Planning Team are to direct the overall planning, coordination, and implementation of the planning effort, including additional hardware requirements, software, and staff; new systems development; and proposals to enhance or discontinue systems.

Composition of the Team

The IT planning team should be composed of personnel who are qualified and authorized to represent the overall interests of the financial institution. For maximum effectiveness, the team should consist of five to seven members, including the chairperson, that fairly represent existing and potential users of automated systems. A single department should not have more than one representative on the team. The IT planning team is structured so that the chairperson is from the user community, preferably in an executive management position, and has direct management responsibility for the success of the planning project. Team members might also consist of key personnel in other departments in the organization that may be affected by future automated systems, plus managers or key users in departments that will be involved in the operation of the system, and a representative from the Management Information Systems function. The MIS director should also be a member of the team.

The team, as a whole, should have the following qualifications:

- An understanding of the objectives and philosophies of the organization.
- General understanding of information technology techniques and services.
- Awareness of, or the ability to understand, the operational needs and desires of various existing and potential users of automated systems.
- Independent viewpoint regarding information technology issues.
- Ability to evaluate information technology alternatives.

Figure 2.3 (Continued)
Sample Description of the IT Planning Team

Each team member will be liaison to a specific number of functionally related departments within the financial institution and will represent them and their interests on the team.

Responsibilities of the Team

The team is responsible for determining the financial institution's information technology objectives, policies, and goals. Its basic responsibilities are to:

- Promote the effective, economic use of information technology.
- Establish and coordinate the schedule for the planning process. The schedule should be segmented so that decisions related to the plan can be made at several successive checkpoints.
- Develop an understanding of the information requirements of all functional areas of the financial institution.
- Assure that proper resources are allocated for successful completion of the plan.
- Review and propose solutions to territorial, political, departmental, or functional conflicts relating to information technology matters.
- Provide the basis for recommending to the financial institution, its executive management and directors, a course of systems action.
- Provide management direction to the planning team.
- Provide periodic project status reports to executive management.

Specific Functions of the Team

- Develop project plans and timetable.
- Communicate the key conceptual design considerations and requirements as a result of the planning process.
- Schedule time for handling necessary planning activities.
- Maintain the unity of direction of the planning team.
- Guide and direct user department(s) and MIS personnel in the evaluation, selection, conversion, and implementation of the new or enhanced systems.
- Monitor and guide other related systems activities.

Figure 2.3 (Continued)
Sample Description of the IT Planning Team

General Operation of the Team

Success of the team depends largely on the clear understanding that the chairperson is directly responsible to executive management for successful completion of the plan.

The IT planning team should meet on a regularly scheduled basis at an appointed time and place. The frequency of meetings will depend on the urgency and complexity of the situation. The agenda for meetings should be structured to minimize the time consumed. Status reports, proposals for new projects, and other pertinent materials should be distributed in advance and minutes of the meetings should be documented and retained by the secretary to the president.

By clearly designating the planning team as having responsibility for the successful development and presentation of the plan, certain pressures on the MIS function are reduced and additional attention can be focused on allocating proper MIS and technical support personnel to the plan.

The user departments also receive major benefits from the planning process. Review by the planning team helps ensure that the conceptual design specifications meet user requirements, that adequate evaluation and selection activities are performed, that the proper resources are available at the right time, and that a feasible schedule for implementation of the plan is developed. In addition, user department personnel retain cost awareness of the plan because of a clear insight into the one-time and ongoing expenses associated with the systems involved.

Figure 2.4
Strategic Information Systems Planning
Sample Project Schedule

	Month					
	1	**2**	**3**	**4**	**5**	**6**

PHASE I: ORGANIZATION ASSESSMENT

A.   Analyze Organization Goals and Objectives

B.   Structure the IT Planning Team

C.   Develop MIS Mission Statement

D.   Evaluate MIS Function

PHASE II: INFORMATION REQUIREMENTS

A.   Perform Information Needs Assessment

B.   Classify Needs

C.   Determine Priorities

D.   Develop the Systems Plan

PHASE III: RESOURCE DETERMINATION

A.   Perform Research

B.   Develop Hardware and Communications Plan

C.   Develop Software Plan

D.   Develop Staffing and Education Plan

PHASE IV: IMPLEMENTATION PROCESS

A.   Establish Control Policies

B.   Use Project Control Procedures

C.   Develop Projected Budgets

D.   Plan the Implementation

Figure 2.6
Strategic Information Systems Planning
Sample Project Status Report

Project: Strategic Information System Planning   Status as of:_____

Prepared by:_____   Date prepared:_____

Accomplishments During Last Reporting Period:

_____
_____
_____
_____
_____

Overall Progress:

_____
_____
_____
_____

Estimated Percentage Completed:___ (Based on project hours)

Attention Items:

Problems/Opportunities Developing or Anticipated:

_____
_____
_____

Goals for Next Reporting Period:

_____
_____
_____
_____
_____

Distribution: Executive Management
                       IT Planning Team

CHAPTER 3
ORGANIZATION ASSESSMENT

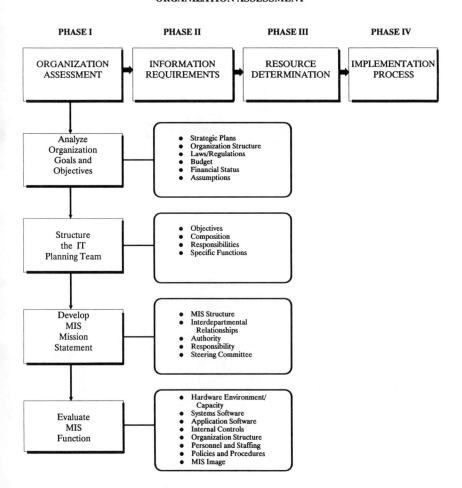

PHASE I   PHASE II   PHASE III   PHASE IV

| ORGANIZATION ASSESSMENT | INFORMATION REQUIREMENTS | RESOURCE DETERMINATION | IMPLEMENTATION PROCESS |

Analyze Organization Goals and Objectives
- Strategic Plans
- Organization Structure
- Laws/Regulations
- Budget
- Financial Status
- Assumptions

Structure the IT Planning Team
- Objectives
- Composition
- Responsibilities
- Specific Functions

Develop MIS Mission Statement
- MIS Structure
- Interdepartmental Relationships
- Authority
- Responsibility
- Steering Committee

Evaluate MIS Function
- Hardware Environment/ Capacity
- Systems Software
- Application Software
- Internal Controls
- Organization Structure
- Personnel and Staffing
- Policies and Procedures
- MIS Image

3 ORGANIZATION ASSESSMENT

The first phase of strategic information systems planning involves an assessment process that should analyze organizational goals and objectives, the financial institution's overall mission statement, and should include a detailed review of the current information systems in use within the financial institution. As the assessment process is initiated, a planning team should be identified, which will ultimately be responsible for the successful completion of planning activities.

ANALYZING ORGANIZATION GOALS AND OBJECTIVES

The organizational assessment process begins with the identification of organization goals and objectives. The planning team should understand the overall objectives of the organization and then attempt to align the information systems plan with these objectives. This can be accomplished by reviewing the existing strategic plan or, if one does not exist, identifying existing organizational goals, plans, and strategies through interviews and discussions with key management personnel.

In many cases, an organization-wide strategic plan may not have been developed, but through research and discussion with the planning group and other key personnel within the organization, it is possible to ascertain the key strategies and goals to which the information systems plan should be aligned. If the information systems plan does not complement and agree with the strategic direction of the financial institution, it will be difficult to obtain the support of the organization, which is critical for success during the implementation phase.

Following are the major components of the financial institution's overall strategic plan that may have relevance as the IT plan is developed. These components should be reviewed and understood by the planning team prior to proceeding with the strategic information systems plan. In the event the following components do not exist, the planning team should work with management in developing this basic information.

Position statement

The position statement should provide a picture of where the financial institution is today and identify the major issues and challenges facing the financial institution in today's climate. Understanding the current position is the basis of the strategic plan and is critical to the development of sound strategies, goals, and objectives. Some key components of the position statement include the following:

- History of the financial institution's business development and growth.

- Current status of the financial institution in the industry and in the marketplace (i.e., community, state, or region(s)). Current status can include such items as:

    - Financial position and profitability.
    - Degree of diversification.
    - Products and services provided.
    - Customer base.
    - Market share.
    - Industry/competitor considerations.
    - Image.

- Future outlook for the financial institution based on recent performance and direction.

- Major challenges that must be met for long-term success.

Strategic planning assumptions

The financial institution's strategic plan is based on a series of assumptions that were developed as a result of analyzing the current business environment and researching a variety of external factors that could impact the future business direction of the financial institution. Planning assumptions are typically developed to provide direction and control during the planning process and often to address external economic factors and critical internal forces that could significantly impact the financial industry and the institution itself. Assumptions help outline management's best picture of the business climate at the time the process is undertaken and for some time into the future.

Planning assumptions are typically classified in broad terms, such as:

*   National economic conditions.

    National economic conditions include such factors as interest rates, growth in the gross national product (GNP), unemployment, population growth, and other factors.

*   Local economic conditions.

    Local economic conditions address locally sensitive factors, such as housing starts, availability of business development funds, local unemployment, and other local economic conditions.

*   Market conditions.

    Market conditions include such factors as market segments served, opportunity for increased market share, competitive environment, and typical customer profiles.

*   Organizational considerations.

    Some assumptions relating to factors within the organization are also appropriate, such as staffing requirements, organization structural changes, ownership structure, and skill requirements.

*   Political/regulatory considerations.

    These considerations include assumptions relating to future regulatory changes, political attitude toward the industry, and other considerations.

*   Financial considerations.

    Certain financial assumptions are appropriate, dealing with issues such as return on assets, profitability, availability of funds, liquidity, investment yields, margins on products and services, and other financial considerations.

- Technological considerations.

  The advent of new technologies and their implementation within the financial industry is relatively predictable. As cost-effective tools are developed, their application at the financial institution and branch levels can be assumed. Such technologies as imaging, systems integration, and client/server architecture may impact the planning process.

Mission statement

The mission statement is a definition of the basic purpose of the organization. It represents the organization's broadest strategic planning choice or decision. It serves the dual purpose of answering the questions:

- What business are we in?

- Where do we want to go?

In answering these questions, the mission statement should define:

- What the organization is.

- Why it exists.

- The unique contribution it desires to make in the future.

While mission statements can be written in many different terms, the following items are normally included within the mission statement:

- A general statement about the financial institution's type of business.

- A definition of the basic purpose of the organization.

- Top management's vision, values, and priorities.

- Philosophy and value statements that will guide future actions.

- A description of the image the financial institution would like to project.

- Key strengths that have led to the financial institution's success and that the financial institution would like to continue to build upon.

- Critical issues relating to the business climate that should be considered as the plan is developed.

- Markets and geographical areas that are and will be served.

- A list of current and future products/services that will be provided and their method of delivery.

- Statements describing the desired relationship between the financial institution and its employees, customers, and the community.

- Statistics relating to the financial institution's market share, growth, and profitability.

- Broad strategies and longer-term direction of the financial institution.

The mission statement should be broad enough to allow the bank and its personnel the flexibility to address new markets, products, and services that represent opportunities for growth. However, it should be narrow enough to prevent the organization from adventuring into "incompatible" businesses, which could divert the organization's attention and focus from its real business objectives.

Some literature suggests that the mission statement should be no longer than a paragraph, while other literature suggests a maximum of two to three typewritten pages. As long as the statement's content delivers a concise message to financial institution personnel that can help guide their actions, then it is at an acceptable level of detail.

Major strategies

Major strategies address the primary direction(s) the financial institution will take to achieve its mission and long-term goals and objectives. Major strategies are typically developed for the overall organization as well as for each of its operating divisions. Strategies often deal with the following areas:

- Maintaining present business levels and customers.

- Growing products and services within the present customer base.

- Extending products and services to new, add-on markets.

•   Generating new business outside the current customer base.

Long-range goals and objectives

Long-range goals and objectives help the financial institution move from its current situation, as defined in the position statement, to its desired position, as defined in the mission statement.

Objectives are broad statements describing activities that need to be performed to accomplish the mission statement. Objectives have a qualitative versus quantitative orientation and should serve as a general guide in setting measurable goals. Objectives often address the following broad topics:

•   Growth
•   Profitability
•   Return on investment
•   Geographic coverage
•   Product and service development
•   Technology
•   Market position
•   Diversification
•   Innovation

Goals are statements that typically address specific business attributes. They are measurable and dated. Goals describe "what" will be done, while objectives describe "how" they will be done. For each objective identified above (i.e., growth, profitability, etc.), several goals may be developed that will help measure success in achieving the objective.

Short-range goals and objectives

Ultimately, the financial institution's strategic plan must be reduced to short-term activities and goals that complement the broader strategies, goals, and objectives of the plan. Short-range goals and objectives should address areas that are most critical to achieving longer-term plans and that must be started or completed within the next twelve months. This equates to an annual business plan with detailed activities, responsibility assignments, and targeted completion dates during the next year. The detailed activities should correspond to specific short-term goals and objectives, which in turn correspond to specific longer-term strategies, goals, and objectives.

STRUCTURING THE PLANNING TEAM

Following the initial assessment of organizational objectives and strategies, it is necessary to structure the planning team. Many organizations may have already established a committee or team in which selected department heads provide input to the systems planning process on an ongoing basis. However, if a team is not established, it is important to structure a team before continuing with development of the plan. Planning team considerations include:

- Objectives of the team.
- Composition of the membership.
- Responsibilities of each member.
- Specific functions of the team.

The team should consist of at least one person from the following areas:

- Management.
- Management Information Services (MIS) function.
- Users--key departments and functional areas.

The team should be structured so that its leader has direct responsibility for the success of the project. Total membership should be between five and seven persons, with involvement from others on a periodic basis as particular topics of interest and relevance are discussed. For example, internal audit personnel should be involved in assessing the general and application control environment relating to data entry, processing, and report production as well as audit trail and on-line security. Telecommunications personnel should be involved in assessing current communication network capacities and evaluating strategies for future voice and data communications.

General responsibilities of the team should include:

- Establishing the project schedule.
- Assigning project responsibilities for major tasks and activities.
- Ensuring that adequate resources are committed to the project.
- Resolving differences relating to departmental or application priorities.
- Reviewing situation analyses, research information, requirements lists, general design documents, and vendor technical information.
- Preparing a management summary indicating the overall recommendations of the group.

- Coordinating the planning process.
- Providing periodic status reports to management.

The IT planning team should be involved in the implementation process, but the organization may determine that an implementation committee, consisting of MIS and user support personnel, could best fulfill the responsibilities relating to the implementation process.

DEVELOPING THE MIS MISSION STATEMENT

After structuring the planning team, it is necessary to establish a mission statement for MIS. The MIS mission statement may differ significantly from the mission statement developed during the strategic planning process. The primary reason for the difference is that the MIS function typically is viewed as a service and support organization for the various operating entities within the financial institution. Therefore, the MIS mission statement will normally be written with technical service and support issues in mind.

Before developing the MIS mission statement, the planning team should have an understanding of the MIS organization structure, including authorities and responsibilities of the various department managers within MIS. The typical MIS organization structure includes the following major elements:

- MIS administration and planning
- Security and control
- Operations
- Applications systems development
- Applications systems maintenance
- Quality assurance

- Systems programming
- Communications
- Help desk (i.e., end-user support)

A significant difference exists in the number of personnel performing these functions in a large institution versus a small institution. Interdepartmental relationships should also be explored to fully understand the division of authority and responsibility. For example, facility security is often a responsibility held outside the MIS function, yet the MIS operations function may have responsibility for computer room and vault storage access. Similarly, voice communications may be assigned outside the MIS organization, while data communications may be assigned within MIS. These interrelationships should be known, as they will impact assignment of team responsibilities during the planning and implementation process.

The content of the MIS mission statement is often a reflection of the current MIS organization. Responsibilities assigned within the MIS function tend to form the basis for the mission statement. Drawing a parallel between the mission statement from the strategic plan and the MIS mission statement, the following questions can be restated:

Financial Institution Mission Statement	MIS Mission Statement
• What business are we in?	What is our primary role within the financial institution?
• Where do we want to go?	How can we best serve the user departments (i.e., our customers) in the future?

However, some questions are similar in both levels of planning:

• What is the organization's purpose?

• Why does it exist?

• What unique contribution can it make in the future?

The MIS mission statement could include the following descriptions:

• A general statement about the primary service areas of the MIS function.

• A statement of the basic purpose of the organization.

• A restatement of top management's priorities in MIS terminology.

• Philosophy and value statements that will guide future actions within the MIS function.

• A description of the image the MIS function would like to project to its customers--that is, the user departments.

• Key strengths that have led to the department's success and that could lead to future successes.

- Critical issues relating to MIS culture that should be considered as the plan is developed.

- Departments and locations that are and will be served by the MIS function.

- A list of current and future MIS-related services that will be provided and their methods of delivery.

- Statements describing the desired relationship between the MIS department and its users.

- Statistics relating to the MIS department's performance (i.e., uptime, deliverables, systems supported, etc.).

- Broad strategies for sustaining a technological edge and maintaining a leadership role in technology issues within the financial institution.

The MIS mission statement should be flexible enough to allow the department to perform additional support functions in the future and to use new and emerging technologies. Most importantly, it must be compatible with the overall mission, strategies, goals, and objectives of the financial institution.

Once the MIS mission statement has been developed, the remainder of the first phase of the planning process centers upon the assessment of the current MIS environment (e.g., existing capabilities, personal skills, image within the organization, technology, etc.) and the development of MIS policies, objectives, and strategies.

EVALUATING THE MIS FUNCTION

An important step in developing a strategic information systems plan is to solicit input from various departmental entities regarding their assessment of the information systems and the MIS function within the organization. This can most easily be accomplished using a survey questionnaire which, if properly designed, can provide an initial assessment of the use and degree of satisfaction by users of information technology resources. In addition, the questionnaire will help determine if existing automation efforts are properly addressing and satisfying current needs and objectives and whether additional resources are necessary in addressing the need for change in current and future systems.

The purpose of the questionnaire is to provide each department of the financial institution with an opportunity to be involved in the planning process. This is very important to the overall success of this project. The questionnaire can also help identify specific individuals who can and should participate in the planning process. These potential sources of information are not intended to judge past decisions regarding automation, rather the intent is to focus on the future. Results from the questionnaire should be summarized and provided to each respondent in an effort to keep them involved in the planning process.

Although the questionnaire should be customized to fit the scope of the planning project, information relating to the following subjects is typically requested:

- Present hardware and peripheral devices
- Software packages
- Manual systems and procedures
- Quality and level of MIS department services
- Information availability
- User training and support
- Current uses and needs for future computing
- Information systems administration
- General comments regarding information systems

The systems planning questionnaire can provide the following benefit to the planning project:

- Provides users and potential users an opportunity for input into the planning process.
- Identifies specific departmental needs.
- Identifies existing and potential problem areas.
- Helps determine if current user needs and objectives are satisfied.
- Provides feedback on the effectiveness, efficiency, and general direction of the information systems function.

See Figure 3.1 for a sample strategic information systems planning questionnaire.

Concurrently with the systems planning questionnaire, the planning team can begin the organization assessment process relating to the MIS function itself. During this process, the planning team should review and evaluate the following:

- Hardware environment and capacities
- Systems software
- Application software
- Internal controls
- Organization structure
- Personnel and staffing
- Policies and procedures
- MIS image

For each of these topical areas, a brief overview of background and history as introductory information is beneficial to the planning team. This background information often tells a story of progressive events in the financial institution's history that significantly impacted the direction of automation and information systems. The background information should summarize key events as they occurred during the last 5 to 10 years, such as hardware migrations, application system development and/or acquisitions, personnel and staffing changes, introduction of new policies and procedures, internal control enhancements, and other key events.

1.   Hardware environment and capacities

A.   Background hardware environment information

The history should include the replacement and upgrades of mainframe and midrange computer(s) as well as any departmental systems, networks, teller terminals, and other equipment which may have been implemented during the last 5 to 10 years. Summary information relating to the acquisition, rental, or leasing of equipment may also be appropriate.

B.   Equipment capacities

Growth or changes in equipment capacities should be addressed, including:

- CPU memory
- Communications activity
- Disk (DASD) storage
- Off-line storage
- Printer(s) and speeds
- Workstations and PCs
- Transaction volumes

These changes should be tracked along a time line, which will indicate trends in capacity changes due to transaction volume increases and the addition of new major application areas.

C.   Changes in processing mode

Changes in processing mode should also be noted, such as moving from a service center environment to an in-house system or the implementation of specific departmental systems, such as a trust system or platform automation. Additionally, it is important to identify whether MIS structure and processing is generally centralized or decentralized. Both structures have advantages and disadvantages that can impact the planning process, especially if management states a clear preference for the method of structure and processing.

D.   Performance analysis

For in-house systems, performance analysis tools are often available from the equipment manufacturers that allow the tracking of hardware utilization during certain periods of time. This is especially relevant when analyzing hardware/CPU capacities during peak processing periods, such as end-of-day or end-of-month. Some performance analysis packages also track usage of the communications network. Heavy communications and transaction activity are often associated with late morning, end of the business day, and end-of-week processing.

Obviously, equipment and network capacities should be at such levels that peak volumes can be processed without significant delay from the user's and/or customer's viewpoint. Response time measurements should be a part of normal operational reporting in larger MIS departments.

Once hardware and communications performance has been analyzed for a reasonable period of time, the planning team should summarize this information and place it in a format that can be used to identify trends and potential problem areas. Most evaluations include graphical representation of the periods under analysis, which tend to be a more suitable method of presentation for nontechnical personnel involved in the process. These graphical representations often allow the evaluator to overlay peak transaction volumes over a larger or faster configuration of equipment to assist in estimating the impact of equipment upgrades on peak usage and response time.

2.   Systems software

A.   Background systems software information

A history of the addition and upgrade of systems software is also relevant to the MIS assessment process. Once again, a 5- to 10-year period will help indicate trends relating to changes in systems software.

B.   Current systems software assessment

Several different types of systems software should be included in this analysis:

- Operating software
- Communications software
- Source program maintenance software
- Database management system(s)
- Screen design aids
- Librarian software (tape and disk)
- Program compilers/interpreters
- 4th generation languages
- Access security software
- File transfer software

- Terminal emulation software
- Performance analysis tools
- CASE tools
- Scheduling software
- Documentation software
- Report writers
- Productivity aids
- Job accounting reporting systems

Current release levels and release dates should be identified as well as an assessment of the useful life of the various levels of systems software. If new releases are planned for implementation in the near future, this information should also be noted along with the related time frame.

3.   Application software

A.   Background application software information

The following information is of special significance relating to the background of application systems in use by the financial institution:

- Application name
- Purchased or internally developed
- Date originally implemented
- Source language
- Major enhancements and related dates
- Degree of modification, especially if purchased
- Degree of integration with other application software (specify application interfaces)
- Dependencies (on development tools, operating software, custom code, other applications, etc.)

B.   Current application software assessment

To begin the application software assessment process, a detailed list of functions, features, and capabilities should be developed by application area. This list of features will become the basis for evaluating the capabilities of present software and for comparing it to similar software available from turnkey suppliers of financial industry systems.

Once the basic list of software features has been developed, the assessment process can continue. Several analyses should be performed, including:

- User assessment
- Technical assessment
- Competitive analysis

The **user assessment** is a summary of the "condition" of the application system from the user's perspective. Some factors that may be appropriate in the user assessment process include:

- Additional features necessary to meet current needs.
- Flexibility in meeting future business and operational objectives and requirements.
- Degree of satisfaction with current capabilities and reports.
- Availability and quality of user documentation.
- Availability of training materials and a test database for training new employees.
- Availability of audit trail and balancing summary information.
- Presence of on-line edits and controls to reduce the frequency of errors.
- Ease of error detection and correction.

The user assessment should also include a compilation of functions, features, and reports by application area that current software cannot immediately provide without programming effort or purchase of additional database or reporting tools. The list can be developed using several sources of input, including:

- Responses to the systems planning questionnaire.
- Backlog of user requests for application changes.
- Interviews with key user personnel.

Some effort should be focused on prioritizing the various needs documented through this process. It may also be appropriate to initially identify the degree of complexity in achieving, acquiring, or developing each feature as well as the time and potential cost involved.

The **technical assessment** is a result of evaluation of the various application systems by technical personnel within the organization. Oftentimes, an application system may be in good "condition" from a user's perspective, but the source code may have had several modifications and fixes applied over time that significantly increase the effort involved in maintaining the application. To assess the technical condition of the application, the following factors should be considered:

- Level and degree of modification.
- File structures.
- Redundancy of information.
- Effort involved in maintaining and changing the application.
- Quality of technical documentation.
- Interdependence on other systems.
- Number and seriousness of problems associated with day-to-day processing.
- Ability to restart/recover the application when processing problems occur.
- Programming language(s) and/or CASE tools used during development.

The technical assessment should ultimately yield an overall rating of the condition of the application-- excellent, above average, average or fair, and poor. Individual ratings by the categories stated above should provide a basis for this assessment and can be used to supplement the assessment process. The technical team may also have comments regarding the necessary actions that could significantly improve the condition of current application systems.

The **competitive assessment** is a comparison of current application functions, features, capabilities, and reports with application systems that are generally available from turnkey vendors in the financial industry. To obtain the information necessary for this assessment, the planning team can perform one of the following activities:

- Submit the list of functions and features to turnkey vendors. The list could include desirable functions that current application software cannot provide, as well as present capabilities of various systems.
- Request documentation manuals from turnkey vendors and identify capabilities from the documentation. This could be a fairly time-consuming process, as documentation may not be in a format to facilitate this effort.
- Submit the features list to current users of competitive systems. This is most easily accomplished by contacting area financial institutions that are using competitive systems.

The competitive assessment should provide a basis for understanding how well current systems meet "state-of-the-art" requirements. If the gap is very large, this will undoubtedly influence the planning team's view of the need for replacement systems.

4.   Internal controls

Internal controls are regularly evaluated by internal and external auditors as a part of normal audits and reviews. Likewise, various regulatory agencies will perform compliance audits of the control environment during their regular or periodic examinations.

Several sources of information can be used to assess internal controls relating to automated systems within the financial institution:

- External auditing firm's management and control letters.
- Findings relating to reviews or examinations by regulatory agencies.
- Internal audit findings and recommendations.

- Third-party reports describing the control environment of the data center and/or controls relating to the application software.
- Completion of internal control questionnaires.

Internal controls relating to automated systems are generally classified into two distinct areas:

- General controls.
- Application controls.

General controls are those controls which impact all computer systems and application controls are unique to specific applications. The major components of general and application controls are described in Chapter 10--Security and Control Requirements.

5. Organization structure

A. Background organization structure information

As with the other categories of MIS assessment, recent changes in authorities, responsibilities, and reporting relationships may be relevant to the organization assessment process. Using a time line will help outline this information.

B. Organization assessment

The current organization structure of the MIS function should be documented, including job titles, reporting relationships, and job responsibilities. A current organization chart is usually the starting point in assessing existing MIS organizational responsibilities and reporting relationships. Some sample areas of MIS responsibility may include:

- MIS administration, planning, and budgeting
- Security and control
- Production control and job scheduling
- Computer operations
- Capacity planning
- Item processing
- Data entry
- Proof

- Account services (i.e., research, statement rendering, exception item processing, bulk filing, microfilming, merchant services, etc.)
- Remittance processing and lockbox processing
- Applications systems development
- Applications systems maintenance
- Quality assurance
- Systems programming
- Communications--voice and data
- Network services--ATMs
- Network services--LANs/WANs
- Help desk (i.e., end-user support)
- Receiving and distribution
- Contingency planning

As mentioned during the discussion of the MIS mission statement, interdepartmental relationships should also be explored to fully understand the division of authority and responsibility. As discussed earlier, responsibilities for facility and computer room security may be separated and responsibilities for voice and data communications may also reside with different persons. These interrelationships should be known, as they will impact the teams assigned to implementation activities as a result of the planning process.

6.   Personnel and staffing

A.   Background personnel and staffing information

Of particular interest during the MIS organizational assessment process are changes in personnel and staffing over the past few years. An analysis of FTEs (Full-Time Equivalents) by job category is important in identifying trends in hiring additional technical personnel and potential changes in responsibilities of the MIS function. Some possible trends that may be important include the following:

- Additional programming personnel to maintain existing systems.

- Changes in systems programming staffing levels as more complicated environmental software (i.e., development tools, security packages, database management systems, etc.) are purchased and implemented.
- Changes in user support personnel, potentially indicating an increased role by MIS in training user personnel on automated applications.
- Increases in microcomputer and LAN staffing levels as the number of these systems increase within each department of the financial institution.
- Changes in technical specialties--perhaps additional communications personnel, but a reduced number of application development personnel.
- Reduction in programming personnel, as a reflection in the increased use of purchased packages and/or the use of CASE development tools.
- Movement of certain responsibilities outside the MIS department as those positions require greater responsibilities in working with all departments of the financial institution (e.g., security administration, contingency planning, etc.).

B.   Current personnel and staffing assessment

The personnel and staffing assessment should identify the qualifications of current personnel as they relate to their current job assignments. Employee longevity is an important factor to consider when assessing current personnel. While MIS positions have higher turnover rates than other positions within an organization, the financial industry has experienced even higher turnover rates in these technical positions, primarily because of current trends in outsourcing and financial institution mergers.

However, if turnover rates are low in the MIS department, the financial institution runs the risk of "technology stagnation," especially if budgetary constraints impact the ongoing professional education of technical personnel. Also, a low level of technology change in hardware, operating software, and development tools can negatively impact the total technical knowledge within the organization. This can contribute to limited vision relating to the implementation of new technologies within the financial institution--through no fault of the personnel within the MIS organization. Exposure to new technology is most beneficial when it is "hands-on" and part of the implementation of the technology within the organization.

To overcome this potential pitfall, management can promote the attainment of technical certifications, subscriptions to current publications, participation in continuing education programs, and more structured staff development programs.

Some organizations also include an assessment of the current salary and compensation structure of MIS professionals in comparison to local, regional, and national survey information. Assuming that the survey information can be applied to the financial industry and that geographic factors are also considered, the level of compensation can be a major factor for high or low employee turnover.

Another factor to consider in assessing the current MIS organization is dependency on key technical personnel. This dependency typically results from reliance on one or two persons in a specific technical or application area and a general lack of cross-training within the MIS function. The lack of good technical documentation is also a key factor in sustaining heavy dependencies on key personnel.

7.   **Policies and procedures**

Current policies and procedures relating to the MIS function should be reviewed by the planning team. The formality of procedures is a first indication of whether the MIS function is structured to the degree necessary to meet project deadlines or other commitments relating to deliverables for management and user departments within the financial institution. A formal policies and procedures manual should exist that will provide guidelines for all facets of information systems operations and performance.

Specifically, the following written procedures should be reviewed by the planning team:

- Systems development project control
- Program change procedures
- Systems development standards
- Software acquisition standards
- Librarian control and maintenance of software and documentation
- Physical security plan
- On-line security plan
- Data security plan

Figure 3.2 contains a list of procedures that are often found in an MIS policies and procedures manual.

8.   **MIS image**

The general satisfaction of the organization with the MIS function can be measured relatively easily with the use of a user survey. Generally speaking, the image of the MIS function has changed over the last decade from one of initiator of systems changes within the organization to a technical support role--with the impetus for leadership moving to the user departments. The current trend in information technology is for the user to have control over and ownership of application systems. The MIS function has become a servicing organization and, as such, must be responsive to user requests for service or it will find that outside servicers and consultants are used to deliver systems solutions as they are needed.

A need still exists for technology leadership by the MIS function. Formalization of MIS standards at the mainframe level, midrange level, network level, and PC level will help shape the organization's various hardware and operating environments into an architecture that is compatible with the overall information systems needs of the organization. The MIS function can still perform a "knowledge-based" service for the various departments within the organization by providing guidance to users who are investigating departmental systems and ensuring that MIS and organizational standards are properly considered.

9.   Other relevant issues

The assessment process as described in the above paragraphs should lead the planning team to the proper perspective of the organization's ability to meet user and management demands for additional information. Some other key MIS issues and considerations include the following:

- What is the basic philosophy of the current automation strategy: centralized computer, decentralized processing, service center, or combination?
- What is the nature of the computer hardware environment: single vendor or multiple vendors?
- What is the nature of the computer operating software: vendor dependent, vendor independent, or hardware independent?
- How is the communications network designed: application specific, vendor specific, network specific, or independent of application, vendor, and network?
- What is the preferred processing mode: batch, on-line, interactive, or real-time?
- What is the preferred approach for application software: purchased, turnkey, modified, or internally developed?
- What generation of software is the financial institution using?

Figure 3.1
Strategic Information Systems Planning Questionnaire

Location: _____   Date: _____

Department: _____

Responder's Name   Title

_____   _____

_____   _____

_____   _____

_____   _____

Background and Purpose

The financial institution is in the process of developing a strategic information systems plan (3-5 years) to provide direction for achieving optimal usage of information and technology resources. In addition, the study will determine if the existing automation efforts are properly addressing and satisfying current needs and objectives and that there is a proper direction for maintaining current systems and addressing future needs. The study is not intended to judge past decisions regarding automation, rather the intent is to focus on the future.

The purpose of this questionnaire is to provide each department of the financial institution an opportunity for their input into the planning process. We believe this is very important to the success of this project. We are planning to follow the questionnaire with interviews of several departments.

Instructions

Please complete this questionnaire and return it sealed in the attached envelope to _____ on or before _____. Please read each question carefully and provide answers as indicated. Certain questions may not apply to your department; please indicate N/A if appropriate. If there is not enough room provided with the question for your answer, please use the back of the question sheet or additional sheets as necessary. Your individual and specific responses will be summarized and used by the planning team as appropriate. If you have questions, please call _____, at _____.

Figure 3.1 (Continued)
Strategic Information Systems Planning Questionnaire

I.   **GENERAL**

1.   How could your area benefit from additional technology (i.e., hardware, software, etc.)
     to facilitate your department's operation or to help you do a better job?

     Consider: Are there technologies other than traditional computers that could be
                   used?
                   What operations of the department lend themselves to utilization of
                   technology?

     Please explain:

     _____
     _____
     _____
     _____

2.   How could your area benefit from increased use of technology for the administration
     and management of your department?

     Please explain:

     _____
     _____
     _____
     _____

3.   How could the financial institution better facilitate the transition to improved computer
     technology?

     Please explain:

     _____
     _____

Figure 3.1 (Continued)
Strategic Information Systems Planning Questionnaire

4. Are your employees receptive to computer-based applications to help solve their problems?

    _____ Yes   _____ No   _____ Don't Know

    Please explain:

    _____

    _____

    _____

5. Do you plan on integrating computers and associated technology into your departmental operations?

    _____ Yes   _____ No   _____ Don't Know

    If so, explain:

    _____

    _____

    _____

II. **HARDWARE AND SOFTWARE**

6. What hardware do you have in your area?

    A.   Mainframe terminals?

Model	Quantity	Hours Used Per Week

Figure 3.1 (Continued)
Strategic Information Systems Planning Questionnaire

B.   Personal Computer?

Vendor/Model	Quantity	Hours Used Per Week

C.   Printers?

Vendor/Model	Quantity	Hours Used Per Week

Figure 3.1 (Continued)
Strategic Information Systems Planning Questionnaire

D.   Modems?

| | | Hours Used |
Vendor/Model	Quantity	Per Week

E.   Other Peripherals

| | | Hours Used |
Vendor/Model	Quantity	Per Week

7.   What percentage of time during an eight-hour day is the equipment being used?

User	Percentage

8.   Is there a need for updated equipment in your area?

_____ Yes   _____ No

Please explain:

_____

_____

_____

_____

Figure 3.1 (Continued)
Strategic Information Systems Planning Questionnaire

9.   Is there a need for additional equipment in your area?

_____ Yes   _____ No

Consider: Is time lost waiting for a terminal or PC to become available?
             Is there easy access to computer equipment at this time?
             Could productivity be improved with additional hardware?

A.   Number of additional printers needed: _____
B.   Number of additional mainframe terminals needed: _____
C.   Number of additional PCs needed: _____
D.   Comments: _____
      _____
      _____

10.   Should additional PCs be portable versus desktop?

_____ Yes   _____ No

Please explain:

_____
_____
_____
_____

11.   Is there unused equipment in your area?

_____ Yes   _____ No

A.   Number of unused printers:_____
B.   Number of unused mainframe terminals: _____
C.   Number of unused PCs: _____
D.   Reason for non-use? Indicate with (x).
      ( ) Obsolete   ( ) Inappropriate software
      ( ) Surplus   ( ) Other_____

Figure 3.1 (Continued)
Strategic Information Systems Planning Questionnaire

12. What commercial PC software do you have in your area? (Note: Please include all word processing, database, spreadsheet, desktop publishing, communications, graphics, statistics, desk organizers, and any other packages. Attach additional sheets if necessary.)

Vendor	Software Product	Version Number	Application	Quantity	Spec. Use

13. Can the existing programs and systems on the mainframe be improved?

_____ Yes _____ No

Consider: Could the system be faster or more efficient to use?
Are the displays and reports easy to understand and use?
Could the system do more to help you with your job?

Suggested Improvements Description	Potential Benefits

14. What software are you familiar with that would aid you in doing a better job in the future?

Suggested Software	Potential Benefits

Figure 3.1 (Continued)
Strategic Information Systems Planning Questionnaire

15. Does your area need a local area network (PCs connected together to share hardware, programs and data) to more effectively communicate within the organization?

    _____ Yes   _____ No   _____ Don't Know

    _____ Number of workstations required

16. Are computers used more for administration functions versus delivery of customer service?

    _____ Yes   _____ No

    Please comment:

    _____

    _____

III.   **MANUAL SYSTEMS AND PROCEDURES**

17. Should any of the present manual systems and procedures be automated?

    _____ Yes   _____ No

    Consider: Are some tasks very repetitive and detail-oriented?
                  Are some tasks dependent upon computer-produced records and reports?
                  Are there related areas that are already automated?
                  How can computer technology be used to make reporting tasks easier?
                  Are you required to collect information and report it to other departments?

Figure 3.1 (Continued)
Strategic Information Systems Planning Questionnaire

Potential Functions to Be Automated

Description	Estimated Volume/ Activity	Hours Saved Per Month (If this task is no longer performed manually)	Other Benefits

18.   Is there a need for better computer programs for the customer service in your area?

_____ Yes   _____ No

Please explain:

_____
_____
_____

IV.   INFORMATION AVAILABILITY

19.   Is there specific information that is not now readily available that would enable you to better perform your duties?

_____ Yes   _____ No

Consider: Do you wait for various information?
              Is it time-consuming to obtain various information?

Specific Information	Use of Information

Figure 3.1 (Continued)
Strategic Information Systems Planning Questionnaire

20. Are there sources of information that you know about but are not able to use because you cannot readily access them?

_____ Yes   _____ No

_____Specific Information_____   _____Use of Information_____

_____   _____
_____   _____
_____   _____
_____   _____

V. **USER MANUALS, TRAINING, AND SUPPORT**

21. In general, what level of computer proficiency is representative of staff members in your area?

_____ High   _____ Medium   _____ Low

22. Do you have a user's manual for each system you are currently using?

A. PCs   _____ Yes   _____ No
B. Printers   _____ Yes   _____ No
C. Software   _____ Yes   _____ No

23. Do you use the user's manual?

A. PCs   _____ Yes   _____ No
B. Printers   _____ Yes   _____ No
C. Software   _____ Yes   _____ No

24. Have you received adequate training in the use of the hardware and software?

_____ Yes   _____ No

Figure 3.1 (Continued)
Strategic Information Systems Planning Questionnaire

25.   Has training kept up with staff needs and desires?

_____ Yes   _____ No

26.   Are at least two people in your area trained to use the hardware and software?

_____ Yes   _____ No

27.   What type of training is needed for the staff in your area?

A.	Basic computer concepts	_____ Yes	_____ No
B.	Operating system	_____ Yes	_____ No
C.	Spreadsheet	_____ Yes	_____ No
D.	Word processing	_____ Yes	_____ No
E.	Database	_____ Yes	_____ No
F.	Electronic mail	_____ Yes	_____ No
G.	Local area network	_____ Yes	_____ No
H.	Computer programming	_____ Yes	_____ No
I.	Other _____		

28.   Have you taken any formal computer training?

Internally provided training?   _____ Yes   _____ No
Externally provided training?   _____ Yes   _____ No

Please explain:

_____

_____

Figure 3.1 (Continued)
Strategic Information Systems Planning Questionnaire

29.   What factors prevent you from integrating automation into your area more than you currently do?

      A.   Unfamiliarity with applications   _____ Yes   _____ No
      B.   Availability of training   _____ Yes   _____ No
      C.   Time to learn   _____ Yes   _____ No
      D.   Availability of the computer   _____ Yes   _____ No
      E.   Availability of practical
           applications   _____ Yes   _____ No
      F.   Other _____

30.   Do you have a source for acquiring assistance with computer problems?

                _____ Yes   _____ No

Please explain:

_____
_____
_____
_____

VI.   ADMINISTRATIVE STRUCTURE SUPPORTING TECHNOLOGY UTILIZATION

31.   Is there an adequate planning process for users to communicate their information and technology needs within the financial institution?

                _____ Yes   _____ No

32.   Please state any other concerns and issues related to the strategic information systems planning process.

_____
_____
_____

Figure 3.2
Sample Contents of an MIS Policies and Procedures Manual

I.   Systems Development
      •   Project Control
      •   Program Change Procedures
      •   Systems Development Standards
      •   Software Acquisition Standards
      •   Programming Standards
      •   Testing Standards
      •   Systems Implementation
      •   Software Maintenance

II.   Documentation
      •   Documentation Standards
      •   Systems Documentation
      •   Programming Documentation
      •   Operations Documentation
      •   User Documentation
      •   Purchased Software Documentation
      •   Librarian Control & Maintenance of Documentation

III. Operations
      •   Control of Storage Media
      •   Equipment Maintenance
      •   Scheduling of Personnel
      •   Contract Services
      •   Output Distribution & Control

IV.   Security
      •   Security Plan
      •   On-Line Security
      •   Program Security
      •   Emergency Procedures
      •   Building Security
      •   Computer Room Security
      •   Vault Security
      •   Data Security
      •   LAN/WAN Security
      •   Checks & Negotiable Forms
      •   Backup and Contingency Planning
      •   Insurance
      •   Records Protection and Retention

CHAPTER 4
INFORMATION REQUIREMENTS

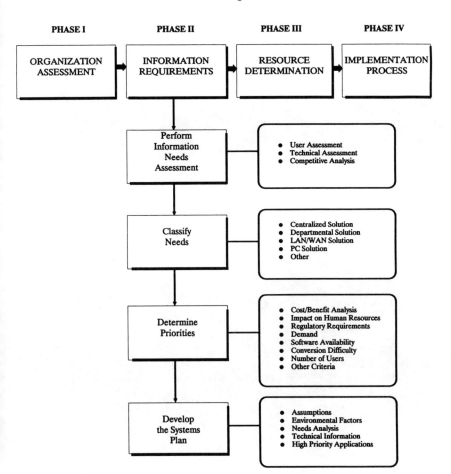

PHASE I	PHASE II	PHASE III	PHASE IV
ORGANIZATION ASSESSMENT	INFORMATION REQUIREMENTS	RESOURCE DETERMINATION	IMPLEMENTATION PROCESS

Perform Information Needs Assessment
- User Assessment
- Technical Assessment
- Competitive Analysis

Classify Needs
- Centralized Solution
- Departmental Solution
- LAN/WAN Solution
- PC Solution
- Other

Determine Priorities
- Cost/Benefit Analysis
- Impact on Human Resources
- Regulatory Requirements
- Demand
- Software Availability
- Conversion Difficulty
- Number of Users
- Other Criteria

Develop the Systems Plan
- Assumptions
- Environmental Factors
- Needs Analysis
- Technical Information
- High Priority Applications

4 INFORMATION REQUIREMENTS

The second phase of the information systems planning process involves an evaluation of the financial institution's information requirements. During this phase, the planning effort focuses on assessing current and future information needs in supporting the management and operation of the organization. During this process, an overall information architecture and systems plan for the financial institution should be developed and refined. This phase requires an analysis of the present applications being processed, potential future application, which should be considered for automation, current and future equipment requirements, file sizes and storage requirements, computer usage estimates by application area, and the procedures involved in operating various financial institution systems.

PERFORMING INFORMATION NEEDS ASSESSMENT

In developing the financial institution's future information architecture, individual departmental needs should be evaluated in an effort to identify their functional objectives and requirements. Information needs can best be determined by working with key management and user department personnel in identifying functions and capabilities that are needed to help them perform their daily work. Information may be needed to:

- Facilitate the decision-making process (i.e., management activities); or,
- Assist in operational activities.

In Chapter 3 of this book, the following assessments of current application systems were described:

- User assessment   An assessment of the "condition" of application systems from the users' perspective.

- Technical assessment   An assessment of the internal "condition" of application systems from a technical perspective.

- Competitive analysis   A comparison of application systems to features available from turnkey software providers.

The user assessment helps answer the question,

> *"How well do existing application systems satisfy management, operational and departmental needs?"*

The user assessment forms the foundation of the needs assessment process by identifying strengths and weaknesses of current application systems. If the user assessment process did not yield detailed lists of required and desired functions, features, and capabilities, then this information will need to be obtained at this point in the planning process from one of the following sources:

- Application survey questionnaires.
- Management and user interviews.
- Function lists, which may be available from outside consulting firms or turnkey software vendors.
- Financial industry publications.

The question is often asked,

> *"How can a user know what to ask for without knowing what is available?"*

This points to the fact that the interviewer(s) must have a broad knowledge and exposure to applications and systems generally available in the financial industry and also be knowledgeable about data processing and technology trends. The interviewer(s) can prepare for this process by researching vendor information, reading current industry publications, attending seminars, conferences, and trade shows. Having several persons involved in these activities can be beneficial because each person may provide a different background and experience level during the process. The net cumulative knowledge base of all participants will tend to grow significantly as the project progresses and alternatives are identified, researched, and analyzed.

Also, the involvement of outside, independent financial industry consultants in the interview and needs assessment process can significantly reduce the time and effort involved in investigating alternatives. The qualifications of the consultant and the consulting firm should be known and references of similar systems planning engagements should be checked before engaging outside involvement.

Vendors can also be used in this process, with the caveat that most vendors will recommend their own solution. However, if the process is closely monitored, some benefit can be obtained from this type of involvement. Turnkey vendors may perform initial analysis and assessment activities at no charge, with the hope that they will be considered as a potential solution.

Several different analyses of currently automated applications can be performed. The planning team should determine which of the following analyses will be most useful in the current operating environment of the financial institution.

- Data usage analysis

    The data usage analysis lists various groups of information and indicates the major users of that information. This analysis should help identify the need for additional on-line workstations or perhaps identify systems that could be departmental in nature versus organization-wide. It may also indicate data that are not generally used or data that may be provided from multiple sources.

•   Function/organization analysis

The function/organization analysis lists major business functions and identifies the organizational entities that perform those functions. This analysis helps identify important business functions and the ultimate authority for executing each function.

•   Function/system analysis

The function/system analysis lists major business functions and identifies the degree of automation of those functions as well as the automated systems that support each function. Functions are generally classified as fully automated, partially automated, or manual. This type of analysis can help identify areas where additional automation may be appropriate.

•   Function/data analysis

The function/data analysis identifies the business functions that are responsible for creating and maintaining information within the organization. Ideally, no data should be created by more than one business function or its integrity could be in question. This implies that the business function is the "owner" of the information and, therefore, responsible for its integrity.

•   Data flow analysis

The data flow analysis should indicate the relationships between data and business functions. Certain groups of data represent the "inputs" to a particular business function. Likewise, that data is an "output" from some other business function.

•   System/organization analysis

The system/organization analysis identifies the number of users of each application system in each organizational entity. It is also useful in identifying systems that could be local or distributed in nature.

- System/data analysis

    The system/data analysis identifies major groups of data and the level of support in obtaining that data by major application area. This, in combination with the function/system analysis, could help identify additional capabilities that are not currently automated.

One of the more difficult aspects of information needs identification is the potential limitation of traditional boundaries. As an example, financial information systems traditionally are classified by "standard" application modules, such as:

- Demand deposit accounting
- Savings accounting
- Certificates of deposit accounting
- Installment loan accounting
- Mortgage loan accounting
- Other application systems/modules

Traditional application design techniques used account numbers as the primary access path into deposit or loan information. Why not? After all, item processing systems were also account-number driven. Therefore, all functions within these application areas tend to be account-number dependent--that is, inquiries, financial transactions, file maintenance, etc.

Yet, when financial institutions realized that information in a different format was needed for marketing additional services to present customers, the ability to determine account relationships and to market by household became important.

"How many account holders live at a particular address on average? Who are they?"

"Which DDA account holders also have CDs or IRAs with our bank?"

"How many account holders with total deposit balances in excess of $10,000 also have safe deposit boxes with us?"

"How many mortgage loan customers also have deposits with us?"

Yet this information was not readily available because of the account-number orientation of past systems. Then came an interim solution from the vendors--the Central Information File (CIF) module. The CIF module can eliminate the redundancy of storing the same name and address information for persons with multiple accounts with the financial institution. It can also assist in "cross-selling" services by indicating other account relationships within the financial institution. In addition, it can provide a single statement listing the status of all accounts on one monthly statement.

What is wrong with this? CIF systems are still account and/or name driven. The financial industry needs more than this to assess the performance of its marketing efforts in its local or regional markets. The industry needs more than this to evaluate the cost of services and the productivity of its labor force.

What is needed? System designers need to have a vision beyond the traditional uses of information technology in the financial environment. Future systems and applications must be able to:

- Integrate information with other systems.
- Provide multiple (and perhaps unknown at the time of design) access paths to that information.
- Provide ad hoc reporting for the nontechnical user.
- Allow movement of data to and from other vendor platforms.
- Allow user-defined information to be stored relating to each customer and/or transaction.

These are just a few of the capabilities that should be considered as part of the information architecture during the planning process. Traditional application designers may not foresee the variety of needs that information systems must deliver in the next 5 to 10 years. But they should design systems with the flexibility to address those future requirements.

The output from the needs assessment process should be a list of desirable functions, features, capabilities, and reports categorized to the degree possible by application area. Some items on the list may be very broad, such as a "household marketing database," while others may be quite descriptive, such as a special report requirement for the mortgage loan application.

Information system needs may or may not be provided by current systems. Some needs may be met through the use of ancillary or ad hoc systems or manual systems and ticker files. However, each requirement should be reviewed and evaluated to determine:

- Potential for automation
- Estimated costs of automation
- Anticipated benefits (quantified, where possible)
- Alternative processing methods

This evaluation will assist the planning team in prioritizing needs at a later point in the process.

CLASSIFYING NEEDS

Information system requirements can be obtained from a variety of sources and/or platforms. It may be useful to classify the various needs using the following major categories:

- Centralized solution
- Departmental solution
- LAN/WAN solution
- PC solution
- Other solutions

1.   **Centralized Solution**

Application requirements with higher volumes, large numbers of users, and significant storage requirements may best be satisfied by a centralized solution. This includes some of the "traditional" application areas, such as deposits, loans, etc., that can best be addressed by a centralized system because of the large number of users and heavy resource requirements in processing large transaction volumes.

The centralized solution may be a mainframe computer system for larger financial institutions or a midrange system for moderately sized organizations. Most introductory midrange systems have sufficient growth capability to handle the needs of a smaller institution in a cost-effective manner. For the purposes of this discussion, we are considering a service center solution as a centralized solution, as well as in-house systems or facilities management alternatives.

If the centralized system appears to be the most appropriate solution, the individual information requirements should be further classified as:

- New application or system.
- Major or minor software enhancement to existing systems. For example, enhancements requiring more than 100 hours of programming time are usually classified as major enhancements.
- Potential software package acquisition.
- Probable internal development. Certain needs are unique and can only be satisfied by special programming since turnkey application systems may not be readily available to meet this need.

Multiple classifications will occur using this scheme; that is, requirements may be part of a new application, but the application may be developed internally.

2.   Departmental Solution

Some applications may be used only by a particular department. For example, a fixed asset package or a lockbox application may be used only by one department within the financial institution. Consequently, a departmental solution may be appropriate. Again, the level of transaction activity and the need for computing resources will dictate whether this departmental solution is a mainframe or a midrange system.

In some larger financial institutions, departmental systems are often installed for MCIF, mortgage servicing, trust accounting, or other similar applications. The need for multi-department access to this information may indicate the level of equipment that could be used to satisfy the application requirements.

3.   LAN/WAN Solution

The LAN/WAN solution may be appropriate for generalized software packages that support basic office functions. Some examples of these are:

- Electronic spreadsheets
- Word processing
- Database management systems
- EMail (Electronic Mail)

This architecture could also provide the computing resources for departmental and/or organization-wide solutions. However, the availability of application software may impact the feasibility of using a LAN/WAN in this capacity.

LAN/WAN alternatives are often used for platform automation applications and will continue to be used as "gateways" into mainframe and midrange centralized solutions.

4.   PC Solution

Many needs can be satisfied for individual users by using PC technology. If the use of PCs appears to be the best solution, the need should be further classified as:

- Electronic spreadsheet
- Word processing
- Database management system
- Specialized package

PCs and LAN/WAN alternatives are also quite adaptable in using file transfer capabilities, downloading centralized information for further manipulation to meet specific departmental needs. File upload capabilities are often used in file maintenance activities or special application processing, such as budgeting.

5.   Other Solutions

Several other potential solutions are available, including specialized proprietary hardware and/or software for stand-alone functions (e.g., teller functions, research, optical scanning, etc.). Also, combinations of several types of processing may be used in some situations. For example, a service center may upload item processing files from a financial institution's back office system and transmit spooled print files back to the financial institution after mainframe processing. The print files may be sent to the back office system, a LAN server, an optical disk system, or a PC.

The above discussion indicates that a variety of factors leads to the classification of specific applications by type of platform. Realizing that an application can be delivered on small systems or large systems, several factors may affect how it is classified, including:

- Transaction volumes
- Number of users
- Location(s) of users
- Storage requirements
- Output requirements
- Complexity of systems
- The need for ongoing maintenance and technical support

Transaction Volumes

Although internal speeds of microcomputers have increased dramatically during the past 5 to 10 years, applications that process high-transaction volumes are still better suited for the mainframe and midrange computer environments. These systems, with their ability to multi-task, multi-process, multi-program and dynamically allocate resources, offer the sophistication necessary to serve the needs of medium to large financial institutions. Today's mainframe systems use a series of processors to handle independent, but interdependent, tasks--all managed by very sophisticated operating software. Some processors handle complex communications tasks while others are dedicated to storage management.

The operating software for these systems contains complex algorithms that schedule and allocate resources as needed and set processing priorities. The operating software monitors processing, tracks resource usage, reports exception conditions, performs self-diagnostics, tracks hardware failures, and, in some cases, bypasses faulty circuitry when hardware errors are detected.

The difference in application design and related transaction volumes becomes apparent when reviewing the capabilities of turnkey banking systems versus systems designed for the thrift industry. Banking systems tend to be high-volume, transaction-oriented systems. Items are captured in batches during and following the business day by large, high-speed item-capture equipment, which then transmits an electronic file to the centralized system for batch processing and updating. These systems have the appearance to the casual user of being on-line, although most are "memo post" systems which are actually updated during end-of-day processing. Batch processing is not an obsolete technique--especially as it applies to high-volume transaction processing applications.

Thrift systems, which tend to be designed to capture items over the counter, update master files in a real-time mode at the time of entry, rather than in batch at the end of the day. These systems typically cannot handle the transaction volumes involved in bank processing, since each over-the-counter and ATM transaction updates master files at the time it is processed.

Number of Users

The number of users will significantly impact the level of hardware required to support the operating environment of the financial institution. Although the number of users is important, because it directly correlates with the number of ports (i.e., connections for workstations and printers) that are offered by hardware manufacturers, it is not the only factor. The manner in which the workstation is used is also important.

A workstation that is on-line but not in use may require less systems resource than a heavily used workstation. Likewise, a workstation connected to a smaller application system may require less resource (i.e., smaller memory requirements) than the same workstation connected to a larger, more complex application.

Equipment manufacturers have established theoretical limitations on the numbers of workstations and printers that can be supported by one model versus another. Factors, such as the target market, competitive systems, costing and pricing considerations, etc., impact their decision to limit peripheral devices for one model or another. These factors also impact whether a computer system is "field upgradeable" or has to be "swapped out" with a larger replacement unit. But, ultimately, the number of on-line users and the type of use will impact systems performance and response time--which impacts the level of hardware necessary to meet application and system requirements.

Location(s) of Users

Similar to the number of users, locations of users will also impact the level of hardware needed to process various application systems. Hardware manufacturers have also placed limitations on the number of remote users that can be connected to each model of computer. Some systems require separate lines for each remote workstation and printer, while others use a multiplexing scheme, where multiple workstations and printers are connected to a remote control device on a single line, which is periodically polled by the mainframe system. Whether the user is located across town or in another part of the world is usually not relevant, although costs for dedicated communications lines may be considerably higher in the second case. However, the number of remote users versus local users could impact hardware requirements.

A second area that could impact level and type of hardware relates to the location of computer operations personnel. Many data centers are moving toward "lights out" operations, in which the computer hardware is located in a dimly lit, protected room miles from the operations staff that runs the systems. This is possible now because of "channel extension" capabilities offered by several vendors. This capability allows peripheral equipment that is needed for normal computer operations, such as tape drives, printers, and operator consoles, to be remotely located. This eliminates the distance limitations of the past, when these devices had to be located within several feet of the central processor(s) and disk drives.

The implications of this from a computer operations and contingency planning standpoint are very important. Computer systems can now be located in geographically "safe" areas--out of earthquake zones and away from hurricane-susceptible locations. Operations staff can be located in low-cost employment markets and/or next to user department personnel to facilitate better support. If a disaster strikes the data center, operations staff could, through line re-routing services, operate computers at a hot-site without needing to relocate.

Storage Requirements

Storage requirements are typically a function of three characteristics:

- Transaction activity;
- Complexity of the transaction; and
- Amount of transaction history to be maintained.

Transaction activity is the volume of transactions. Financial institution transactions are higher at the end of the week and end of month. Large financial institutions typically have higher transaction volumes than small financial institutions.

Complexity of the transaction is the amount of detailed information maintained within the transaction. A financial transaction may have an account number, a date, and the debit or credit amount. Some financial transactions also have the ID of the data entry person, the workstation ID, the general ledger account(s) impacted by the transaction, etc. Text typically requires more space to store than numeric information--hence, older systems used numeric codes in an effort to save storage space to indicate what is described in text today.

The amount of transaction history maintained equates directly to mass storage requirements. For example, if a financial institution processes 10,000 items per day and is open six days per week, this equates to 3.1 million transactions per year. If each transaction requires 90 bytes (or characters) of storage, then 281 MB (million bytes) of storage will be required to store a full year's history. If a service center processes for 100 financial institutions, then it is relatively easy to understand why they purge detailed transactions after each monthly statement run or charge a considerable fee for maintaining additional detail on-line.

Computer technology now allows numeric and alphanumeric data to be compressed. Software packages are available to further compress data. Newer file storage techniques do not require the same disk space to store a five-digit number and a ten-digit number in a similar field of a record. Modern disk access is many times faster than previous technologies, and disk storage devices are extremely reliable. In conclusion, disk storage is currently inexpensive in comparison to past technology and other systems cost. Although it is a factor in the level of hardware necessary to process an application, it is fast becoming a nonfactor.

Output Requirements

Larger computers can attach greater numbers of printers than smaller computers. Some large systems use specialized on-line or off-line laser printers for output production. Some large data centers use hydraulically lifted, roll-fed paper containing the equivalent of 70,000 sheets of paper per roll, feeding multiple printers that are programmatically controlled to fold and cut each report. These huge printers are attached to conveyor belts, which move printed output across scanners to the proper output distribution bins. Hard copy reports have been replaced with microfiche, which is being replaced with optical disk technology. Each of these new technologies requires greater computing power, whether through stand-alone, dedicated systems or mainframe processors.

Complexity of Systems

The complexity of an application system will vary with the sophistication of its users. Financial institutions that were introduced to a "basic" computer system or service center soon developed an understanding of the system's capabilities and its lack of functionality. The next time a system was considered, the list of required and desired features became longer--because the user was more sophisticated and knew what to expect and what was needed to do the job more efficiently and effectively. More complex applications generally cost more to develop and require greater computing power to process.

The Need for Ongoing Maintenance and Technical Support

The relationship between application complexity and computing power is similar to the relationship of complexity and the need for ongoing maintenance and technical support. The more complex an application, the more effort will be required to support the application. The need for technical support can be caused by the following reasons:

- "Bugs" or fixes.
- Enhancements requested by users of the application.
- Changes to meet regulatory requirements.
- Improvements for more efficient operations.

Program "bugs" more frequently appear in new application software and the quantity of bugs is usually inversely related to the degree of testing. The availability of enhancements and improvements is related to the following factors: the user group, the industry, and the quality of the vendor who develops and maintains the software. A program with 10,000 lines of source code may be much more difficult to maintain than a program with 2,000 lines of code. The learning curve and the relearning curve influence this fact. Programming languages influence the level of effort required to maintain programs as do the implementation of standards and level of documentation. But whether a program is written in a fourth-generation language or developed using CASE tools, more complex applications generally require greater effort to maintain, and they require more computing resources to run.

DETERMINING PRIORITIES

Both automated and manual applications need to be prioritized based on user need, potential cost/benefit, impact on personnel resources, conversion difficulty, software availability, projected growth and other criteria. The 80/20 rule is a good approach in that 80 percent of the high-priority applications usually result from 20 percent of the needs. The priority list, subject to short-term review and change, becomes the systems plan.

Several methods can be used in setting priorities. The planning team should identify the method(s) to be used prior to initiating the process. If the process "feels good" at its conclusion, then no adjustments will be necessary. However, if the intuitive sense of the group is that the priority-setting method has not helped the organization arrive at the proper answer, then changes must occur. This may seem like adjusting the equation to obtain the right answer, but the team should realize that the right answer may vary with the situation and timing.

The following criteria may be used in setting architectural priorities:

- Perceived value by the user.
- Impact on functions, people, processes, and data.
- Probability of successful implementation.
- Demand.
- Costs.
- Impact on profitability.

Perceived Value by the User

The perceived value by the user in solving the business problem or in automating the application area can be based on user interviews, survey questionnaire responses and follow-up interaction. Users may have direct costs in mind that relate to:

- Fees for internal/external services that are purchased to provide this information.
- Direct labor hours involved in performing the activity at normal salaries plus benefits.
- Direct labor hours involved if the function is not performed but would have to be performed to obtain the information.
- Subscriptions to publications or database services providing this information.
- Costs potentially associated with the delay in hiring additional personnel to perform the task.
- Potential costs to modify an existing system--by contract programmers, the software vendor, or internally.
- Potential costs to purchase a turnkey system, including hardware and software, to meet the specific requirement.

Similarly, the user may consider the intangible benefits of having the information, including:

- Improved decision-making capability.
- More efficient management reporting.
- Potential productivity improvements.

Intangible benefits are difficult to quantify, but may considerably impact the value to the user.

Impact on Organizational Entities, People, Business Processes, and Data

The several analyses described earlier in this chapter can assist in identifying the impact of an application system or a major change on the organization. The impact can affect:

- Individual organizational entities or departments
- People
- Business processes or functions
- Data

An example of determining impact using these factors is described below:

> *We find that 6 departments and 32 people are impacted by this information requirement. Twelve business processes and four classes of information (data) are also impacted by not having this information on a timely basis.*

The greater the impact on the entities described above, then the greater the impact on the whole organization. If the impact is high on the organization, then the priority should be high for the application.

Probability of Success

Unfortunately, not every good idea and recommendation is successfully implemented. The probability-of-success rating considers the probability of acceptance and degree of risk associated with the implementation of a given systems change. Cultural factors will influence this rating as well as the people who will be involved in the implementation process. A good idea may not be implemented if all users do not believe in it. This criterion gives the planning team the opportunity to change priorities because change may not be readily acceptable by all or a part of the organization. The most appropriate approach is to concentrate on the areas that have the most likely chances of success.

Demand

Demand is the degree of need for the change in question. It is typically based on interview responses, number of users affected, and the extent that the proposed change supports the organization's goals and objectives. Demand represents popular opinion regarding the systems change. Without a relatively high demand, there is little need for action on the item in question.

Costs

Costs represent an estimate of the resources required to deliver the desired systems change. While costs may be difficult to estimate, they can be the most influential factor in setting application priorities. A zealous department head can totally redirect the priority setting process with claims of low cost and high benefit.

Whatever technique is used for developing time and cost estimates, the planning team should review the estimates to ensure that assumptions, estimates, and methodology are consistent with the nature of the planning process.

Impact on Profitability

A change that could increase revenues, decrease costs, improve margins, enhance employee productivity, reduce work effort, etc., will have a positive impact on profitability of the financial institution and, accordingly, be a high priority. This, of course, assumes that the proposition is legitimate and that implementation of the recommended systems change is feasible.

DEVELOPING THE SYSTEMS PLAN

Although the financial industry is one of the most automated industries, additional automation of various service areas can positively impact profitability and quality of customer service. However, because of the degree of automation, financial institutions have increased their dependence on automated systems and procedures. One of the goals of management is typically to utilize computer technology within each department to the degree necessary to satisfy operational requirements and, hopefully, reduce the need for additional employees as regulations and other factors influence the type and amount of information that must be maintained. Increased internal and external reporting requirements have expanded the need for more comprehensive application and departmental systems. Many of these information needs can be satisfied in a cost-effective manner through increased use of data processing resources--whether at the department level or through financial-institution-wide systems.

The data processing environment has been subject to rapid change due to technological advances associated with the industry. Because most financial institution budgets are limited and opportunities for cost control continue to consume management's attention, a plan to optimize data processing expenditures within the financial institution is a requirement in today's environment.

Developing the systems plan is the most time-consuming and critical portion of the strategic information systems planning effort. There must be a clear understanding of the financial institution's organizational structure, the various interrelationships of departments, and the existing automated systems that support these functions. The systems plan is a description of the existing and planned application systems, including solutions to needs that appear to be feasible for automation.

Application systems are the driving force behind the strategic information systems plan. Application systems development, implementation, and maintenance are the primary sources of requirements for hardware, software, personnel, and facilities. The term *application system* is used broadly to mean a process for performing a function, exclusive of the computer functions that support the application system.

The systems plan includes the following major components:

- Systems plan assumptions
- Factors affecting the systems plan
- Departmental needs analysis
- Supplemental technical information
- High-priority applications

1.   Systems Plan Assumptions

It is important to document the assumptions used in developing the systems plan. Some typical assumptions that should be carefully analyzed in the planning process are described below.

- **Centralized planning and control**

  Assumption: *Centralized planning and control is necessary for implementation of future technologies within the organization.*

  Planning and control as well as the development of overall policies and procedures that impact the entire organization may be easier to implement with a centralized approach. Specific tasks that can be coordinated and accomplished better with a centralized approach could include:

-      Establishing, modifying, and approving the
       contents of annual systems plans.

-      Developing a financial-institution-wide plan by
       documenting, accumulating, and prioritizing
       information system needs.

-      Reviewing project proposals and major
       equipment changes.

-      Considering and contracting for outside services
       as appropriate.

-      Reviewing security and control considerations.

•   **Centralized MIS function**

Assumption: *A centralized MIS function is*
                               necessary to support the
                               information system needs of the
                               organization.

Application systems typically cross departmental lines of
authority and responsibility. One department may be
responsible for establishing new accounts, while another
department actually enters financial transactions that
affect that account.

A centralized MIS function can provide the following
advantages:

-      Developing standards and procedures for
       feasibility studies, programs, documentation, and
       operating policies relating to the MIS function
       and monitoring adherence to these standards and
       procedures.

-      Monitoring staff development activities in
       information systems and arranging for necessary
       training programs.

-      Reviewing, on a continuing basis, the conduct
       and progress of major projects.

- Acquiring, maintaining, and providing specialized staff expertise for the appropriate departmental areas.

- **Centralized technical support**

Assumption: *Systems design, development, implementation, and maintenance activities for application systems should be centralized.*

Some organizations assign specific technical personnel to each department from a centralized pool of resources to support specific departmental requirements. The major advantages of centralized technical support include:

- Better utilization of personnel. A larger pool of technical personnel could be available to staff projects and to better match their skills with specific project needs.

- Capability to attract and retain competent MIS staff. A larger group can provide more career path options and opportunities for advancement.

- Better opportunity for specialization. Although cross-training is important in minimizing the organizational impact following the loss of key personnel, technical personnel can develop specialist roles in such areas as communications, systems programming, performance analysis, security, disaster recovery, etc.

- Facilitate backup of critical functions in the event of employee turnover or separation.

- Opportunities to develop applications that serve more than one department.

- Easier to develop and monitor adherence to standards for system, programming, operations, and user documentation and to monitor adherence with established programming standards and change controls.

- Lower number of total technical specialists will be required as the group can support the needs of several departments.

- The purchase cost of special-purpose software, such as performance measurement tools, systems software, application software, etc., can be spread among several departments.

• **Mainframe system(s)**

Assumption: *The mainframe system(s) will be the primary processing platform for financial-institution-wide applications.*

An investment in time and dollars may have been incurred in the development and enhancement of the organization's mainframe system. The system may continue to meet the needs of financial application processing into the foreseeable future, especially as the primary hardware manufacturer introduces upgrade options that have superior performance at lower or similar costs. Most mainframe computers have a variety of microcomputers accessing mainframe databases, and departmental systems are generally available, and meet specific departmental needs.

• **Decentralized hardware**

Assumption: *Decentralized hardware, such as departmental systems, LANs, or PCs, will be considered in satisfying departmental needs when economically feasible.*

Advantages of using decentralized systems include the following:

- Certain applications are processed more cost effectively on smaller systems using intelligent workstations or microcomputers (e.g., spreadsheets, word processing, desktop publishing, graphics, etc.).

- Microcomputers and LANs have the capability to access mainframe systems, to download information from the system for more specific processing, and to process low-volume applications that may not be cost-justified on the mainframe system.

- Greater user control of hardware resources within the department.

• **Local area networks**

Assumption: *Local area networks will be implemented to facilitate shared usage of hardware resources and software and form the basis for additional automation in the platform and teller areas.*

To support planned automation, the addition of microcomputers is typically required. Most financial institutions also consider implementation of local area networks. A local area network environment will facilitate shared usage of software and peripheral equipment, such as printers, and potentially form the foundation for future application automation in such areas as teller and platform functions.

• **Turnkey software packages**

Assumptions: *Use of turnkey software packages should be considered to meet application requirements when available and cost-effective.*

For in-house alternatives, packaged software should be considered where possible. A variety of turnkey packages exist on several hardware "platforms" that offer full functionality in most financial institution application areas. In addition to institution-wide applications, other packaged software alternatives exist to meet specialized departmental requirements. Many of these applications use PCs that do not require the resources available on the mainframe system.

If the financial institution believes that an application must be customized to fit specific requirements, then the availability of the program's source code is important when choosing the best alternative. Because of the effort required to design, program, test, document, train, and implement custom versions of major applications, the development of custom software should be approached cautiously. Figure 4.1 contains sample packaged software selection criteria.

Following are some major advantages and disadvantages of packaged software versus custom software:

Advantages

- Packaged software typically offers a wide variety of functions and features that may not be easily programmed or modified by an internal support staff.

- Turnkey software for financial institutions is readily available on a variety of hardware platforms.

- Costs for packaged software may be moderate compared to the effort involved in custom development.

- Software changes and enhancements are typically provided as part of the ongoing license or support fees.

- Ancillary software modules may be available from the supplier that interface with the primary software applications.

- The time frame for implementation of packaged software could be shorter than custom development of the application.

- Documentation for packaged software tends to be higher in quality than documentation of internally developed software.

-    Software customization, training, and
     implementation could be provided by the vendor.

Disadvantages

-    Packaged software may not offer specific
     functions that may be necessary for the financial
     institution's operations.

-    Some packaged software is written for older
     hardware and operating environments and may
     not take advantage of current hardware and
     operating software architecture.

-    Some packaged software vendors will not
     provide the source code for program
     customization. Also, some vendors will not
     support program source code that has been
     modified.

-    Packaged software may offer functions and
     features that will never be used by the financial
     institution.

-    Packaged software may have to be modified to
     interface with internally developed systems.

-    The financial institution may have to rely on the
     software vendor for ongoing support and
     enhancements. Economic viability of the vendor
     could be a concern.

-    A large financial institution could consume the
     somewhat limited resources of smaller software
     vendors.

-    Packaged software typically requires ongoing
     license fees.

2.   **Factors Affecting the Systems Plan**

A number of cultural and environmental factors may significantly
impact the systems plan. Some factors may be recognized as
constraints due to the current position of the organization
financially or competitively. Other factors were identified in the
strategic planning process, either in the mission statement or
elsewhere. These factors should be identified where possible.
Following is a list of possible factors that may directly or
indirectly impact the systems plan:

- National economic conditions, including such factors as
  interest rates, industry growth or decline, level of
  unemployment, population growth or decline, and other
  factors.
- Local economic conditions, addressing locally sensitive
  factors, such as area trade, transportation, housing starts,
  availability of business development funds, local
  unemployment, etc.
- Local marketing conditions, including such factors as
  customer segments served, opportunity for increased
  market share, competitive environment, typical customer
  profiles, and customer wealth.
- Factors within the organization, such as staffing
  availability, organization structure, ownership structure,
  autonomy of branch or operations within the holding
  company.
- Current or future regulatory climate, including regulatory
  changes, political attitude toward the industry, etc.
- Financial status, including availability of funds, liquidity,
  investment yields, margins on products and services,
  profitability, etc.
- New technologies and their degree of implementation
  within the financial industry. As cost-effective tools are
  developed, their application at the financial institution
  and branch level can be assumed. Such technologies as
  imaging, systems integration, client/server architecture,
  etc., will undoubtedly impact the planning process.

Other factors may also impact the direction and content of the systems plan, including:

- Top management's vision, philosophy, values, and priorities, which ultimately will guide future direction and actions. This may also be reflected in the mission statement of the strategic plan.
- The image the financial institution would like to project in the community.
- Current and future products/services that will be provided by the financial institution.
- Desired market share, growth, and profitability as indicated in the strategic plan of the financial institution.

3.   **Departmental Needs Analysis**

In the beginning of this chapter, several different approaches in identifying departmental needs were discussed. The results of these analyses should be summarized in the systems plan. Although the format of the needs analysis will vary with the type of information obtained, the following components are most often present:

- Department name
- Description of need:
  - Cause of the problem
  - Problem result
  - Value/cost estimated by the user
  - Suggested solution
- Status (i.e., in process, pending, etc.)
- Indication whether the need is maintenance or enhancement of the existing system
- Application system affected
- Degree of complexity (major, moderate, minor)
- If a new system, the probable source for obtaining the system:
  - Internal development
  - Package acquisition
- If a PC or LAN solution, the probable generalized software tool to be used:
  - Database management system
  - Spreadsheet
  - Word processing
  - Special program--internal development
  - Special program--package acquisition

- Need for mainframe or departmental system interface
- User department(s) affected

4.   Supplemental Technical Information

The systems plan should contain summary information relating to the key aspects of the MIS function. This should include the following summary information:

- Application programming time analysis
- Summary of existing applications
- Summary of current MIS projects
- Summary of planned application systems

Application Programming Time Analysis

If the MIS function does not record their time as a part of normal project management procedures, then the planning team may want to determine how technical staff members are utilizing their time. This time analysis may impact opinions regarding the level of maintenance on some application systems. If maintenance time is significant or is increasing at a high rate, then this may indicate that the application(s) should be replaced or rewritten.

Other information that may result from the time analysis includes the following:

- Certain department(s) may be consuming the majority of programming resources.
- Programmer productivity may vary widely within the MIS function or between the MIS function and similarly sized MIS operations in other financial institutions.
- Operational problems may consume an inordinate amount of programming time, which is also an indicator of program or design problems.
- Adequate resources may not be assigned or dedicated to new systems development efforts, indicating that new systems that could significantly impact operational or departmental productivity are not being adequately addressed.

- User requests may be backlogged due to the inability of current staffing levels to complete assigned tasks and address new departmental requests. The net effect of this is that user departments become discouraged with the responsiveness of the MIS function and may search for departmental solutions to the problem.

The time analysis should be performed in sufficient detail to provide the planning team with the information needed to assess the work habits and productivity of the MIS technical staff. The analysis should cover a time span in which a variety of projects and tasks were started and completed. This may be a three- to six-month period--the longer the analysis, the better the information. The analysis should include the following basic information:

- Hours expended by application and within the application by the following activities:
  - Systems design
  - Program coding, compiling, and debugging
  - Conversion
  - Testing
  - Training
  - Documentation
  - Implementation
- Hours expended by department
- Hours expended on administrative tasks
- Changes from the previous year

Comparisons to budgeted hours may be appropriate if the MIS function works with more formal hour and expenditure budgets.

Summary of Existing Applications

A list of current applications should also be developed as supplementary information in the systems plan. Included with this list is the following information:

- Application name
- Primary programming language(s)
- Number of programs within the application
- Database management system
- Resource requirements (i.e., amount of memory, on-line storage, etc.)

- Anticipated resource requirements (in 5 years)
- Major interfaces with other applications
- Source--internally developed or software vendor
- Date written, implemented, or purchased
- Dates of significant changes
- Platform application runs on
- Application dependencies on software or hardware
- Normal hours of on-line activity
- Processing mode (i.e., real-time, memo post, batch, etc.)
- Number of users
- Primary department(s) using the application

Summary of Current MIS Projects

A list of current MIS projects should be obtained for the systems plan. The list should differentiate between general support activities, enhancements, and new development projects. Following is a sample of the information that should be summarized:

- Project number
- Project title
- Requesting department
- Estimated hours
- Category of activity (i.e., enhancement, maintenance, etc.)
- Current status
- Other factors affecting implementation (i.e., additional hardware, software, etc.)

The progress of the MIS function in addressing the current backlog of user requests should be closely monitored. The backlog should be at a sufficient level to allow proper planning for daily programming activities; however, too large a backlog may result in untimely response to user requests.

Summary of Planned Application Systems

A summary of planned application systems should also be developed and included within the systems plan. This summary should describe the purpose of the system, if not self-explanatory, and include the following information:

- Status
- Description of need
- Value (i.e., potential revenue or decline in costs anticipated)
- Priority
- Recommended approach

The description of need may list the specific functionality that the system is intended to include. The recommended approach may include whether the system will be purchased or internally developed and a description of the platform the system will operate on.

5.   High-Priority Applications

Based on the priority-setting criteria set earlier in the planning process, high-priority applications should be identified. The following criteria were described earlier in this chapter:

- Perceived value by the user
- Impact on functions, people, processes, and data
- Probability of successful implementation
- Demand
- Costs
- Effect on profitability

Additional criteria may also be relevant to the process, including:

- Development time
- Implementation time
- Training effort
- Conversion difficulty
- Impact on staffing levels
- Level of user need
- Potential benefit
- Effect on organization growth
- Software package availability
- Data commonality with existing systems
- Systems interrelationships
- Regulatory requirements

The high-priority applications may require additional hardware, systems software, application software, networks, staffing, and facilities. These requirements may in turn suggest new information systems management policies and procedures. The planning team should consider the interdependencies of the various projects and identify a sequence for their implementation. It may be beneficial to identify the criteria that will be used in setting application priorities and assigning points to each criterion. Alternatively, it may be easier to rate the criteria as high, medium, or low for each application or project need. Points can then be assigned to replace the high, medium, or low rating.

The applications or needs having the highest cumulative points, considering all evaluation criteria, then become the highest-priority applications. This method, of course, gives equal weight to each criterion, which may not be in accordance with the financial institution's strategic plan. If higher emphasis should be placed on certain criteria, such as effect on profitability or growth, then weighted criteria can be used in determining application priority. Total scores can then be determined by multiplying the weighted value of the criteria times the ranking.

The planning team should identify projects with the fastest payback. These may be small, simple, and independent projects that can be accomplished quickly and easily with high return and minimal risk. This approach is especially beneficial because these projects promptly demonstrate the value of the planning process.

Figure 4.1
Packaged Software Selection Criteria

Each type of software application will have unique requirements and considerations. However, the following criteria should be considered when evaluating software packages.

Criteria Description	Required	Desired	Optional
A. Requirements Definition			

Prior to the evaluation of a software package, the requirements of the system should be carefully documented and include:

1.   Outputs to be produced by system:

    a.   Reports:

	Required	Desired	Optional
• Information to be contained on report			
• Format of report	_____	_____	_____
• Method of report generation:	_____	_____	_____
- Paper	_____	_____	_____
- Displayed on terminal	_____	_____	_____
- Graphic representations	_____	_____	_____
• Time frame of report:			
- Monthly	_____	_____	_____
- Weekly	_____	_____	_____
- Daily	_____	_____	_____
- On demand	_____	_____	_____
- Etc.	_____	_____	_____

    b.   Other outputs:

	Required	Desired	Optional
• Special forms	_____	_____	_____
• Notices	_____	_____	_____
• Etc.	_____	_____	_____

Figure 4.1 (Continued)
Packaged Software Selection Criteria

Criteria Description	Required	Desired	Optional
2. Inputs to be provided:			
a. Sources of data.	_____	_____	_____
b. Format of data.	_____	_____	_____
c. Volumes of data.	_____	_____	_____
3. Calculations to be performed	_____	_____	_____
4. Software features, functions and capabilities	_____	_____	_____
5. General requirements:			
a. Budget considerations.	_____	_____	_____
b. Systems software considerations (if using existing hardware):			
• Operating system	_____	_____	_____
• Programming language	_____	_____	_____
• Database management system	_____	_____	_____
• Data communications monitor	_____	_____	_____
• Etc.	_____	_____	_____
c. Interface considerations:			
• Compatibility requirements with other software	_____	_____	_____
• Compatibility requirements with other hardware	_____	_____	_____
d. Equipment considerations (if using existing hardware):			
• Internal memory	_____	_____	_____
• Disk	_____	_____	_____
• Tape	_____	_____	_____
• Printer	_____	_____	_____

Figure 4.1 (Continued)
Packaged Software Selection Criteria

Criteria Description	Required	Desired	Optional
e. Processing mode:			
• Batch	_____	_____	_____
• On-line	_____	_____	_____
• Interactive	_____	_____	_____

B.   Software Evaluation

Following the preparation of the requirements definition, appropriate software may be located that appears to satisfy the requirements. Packages and vendors should be evaluated using the following criteria:

1.   Functionality

	Required	Desired	Optional
a. Internal controls provided within the system (i.e., input, processing and output controls).	_____	_____	_____
b. Inputs consistent with requirements.	_____	_____	_____
c. Computational capabilities consistent with requirements.	_____	_____	_____
d. Outputs consistent with requirements.	_____	_____	_____
e. Audit trails and transaction registers provided.	_____	_____	_____
f. Error checking and validity testing.	_____	_____	_____
g. Reports contain:			
• Organization name	_____	_____	_____
• Report title	_____	_____	_____

Figure 4.1 (Continued)
Packaged Software Selection Criteria

Criteria Description	Required	Desired	Optional
• Column heading descriptions	___	___	___
• Processing date	___	___	___
• Page numbers	___	___	___
• Subtotals	___	___	___
• Grand totals	___	___	___
• Numeric data fields properly formatted (e.g., decimal point, commas, sign, etc.)	___	___	___
• Data should be right or left justified as appropriate	___	___	___

h. Report options:

	Required	Desired	Optional
• Available on request (user initiated)	___	___	___
• Different sort sequences	___	___	___
• Selection of a desired range of data	___	___	___

i. Use of special forms minimized. ___ ___ ___

2. Security

a. Package provides means to prevent unauthorized access. ___ ___ ___

b. Package restricts access to certain program procedures and functions. ___ ___ ___

3. Flexibility

a. Capability to change report formats and headings. ___ ___ ___

b. Capability to change screen layouts. ___ ___ ___

Figure 4.1 (Continued)
Packaged Software Selection Criteria

Criteria Description	Required	Desired	Optional
c. Capability to fit current environment without significantly changing current manual procedures (software should adapt to needs, not vice versa).	_____	_____	_____
d. Capability to expand capabilities to meet future needs.	_____	_____	_____
e. Operational flexibility during periods of system failure.	_____	_____	_____
f. All tables stored on external files, accessible to the user to allow for changes without requiring program recompilation.	_____	_____	_____
g. Record layouts should provide for future expansion without increasing the record size (approximately 20%).	_____	_____	_____
h. Software modularity and ease of upgrade.	_____	_____	_____
4. Performance			
a. Terminal response time.	_____	_____	_____
b. Throughput speed.	_____	_____	_____
c. Memory required for optimum results.	_____	_____	_____
d. Disk storage required for present and future volumes.	_____	_____	_____
e. Redundant data should be minimized.	_____	_____	_____

Figure 4.1 (Continued)
Packaged Software Selection Criteria

Criteria Description	Required	Desired	Optional
5. Ease of Operation	_____	_____	_____
a. Menu driven.			
b. Menu items arranged in a logical sequence.	_____	_____	_____
c. Use of cursor prompting.	_____	_____	_____
d. Detailed operator instructions displayed on terminal.	_____	_____	_____
e. Help messages.	_____	_____	_____
f. Sufficient error messages.	_____	_____	_____
g. Capability to bypass menus.	_____	_____	_____
h. Use of preformatted forms for data entry.	_____	_____	_____
i. Date fields in consistent format (MM/DD/YY).	_____	_____	_____
j. Capability to have data entry fields automatically default to a specific value (e.g., date fields should default to the system date when appropriate).	_____	_____	_____
k. Data fields should be entered in the same sequence as arranged on the source document.	_____	_____	_____
l. Display screens should be properly formatted (e.g., field descriptions and properly formatted numeric fields).	_____	_____	_____

Figure 4.1 (Continued)
Packaged Software Selection Criteria

Criteria Description	Required	Desired	Optional
m. Consistent data entry routines.	_____	_____	_____
n. Consistent use of field names and abbreviations.	_____	_____	_____
o. Capability to move cursor:			
• Forward to next field	_____	_____	_____
• Backward to previous field	_____	_____	_____
• Top of screen	_____	_____	_____
• Bottom of screen	_____	_____	_____
p. Capability to easily correct errors.	_____	_____	_____
q. Multiple file keys used appropriately.	_____	_____	_____
r. Turnaround documents used appropriately.	_____	_____	_____

6. File Controls

Criteria Description	Required	Desired	Optional
a. The system should provide an audit trail from program to program.	_____	_____	_____
b. There should be control totals on amount fields and record counts by transaction type.	_____	_____	_____
c. The process control summary should be easy to identify, read, and understand.	_____	_____	_____
d. Appropriate totals and messages should be displayed on the console.	_____	_____	_____

Figure 4.1 (Continued)
Packaged Software Selection Criteria

Criteria Description	Required	Desired	Optional
e. All input/output file sequences should be checked.	_____	_____	_____
f. Control records should be included in each master and transaction file as appropriate.	_____	_____	_____
7. Edit Features			
a. Editing should generally be performed by one program at the beginning of the processing rather than performed by several programs throughout the system.	_____	_____	_____
b. New input data should be completely edited and verified.	_____	_____	_____
c. Each field should be edited for as many error conditions as practical.	_____	_____	_____
d. Errors should be properly designated so that an error condition can be quickly and easily identified in the output.	_____	_____	_____
e. Errors should prohibit further processing.	_____	_____	_____
f. The system should facilitate correction of errors.	_____	_____	_____
8. Processing Features			
a. The first and last records should be properly processed.	_____	_____	_____

Figure 4.1 (Continued)
Packaged Software Selection Criteria

Criteria Description	Required	Desired	Optional
b. Calculation results should be correct for high and low values.	_____	_____	_____
c. Division routines should check for a zero divisor.	_____	_____	_____
9. Reports			
a. All numeric fields should be sign-controlled.	_____	_____	_____
b. Cents and units positions should be zero-suppressed.	_____	_____	_____
c. The current date should be on all reports.	_____	_____	_____
d. There should be provisions for preprinted forms alignment.	_____	_____	_____
e. There should be proper controls included for prenumbered documents.	_____	_____	_____
f. Checks should be check-protected utilizing asterisks to precede dollar amounts.	_____	_____	_____
g. Zero-balance or negative checks should not be printed.	_____	_____	_____
10. Console Messages			
a. Operator intervention should be minimized.	_____	_____	_____
b. Console messages should be short, concise and easy to understand.	_____	_____	_____

Figure 4.1 (Continued)
Packaged Software Selection Criteria

Criteria Description	Required	Desired	Optional
c. Responses to console messages should be easy to enter.	_____	_____	_____
11. Documentation			
a. Installation manual.	_____	_____	_____
b. User manual.	_____	_____	_____
c. Tutorials.	_____	_____	_____
d. Reference cards.	_____	_____	_____
e. Input forms.	_____	_____	_____
f. Source code (as appropriate).	_____	_____	_____
g. Backup procedures.	_____	_____	_____
h. Restart procedures.	_____	_____	_____
i. System documentation.	_____	_____	_____
j. Program documentation.	_____	_____	_____
k. Operator instructions.	_____	_____	_____
l. Structured programming techniques.	_____	_____	_____
12. Vendor Consideration			
a. Software developer:			
• Financial stability, longevity and strength	_____	_____	_____
• Number of installations	_____	_____	_____
• Support provided	_____	_____	_____

Figure 4.1 (Continued)
Packaged Software Selection Criteria

Criteria Description	Required	Desired	Optional
• Update services provided	_____	_____	_____
• Capability to provide modifications	_____	_____	_____
• Date of first installation	_____	_____	_____
• Maintenance of program logic errors (bugs)	_____	_____	_____

b.   Local representative:

Criteria Description	Required	Desired	Optional
• Financial stability	_____	_____	_____
• Number of installations of the product	_____	_____	_____
• On-site training provided	_____	_____	_____
• Classroom training provided	_____	_____	_____
• On-site support provided	_____	_____	_____
• Telephone support provided	_____	_____	_____
• Capability to provide modifications	_____	_____	_____
• User references	_____	_____	_____
• Installation services provided	_____	_____	_____
• Availability of local user groups	_____	_____	_____
• The number, type, and experience of local staff	_____	_____	_____

13. Mainframe Considerations

	Required	Desired	Optional
a. Type of data communications line and line adapter.	_____	_____	_____
b. Type of terminal.	_____	_____	_____
c. Compatible with other special systems software requirements.	_____	_____	_____

Figure 4.1 (Continued)
Packaged Software Selection Criteria

Criteria Description	Required	Desired	Optional
14. Cost			
a. Initial one-time costs.	_____	_____	_____
b. Annual support contracts.	_____	_____	_____
c. Maintenance costs.	_____	_____	_____
d. Modification costs/hourly rates.	_____	_____	_____
e. Training cost.	_____	_____	_____
f. File conversion cost.	_____	_____	_____
g. Forms and supplies cost.	_____	_____	_____
h. Discounts available.	_____	_____	_____
i. Software license fees.	_____	_____	_____
15. Contract Considerations			
a. Terms of payment.	_____	_____	_____
b. Software licenses/copyright.	_____	_____	_____
c. Capability to operate on multiple CPUs.	_____	_____	_____
d. Trial periods/guarantees.	_____	_____	_____
e. Vendor maintenance and enhancement policy.	_____	_____	_____
f. Acceptance testing provisions.	_____	_____	_____
g. Warranty restrictions.	_____	_____	_____
h. Vendor training.	_____	_____	_____
i. Contract monitoring.	_____	_____	_____

CHAPTER 5
RESOURCE DETERMINATION

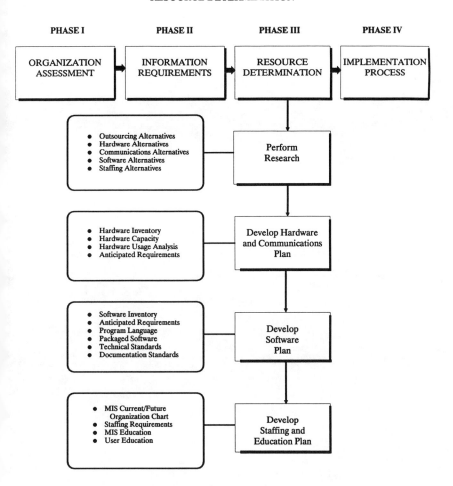

5 RESOURCE DETERMINATION

The third phase of developing a strategic information systems plan includes research and analysis of the service center and/or in-house hardware, software, data communications equipment and lines, personnel, and costs necessary to implement the needs and application requirements prioritized in the systems plan. The hardware, communications, software, staffing, and education elements of the plan are usually developed simultaneously, based on extensive research and analysis activities.

PERFORMING RESEARCH

Before completing the remaining elements of the strategic information systems plan, research should be performed in the following primary areas:

- Hardware alternatives
- Communications alternatives
- Software alternatives
- Staffing alternatives

Given the background information obtained during the MIS assessment, the planning team should be aware of the limitations, if any, of the current hardware and software. An investigation of alternatives should be undertaken to help determine the most cost-effective means to deliver and implement the high-priority application needs identified in the systems plan.

Hardware Alternatives

Identifying hardware alternatives may not be the first item on the agenda because software generally determines the hardware platform and operating environment. However, several options are available, depending on the assumptions in the systems plan and the direction of the planning team.

Alternatives to Consider

The process of evaluating alternatives should include a comparison of the financial institution's current technology capabilities with various alternatives that are available in today's marketplace. The comparison could result in the following options:

*   Continue with the present system, with no significant change in hardware or application software.
*   Upgrade the present hardware, assuming changes in the central processor, memory capacity, disk subsystem, operating system, teller equipment, etc., but no significant change in application software.
*   Replace current systems with hardware and/or fully featured turnkey software for the primary application areas.
*   Use a service center to process the majority of the organization's transactions.
*   Contract with a facilities management firm to operate the internal data processing function.

Each of these alternatives offers a number of advantages and disadvantages as well as complicating issues related to personnel requirements, teller equipment interfaces, communications requirements, disaster recovery backup, etc. Following is a summary discussion of the major alternatives identified above:

1.   Continue With Present System

The first alternative is to continue with the present system with little or no change in hardware, operating software, or application software.

Advantages

*   Assuming a present in-house MIS function, this alternative offers minimal organizational change or personnel displacement. The MIS function could remain intact and continue to support the organization as it has in the past.

- Assuming that no hardware or operating software upgrades are imminent, annual recurring costs could continue at their present levels, which may be lower than other alternatives.
- No conversion would be required.
- User department personnel would not have to be retrained.

Disadvantages

- Application software may continue to lack functionality in comparison to software currently on the market. This may be especially true if present software has been internally developed.
- The present computer system may not provide the financial institution with sufficient hardware growth for future years.
- Hardware maintenance rates may continue to escalate, and some components may no longer be supported by the present hardware vendor.
- The hardware vendor may no longer support the operating system, communications software, or other systems software presently in use.
- The financial institution may continue to be dependent on key technical personnel for support of internally developed application systems.

2.   Upgrade Present Hardware

If the organization's present computer hardware and operating software are not up-to-date or are at capacity limits, they could be replaced with the most current models or releases available. With this alternative, the following minimal changes could be considered:

- Replace the central processor with the latest model or upgrade the system to a faster, higher-capacity model.
- Replace the disk subsystem with smaller, higher-density units.
- Replace the teller equipment with the latest-generation equipment.

- Upgrade the operating software to the latest release levels.

Advantages

- The upgraded system may provide the organization with sufficient hardware growth for the future, with minimal upgrades.
- Present application systems could be enhanced to take advantage of improved hardware capacities and increased capabilities.
- The present MIS function or technical support staff could remain intact and continue to support the organization with a minimal learning curve.
- Annual recurring costs may be able to be reduced because of lower hardware maintenance, restructured software license fees, and reduced power requirements.
- Conversion to new hardware may require minimal effort in comparison to conversion to new software or to a service center.
- User department personnel will not need retraining, since application software will continue to operate in the same manner.

Disadvantages

- Application software may continue to lack functionality in comparison to software currently on the market. This may be especially true if present software has been internally developed.
- The financial institution may continue to be dependent on key technical personnel for support of internally developed application systems.
- The costs to upgrade hardware and/or operating software may be significant, with little additional benefit in functionality and capability.

3.   **Replace Present Hardware and/or Software**

A third systems alternative is replacement of present systems with new hardware and/or software. However, if the financial institution is presently using a certain brand and model of computer system and wants to continue using that vendor's hardware platform, the number of potential software packages available for evaluation may be limited.

Advantages

*   New application software may offer improved functionality.
*   Changes needed to meet regulatory requirements could be provided as part of the annual support and license fees from a turnkey software supplier.
*   Application software enhancements designed to meet current industry trends or demands may also be provided.
*   Program maintenance activities by internal MIS staff could be reduced so that time is available to satisfy custom user requests.

Disadvantages

*   The present MIS staff may have a considerable learning curve in becoming knowledgeable in new hardware and application software.
*   Both one-time and annual recurring application software costs could increase from their present levels.
*   The financial institution may become dependent on one or more outside vendors for support of hardware and/or software.
*   A considerable conversion effort may be required.
*   User department personnel will need training on the new systems.

4.   Service Center Processing

A fourth alternative involves processing the majority of the
financial institution's data through a regional or national service
center. All branches and departments could be on-line to a
service center, supported by high-speed data communications and
a remote technical support staff.

The service center would have the responsibility for maintaining
application software and providing enhancements to meet
industry changes and regulatory requirements. Typically, the
service center would provide all data communications with the
organization's main facilities, branch locations, and ATM
network. This may be through traditional dedicated leased phone
lines or through satellite communications, depending on the
servicer.

Advantages

- Data center operations are the responsibility of the
  vendor (personnel, scheduling, backup, multishift
  operations, etc.).
- Internal technical support requirements will be minimized
  with this alternative.
- Disaster recovery responsibilities are shared between the
  financial institution and the service center.

Disadvantages

- Costs are typically based on transaction and account
  volumes. Therefore, costs will increase as transaction
  volumes increase. However, some service centers offer
  fixed-priced contracts, which may allow for limited
  transaction growth.
- Costs tend to increase substantially when special reports
  and custom requests are not part of the base system.
- Costs are typically tied to inflationary factors and tend to
  escalate over time.
- Smaller financial institutions may have little influence
  over enhancements and the future direction of larger
  servicers.

- Requests for changes may require more time to fulfill than they would with in-house systems.
- A considerable conversion effort may be required.
- User department personnel will need training on the new system.

5.   **Facilities Management**

One of the more popular services available is facilities management (FM) or outsourcing. With a facilities management arrangement, a third-party vendor assumes the responsibilities of the organization's internal MIS function and operates the institution's data center. The vendors provide training for departmental personnel, customization of programs and special reports, enhancements to meet industry changes and regulatory requirements, and all other operational types of services.

Many vendors are willing to use a financial institution's existing technical staff to support operations because of their familiarity with the organization and its personnel.

Facilities management tends to be a higher-priced alternative and is usually available only to larger financial institutions. However, several start-up FM firms appear to be interested in approaching financial institutions with smaller asset sizes.

Advantages

- Facilities management could provide a financial institution with the advantages of an internal MIS function without the administrative responsibilities inherent in its operation.
- FM firms typically provide state-of-the-art application software, since many of these vendors are software suppliers or service centers.
- FM firms will provide fixed-rate arrangements with longer-term contracts.

Disadvantages

- Facilities management costs tend to be higher than costs of other alternatives available to financial institutions today.
- Most FM vendors are interested in providing service to larger financial institutions.
- A considerable conversion effort may be required.
- User department personnel will need training on the new system.

Communications Alternatives

The data communications subject is very complex, but several basic principles should be known when selecting communications alternatives. To send information from one location to another, a transmission device, a receiver, and a transmission medium are necessary. The medium may be a pair of wires, a fiber-optic cable, or the earth's atmosphere.

Two types of transmissions are used in data communications: analog transmissions and digital transmissions. Analog signals use tones to represent data and are continuous in form. The signals tend to fade over longer distances and must be re-amplified along their transmission path. Analog signals can tolerate a moderate degree of distortion or "noise" without losing their message.

Digital transmissions occur in discrete steps or pulses. The signals are seriously impacted by distortion and must be regenerated along the transmission path. Because of this regeneration process, distortion is eliminated, rather than amplified as with analog signals. Analog signals have been the dominant form of data communications in the past, primarily because of low cost, but digital transmission methods are becoming less expensive and more popular, offering greater capacities than analog transmission.

A number of data transmission facilities or routes may be available for consideration, for communicating between the mainframe system and the various financial institution locations, including:

- Leased lines (or nonswitched facilities)
- Dial-up (voice grade) lines (or switched facilities)
- Packet switching

- Microwave communications
- Fiber-optic cable
- Satellite communications

Leased lines are permanent telephone lines connecting two locations. They are generally installed when the line will be used for several hours during the business day. Leased lines are often "conditioned" to compensate for the noise and distortion that may be encountered over public lines. This will ultimately reduce error conditions when data is transmitted from one location to another. Leased lines allow faster transmission of data because of the higher-quality lines, usually 9600 to 48000 bits per second, although faster line speeds are certainly available. Leased lines may be analog or digital and are billed, typically, at a fixed-rate monthly fee.

Dial-up lines are usually voice-grade public lines, such as the lines used during a typical telephone conversation. They are analog or digital lines that go through central switches and can, therefore, be used by a number of parties. Each party is charged based on the length of the call. Dial-up lines are most frequently needed when the connection is relatively short in duration or if the line will have a relative low daily usage. Dial-up lines are less expensive than leased lines. Although line speeds are generally less than those provided by leased lines, usually in the range of 2400 to 9600 bits per second, the quality of telephone circuits and modems has allowed much faster line speeds than in the past.

Packet switching is a service that is provided by various common carriers. Through a packet switching network, data is transmitted in groups of characters, with control information at the beginning and end of the transmission. The control information and data represent the entire packet. The contracted carrier routes the packet through the most efficient path to its destination. The path taken may vary for each packet sent. Consequently, the packet must be numbered so it can be properly disassembled and interpreted at the destination location. Packet switching is most often used for computer-to-computer communications, rather than computer-to-terminal communications, and it is very protocol sensitive.

Microwave communication is actually point-to-point radio transmission. This communication method has become more viable because of equipment cost reductions and technology innovations. Also, this communication technique has become more justifiable since leased-line costs are incurred over extended periods of time versus higher front-end costs for microwave communications for the radio transmitter and receiver--each mounted on a tall building or tower. To be effective, various financial institution locations that intend to use microwave communications must be in "line-of-sight," with no obstruction between facilities or microwave towers. Microwave tends to be less expensive than fiber-optic communication, yet it still allows a wide bandwidth of communications.

Fiber-optic cable offers a significant increase in capacity over copper-based wire. A fiber-optic cable allows a thousandfold increase in the number of calls over what can be carried on copper wire with the same dimensions. With today's technology, signals can be transmitted at a rate of 1 billion bits per second over hundreds of miles without regenerating the signal. Line noise is significantly lessened with fiber-optic cable, and it also offers improved security.

Satellite communication is typically accomplished through geosynchronous communication satellites. It requires an earth station at the source and at the destination of the transmission. The satellite receives, amplifies, and retransmits the transmission to the earth station(s). Satellite communication is typically found in point-to-point communications networks or in point-to-multipoint configurations. More organizations are using satellite communication technology because of the decreasing cost of small earth stations and the high bandwidth capability of the communication method, which allows large amounts of data to be transmitted. To provide for adequate security of these transmissions, the signals should be encrypted.

Wiring and Communications Considerations

When wiring the facility, computer room, and/or office work areas, it is necessary to consider the type of cable that should be used. Some technicians prefer twisted pair; others prefer coax; while some more astute technicians prefer fiber-optic cable. The decision regarding the type of wire to use will be impacted by its relative expense. However, the financial institution should ensure that the wire selected will meet current needs as well as future business requirements. Today's needs may be met with twisted pair, but tomorrow's needs may require greater capacities and speed, so fiber-optic cable may be a better solution. Wiring often lasts longer than the equipment to which it is attached. Industry experts suggest that if a major wiring job is necessary, use fiber-optic and copper cable. You may not need the fiber-optic capacity and speed initially, but, with changes in office technology, it may be needed in the future. Other suggestions include the following:

•   Buy modular equipment whenever possible. In this way it can be changed with minimum disruption to other network components and preserve the investment in current wiring and equipment.
•   Work with a vendor that offers a varied product line and has flexible upgrade policies. This may help to minimize future costs as upgrades are required. If possible, set the price for a future upgrade at the time the order is approved.
•   Document the communications network. The original communications specialist who installed the network may not be available or employed at the time changes are needed. Good network documentation and wire labeling techniques will save considerable time and cost in the future.

The quality of the power in the communications network should also be considered. Central backbone circuits should be supported by an uninterruptible power supply (UPS), which can provide alternative power in the event of short-term power fluctuations or outages.

Wires and Cables

Because most data communications networks have attempted to use voice communications wiring as a cost-reduction technique, twisted-pair is most often used, since this is the type of wiring installed by telephone companies for the last several decades. More expensive coaxial cabling has been used when longer distances or higher speeds are necessary for the connection. Fiber-optic cabling is the newest technology used in communications networks, but also the most expensive alternative. These three types of connecting technology are briefly described below.

• Twisted-Pair Wiring

Twisted-pair wiring has been used the longest period of time. This wiring consists of two (insulated) wires which are literally twisted together. Because of its size and low cost, twisted-pair wiring is most popular. It is very flexible wiring which can be manipulated easily into small spaces. Since only two wires are present, data flow is typically in one direction at a time (i.e., half duplex). It also is quite easy to join two twisted-pair wires together, since only two wires are present.

Twisted-pair wires are usually made of copper or aluminum because of the low resistance of these materials. The wires are used in nearly every home and business. Several thousand twisted-pair wires can be bound together to form a cable for communications between buildings or floors in a building.

• Coaxial Cable

Coaxial cable actually consists of two concentric circles. The inner circle is a conductor, or rod, and is centered inside the cable. It is wrapped by insulating material and surrounded by an outer circle, or pipe, which maintains an opposite charge. The pipe is then further insulated around its exterior. Because of this design, coaxial cable is somewhat self-insulating with the inner signal gravitating toward the outer conductor and vice versa. It is therefore less susceptible to electromagnetic interference.

Coaxial cable can carry higher frequencies of broadband communications, which is its principal advantage over twisted-pair wiring. However, coaxial cable is more susceptible to electronic eavesdropping than twisted-pair wiring because the negative charge is carried on the outer conductor, and it is not grounded. Terminals using coaxial cable require certain alterations to meet government requirements (i.e., Tempest specifications) against electronic eavesdropping.

Coaxial cable cannot be spliced together as easily as twisted-pair wiring. Connectors must be used which clamp over the ends of the cable. They are then screwed together or inserted into one another, depending on the type of connector. Coaxial cable is heavier in construction which makes it more difficult to handle when wiring in tight places.

• Fiber-Optic Cables

Fiber-optic cables consist of small transparent fibers, each surrounded by a layer of glass or quartz which is in turn surrounded by a protective coating. Each cable may consist of approximately a dozen fibers, which are glued together and covered with tape and joined by approximately a dozen similar groups of fibers. The resulting cable then consists of approximately 144 fibers, each at least 10 times faster than coaxial cable but only a half-inch in diameter.

Similar to twisted-pair and coaxial cable, repeaters must be placed at various points in the circuit to repeat the signal before its strength is diminished. The input light source sends analog waves or digital pulses of light down the fiber to a receiving unit that is either a repeater that renews the signal or a receiver which converts the light signal back to an electromagnet i.e., signal for input to the computer or device. The principal advantages of fiber cabling are its speed, clarity, and capacity. The principal disadvantages of fiber cabling are its cost, the cost of repeaters, and its limited flexibility.

Software Alternatives

Once the level of equipment is generally identified, the planning team should refer to published information that describes the prices of hardware and the availability of "industry-oriented" software packages. Information of this type is published by a variety of sources, including:

- Datapro Research Corporation
- Auerbach Publishing
- ICP Directories
- Data Sources
- Various other software selection tools

The planning team may also be able to obtain this information from:

- Hardware and/or software vendors
- Trade publications
- Trade associations
- Consulting firms
- Other financial institutions

From this information, approximate systems costs can be identified and used in developing the hardware and software plans. In addition, these sources can be used to help identify specific products that should be considered and general capabilities of the software. See Chapter 8 for additional information on evaluating and selecting application software.

Staffing Alternatives

The choices available related to staffing include:

- Assign present staff
- Allocate additional internal staff
- Hire additional personnel
- Use vendor personnel
- Subcontract with a third party

Assigning to Present Staff

When reviewing present staffing levels and assignments, consider that most systems projects require a combination of user department personnel and technical personnel. "Ownership" for the project and ultimate project direction should come from the user or operational side of the organization. To have technical personnel lead a new systems project is one of the pitfalls of project management. Since the user department will be the entity that will provide conceptual design criteria, create the database of information, test the completed system, and maintain its information, they should lead the project.

Using present staff to perform activities relating to the systems plan assumes that they have the time available for additional work. While present staff will have less learning curves than new employees or outside contract personnel, the time required for implementation of high application priorities will most likely be longer.

Allocating Additional Internal Staff

A second approach to staffing is the allocation of additional internal staff to the projects at hand. This is especially workable if the organization is seasonal or if some departments, for whatever reason, are temporarily overstaffed. Again, the learning curve in becoming familiar with the application or information needs may be minimized, especially if the individuals involved have had prior experience in other departments in the organization. The pitfalls may be similar to the first alternative-- project implementation may be longer because it still relies to some degree on personnel who have other job responsibilities. Also, allocating additional staff to technical positions will not be successful without sufficient education, training, and experience.

Hiring Additional Personnel

Hiring additional staff can be time-consuming but beneficial if the qualifications are carefully identified and applicants are carefully screened. Technical positions can most easily be filled in this manner in more populous geographical areas that have high concentrations of automated systems. Financial industry experience is a key factor in hiring technical and nontechnical personnel. The financial industry is unique in its requirements and handling of information. The normal sources of recruitment, such as local newspaper advertising, use of recruiting companies, and word-of-mouth through existing employees, can be effective. Unemployment in certain parts of the country may be significantly higher than in others. Likewise, some financial institutions have laid off considerable numbers of personnel due to mergers, acquisitions, cost controls, or takeovers. These geographical areas could have the best supply of workers looking for an opportunity.

Using Vendor Personnel

When a strong relationship has been built with a particular hardware and/or software vendor, then the use of vendor personnel in staffing systems-related projects may be appropriate. This may also be an alternative as a new vendor is selected to provide hardware and software as part of the implementation plan. The use of vendor personnel is particularly advantageous because they (the vendors) may have included the cost of this in their proposal or may be willing to provide this service in the hope of obtaining future business. Vendor personnel also have the advantage of knowing their hardware and/or software better, therefore the learning curve should be minimized in working with and training internal technical personnel. The best place to use vendor personnel is in technical roles rather than roles with nontechnical responsibilities, unless the vendor has certain customer service or support personnel who have experience in the operations of financial institutions.

Subcontracting With a Third Party

Subcontracting for outside services with a qualified third party may also be an attractive solution for staffing. Systems projects require heavy involvement for relatively short periods of time. The use of contract services personnel allows the financial institution to limit their costs to the period of contract or until the systems are implemented. Employee hiring, separation, administration, benefits, and management are responsibilities that can be provided as part of the package by the contractor.

A number of consulting firms specialize in providing project management services or in providing personnel for technical positions, such as systems analysts and programmers, over the duration of a systems project. Some consulting firms specialize in particular platforms, programming languages, and database management systems. Their involvement could result in successful implementation of turnkey or custom-developed systems in the shortest possible time frame.

DEVELOPING THE HARDWARE PLAN

The hardware plan should be based on projections of transaction volumes for current systems, information on present projects in process, and information on new systems and applications from the systems plan. To properly relate to each other, the hardware, communications, software, staffing, and education plans should be developed concurrently.

Recognizing that most computer product lines will be replaced within five years by a new product offering that has greater speed, capacity, and capability for less cost, then a computer system should not be purchased at the end or near the end of its life cycle unless justified by substantial savings.

The hardware plan should identify hardware-related assumptions that may have been stated in the systems plan or were developed as the planning team researched hardware alternatives. The assumptions or strategies within the hardware plan could relate to the following topics:

- Agreement on a specific hardware manufacturer and a statement of the reasons. Some reasons that may be relevant include the following:

    - A wide range of products to meet organization and departmental requirements.
    - High level of maintenance support.
    - Strong presence in the marketplace.
    - Strong financial performance.
    - Investment in existing application software, which may not be readily transportable to other vendor platforms.
    - Investment in current hardware, especially in peripherals that are not compatible with other hardware alternatives.
    - Investment in operating software, environmental software, database management software, etc., which would not be transportable.

- Consideration of "plug-compatible" mainframe hardware because:

    - Costs may be significantly less.
    - Performance may be improved.
    - Peripheral devices may be compatible.
    - Service levels may be adequate.

- Identification of departmental systems needs that would not necessarily be met by the mainframe system, but could be met by departmental systems. Some considerations are:

    - Information may not be needed across departmental lines.
    - Sensitive data could be better secured in a departmental system.
    - Interface requirements with other systems could be minimal.
    - No other departments may perform similar operations.
    - A variety of techniques are available to transfer data to and from other systems.

•   Phaseout of existing technology due to a variety of factors. These
         factors could include:

         -       Downsizing or rightsizing may be the most economical
                 alternative for the organization.
         -       New application systems could be more efficiently
                 developed on other, more current platforms.
         -       Some applications could be processed on PCs, LANs, or
                 smaller departmental systems.
         -       The current technology may not be compatible with
                 primary systems configurations or with future
                 architectures.
         -       Internal controls may be weak with existing systems.
         -       Technical support may be waning for the existing system.
         -       Past technology may be too time-consuming and costly
                 to support.
         -       Older hardware may not be able to perform with the
                 same reliability as newer systems.

The hardware plan should include the following schedules:

•   Hardware acquisition history
•   Current hardware inventory--mainframe system
•   Current hardware inventory--departmental systems
•   Current hardware inventory--workstations and printers
•   Current hardware inventory by department--PCs
•   Current hardware usage and capacity analysis
•   Anticipated computer capacity and requirements--mainframe
         system
•   Anticipated computer requirements--workstations and printers

The plan should contain suggestions relating to current equipment,
identification of the future architecture priorities, judgments relating to the
source of hardware, management's preference toward lease or purchase
of certain components, suggestions relating to the performance of
feasibility studies, evaluation and selection projects, and additional
reviews that may be necessary to complete the planning process.

Immediate needs should be identified and some effort should be focused on delivering solutions in areas that could provide faster payback to the organization. This will improve overall acceptance of the plan by its participants and benefit the organization by more immediate productivity improvements and cost-reduction measures.

The hardware alternatives that were considered should be described as part of the hardware plan, with emphasis on the hardware strategies selected. Strategies should be described for the mainframe system as well as departmental or distributed systems. If branch or office automation is to be considered as part of the plan, then the hardware relating to these strategies should be included. Costs of these strategies should also be outlined and consolidated later with other cost elements in the control plan.

DEVELOPING THE COMMUNICATIONS PLAN

The applications to be processed, along with anticipated trends in hardware and software development, permit the building of the hardware and communications segments of the plan. Hardware and communications requirements can be estimated and present equipment can be evaluated in an effort to predict replacement or upgrade of key components.

The communications plan should include the following schedules:

- Current communications hardware inventory by system
- Current communications hardware inventory by department
- Data communications equipment usage analysis

The communications plan should also include a list of communications-related requirements that were identified during user interviews and the needs assessment process. Communications technology should be described as well as the alternatives considered during the research step of this phase. Costs of the selected communications alternative(s) should also be summarized and consolidated later with other cost elements in the control plan.

DEVELOPING THE SOFTWARE PLAN

The software element of the plan should include both existing and anticipated future software requirements. Provisions should be made for evaluation of potential software packages, if appropriate. Technical and documentation standards should also be part of the software plan. It is important to determine the primary programming language(s) for uniformity and standardization.

Several assumptions or strategies could be considered for the software plan, including the following:

*   Mainframe operating software may be a determining factor in future systems implementations. Migration to the more sophisticated operating software may allow greater capability or allow the use of add-on software products that run only in advanced operating environments.
*   Packaged software solutions may receive first consideration before deciding to develop an application internally. The advantages of this approach should also be documented.
*   Primary programming languages may be identified and the evaluation and use of CASE tools for future development projects may be a desirable strategy.
*   Changes in hardware identified in the hardware plan will impact software strategies. A time line should be developed that indicates software changes that are anticipated over the next three to five years.
*   Consolidation of processing from several computers to a single computer may be a strategic direction that will impact the software plan. Likewise, movement to a distributed processing environment from a centralized processing environment will dictate certain software changes.
*   Implementation of branch or platform automation may be considered as a strategy for implementation. Installation of LANs or WANs will also affect the software plan.

- Development and/or implementation of technical and documentation standards may also be a key strategy within the software plan. Technical standards should address program change controls, systems design, systems maintenance, programming, packaged software selection, testing, training, and implementation. Documentation standards should include systems documentation, programming documentation, operations documentation, and user documentation.

The software plan should include the following schedules:

- Software acquisition history
- Current software inventory--mainframe system
  - Operating software
  - Application software
- Current software inventory--departmental systems
- Current software inventory by department--PCs/LANs
- Current software usage analysis
- Anticipated software requirements

The plan should contain suggestions relating to current software, identification of the future application priorities, high payback areas, judgments relating to the source of software (i.e., internally developed or turnkey package) and suggestions relating to the additional studies and evaluations that may be necessary to complete the software planning process. As with the hardware plan, more immediate needs should be identified and some effort should be focused on delivering solutions in areas that could provide faster payback to the organization. Also, software costs should be itemized and carried forward into the control plan.

DEVELOPING THE STAFFING PLAN

The staffing plan is dependent on the systems plan, the hardware plan, and the software plan. The staffing plan should be shorter-term in nature than other segments of the plan. It should provide for systems maintenance activities, enhancement activities, feasibility studies, and new development work. Time should be allowed for training, conversions, research, and planning.

Certain assumptions will be important to the staffing plan, including:

- Percent of time each person can devote to implementation of the systems plan. Time estimates should be included for MIS personnel and user department personnel. Time should be allowed for training, vacations, sick leave, departmental meetings, and other administrative tasks. Additionally, time should be allocated for efforts that may not relate to the systems plan, including time for regulatory changes, maintenance of systems and application software, loss due to turnover, research, and planning.
- Use of outside contractors or vendor personnel for programming services or technical support.
- Assignment of project director(s) for each major project identified in the systems plan. This may be a full-time position. As discussed in earlier chapters, user department personnel should normally have project direction and leadership, rather than the MIS function.

The staffing plan should include the following schedules:

- Current MIS organization chart
- Future MIS organization chart, depicting major functional changes planned during the next 3 to 5 years
- History of staffing changes over the past 5 years
- Estimated personnel requirements based on workload estimates and current capacity for the next 5 years
- Estimated time by function or activity

New positions or functions within the organization should be identified within the staffing plan. A time line for staffing additions will help in its interpretation. Potential staffing changes can occur in the following areas as the organization grows:

- Data and voice communications
- Microcomputer support
- Database management
- Security administration
- Internal audit
- Librarian

- Documentarian (technical writer)
- Production control
- Network coordination

Changes in reporting relationships, if any, should be identified. Also, personnel costs, including benefits and potential pay adjustments, should be itemized and included in the control plan.

DEVELOPING THE EDUCATION PLAN

The education plan is primarily based on the staffing plan, although the other segments of the systems plan will impact it as well. It should provide for both technical MIS education and nontechnical user education. Attaining the skill levels required to successfully design, program, implement, and support the systems plan will require a continuing training and education program for all personnel in the MIS and user departments. The training program for MIS personnel should be designed to provide a logical and well-defined career path. Applications personnel will require additional specialized skills in programming aids and tools, including CASE tools and, perhaps, training in new development methodologies. Most MIS personnel should have training on new systems architecture and changes in hardware and software capabilities. Operations personnel should have the level of knowledge and skill required to effectively support computer operations.

Minimum continuing professional education standards require at least 40 hours per year of industry-related education and training. This minimum is required for most technical certification programs, including:

- CDP (Certificate in Data Processing)
- CSP (Certified Systems Professional)
- CCP (Certified Computer Programmer)
- CISA (Certified Information Systems Auditor)
- CMC (Certified Management Consultant)

If 40 hours per year is a minimum standard, an additional 40 to 80 hours may be required for some technical personnel in the MIS function while the systems plan is implemented. New hardware, operating software, environmental software, application software, program development tools, etc., will require additional educational time commitments by certain technical positions. Eventually, the organization may desire the education repeated for cross-training and backup of key personnel. Less education and training will be required for computer operations personnel than for programming personnel. As new employees are interviewed, the financial institution should consider technical personnel with the qualifications necessary to support the future operating environment of the financial institution.

User department personnel will also require considerable training as new systems are developed or purchased and implemented. Conversion of existing customer files and financial records is normally required, which means that users must have a clear understanding of application capabilities before the conversion effort can begin. One of the major areas of concern during financial institution conversions is ensuring that control file and parameter file options are properly set. Without this assurance, some functionality that was present in a previous system may not be present in a new system. Or worse yet, interest computations or accruals may not be properly calculated.

If a very large training effort is required, most organizations prefer the "train-the-trainer" approach. In this approach, the vendor performs the initial training of higher-level or more-experienced personnel. The training is then repeated by internal personnel with others in the organization. This tends to be one of the most cost-effective methods of performing large-group training. Naturally, the qualifications, experience, and personalities of the initially selected trainers will be a primary factor in the success of the program.

Throughout the process of hiring and transferring personnel into new staffing positions, the necessity for good, clear job descriptions and performance evaluation criteria will be increased. Spending the time initially in defining job responsibilities, reporting relationships, accountabilities, criteria for performance measurement, minimum qualifications, etc., will provide great benefit to new and present personnel. The need for new positions to fit the current compensation program is also very important--not only for the individual, but also for coworkers.

Education and training can be accomplished in several ways:

- Internal presentations
- Self-instruction materials and courses
- Vendor classes
- Outside classes (non-vendor)
- User groups
- Industry publications

A matrix should be developed as part of the staffing plan. The matrix should list all positions on one axis and the various educational subject areas on the other axis. A similar matrix could be developed listing positions and course alternatives. Obviously, some research will have to be performed to identify the various course options and alternatives, including an evaluation of the course content and review of previous course ratings. Effectiveness of the instructors and educational institutes should also be considered as potential training alternatives are reviewed.

The costs for various education and training should be summarized, including probable travel costs. The cost summary should be included in the projected budgets.

CHAPTER 6
IMPLEMENTATION PROCESS

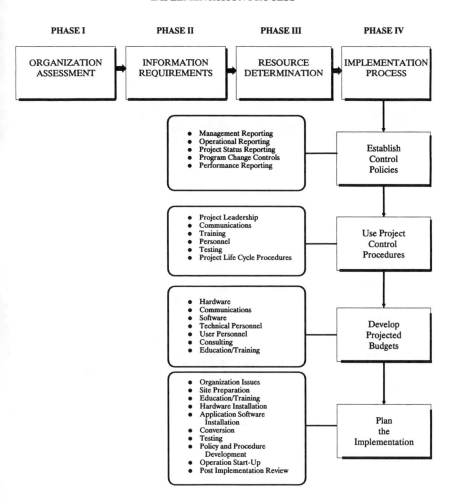

PHASE I   **PHASE II**   **PHASE III**   **PHASE IV**

ORGANIZATION ASSESSMENT → INFORMATION REQUIREMENTS → RESOURCE DETERMINATION → IMPLEMENTATION PROCESS

- Management Reporting
- Operational Reporting
- Project Status Reporting
- Program Change Controls
- Performance Reporting

Establish Control Policies

- Project Leadership
- Communications
- Training
- Personnel
- Testing
- Project Life Cycle Procedures

Use Project Control Procedures

- Hardware
- Communications
- Software
- Technical Personnel
- User Personnel
- Consulting
- Education/Training

Develop Projected Budgets

- Organization Issues
- Site Preparation
- Education/Training
- Hardware Installation
- Application Software Installation
- Conversion
- Testing
- Policy and Procedure Development
- Operation Start-Up
- Post Implementation Review

Plan the Implementation

6 THE IMPLEMENTATION PROCESS

The fourth phase of the strategic information systems planning process includes the policies and procedures for controlling the plan's direction and monitoring actual performance against the plan. The basic components that should be developed during this phase are:

- Control policies
- Project control procedures
- Projected budgets
- Implementation schedule

ESTABLISHING CONTROL POLICIES

The control plan should include the policies, procedures, and techniques necessary to provide management and the planning team with the tools necessary to:

- Control the direction of the project team.
- Monitor the performance of the project team.
- Update the strategic information systems plan.

1.   Management Reporting

The control plan depends on quality management reporting that emphasizes performance evaluation and cost-effectiveness. Management reporting should:

- Indicate results by measuring actual performance against a predetermined standard or plan.
- Be oriented or customized toward the function being measured.
- Cover all functions and activities.
- Predict trends.
- Enable management to anticipate potential problems or unusual expenses.

153

- Be concise and readable, and provide graphical interpretation or presentation when possible.
- Support structural continuity from the lowest level of the organization to top management.
- Be received by management routinely and promptly enough to permit timely corrective action.

An important management report relating to the strategic information systems plan is the project status report. The project status report should indicate:

- Accomplishments during the last reporting period.
- Current status of major tasks.
- Percentage of completion.
- Tasks anticipated for the next reporting period.
- Problems or opportunities.

The percentage of completion should be computed based on either tasks completed or time remaining compared to original estimates. The first method, based on tasks completed, can distort the percentage of completion if less-complex tasks have been completed and major tasks remain. Time estimates, considering time spent and/or time remaining, may provide a more realistic estimate.

More detailed project reporting should also be available for management review, including:

- Tasks completed
- Tasks in process
- Time remaining by task
- Anticipated completion dates
- Assigned responsibilities
- Tasks to be addressed

Project control reports should be generated and distributed at least semimonthly to executive management and team leaders.

Additionally, technical staff time should be summarized on a biweekly, semimonthly, or monthly basis, indicating where each MIS person is spending his or her time. This could be categorized by the type of function (i.e., programming staff, operations staff, communications staff, etc.). Total hours worked by programming staff on identified projects should tie to the project control reports discussed above. Also, programming time used for enhancement and maintenance of existing application software should be identified by application.

2.   Operational Reporting

In addition to management reporting, a number of day-to-day operational reports should exist for use by their functional management. Many of these reports may be available from the current MIS operations reports. These reports help detect trouble spots requiring action and provide capacity utilization trends for long-term planning. They may also be indicators of potential staffing and training needs.

For example, the programming manager should develop and provide the following types of reports:

•   Project control report

        The project control report should show the status of each project, indicating the time estimates for each activity, the targeted completion date, and the accumulated time spent on each activity as of the report date. Some indication of the status of the activity should also be provided. This information may be too detailed for larger projects. In this instance, summary project control reports should be used to provide the above information at the phase level or as it relates to each milestone or deliverable.

•   Change request backlog report

        Some change requests or work orders are not immediately addressed by the MIS function, either because:

        -       Time has not been available.
        -       They may be scheduled for some future date.

-       The project steering committee has not approved the project.
-       Additional information is being obtained so they can be more clearly defined.

The project backlog should be reported and monitored by management to ensure that staffing is at a level that can effectively address change requests in the near future. The backlog reports should indicate the project number, project name, a brief description of the project, estimated hours, impact on existing applications or systems, and probable assignment of responsibility.

The operations manager should develop and provide the following types of reports:

•   Systems downtime report

This report should track systems downtime compared to performance targets, with indication of downtime reason, such as:

-       CPU
-       Peripheral devices
-       Program problems
-       Air-conditioning
-       Power failure
-       Operator error
-       Other causes

•   Rerun report

This report should track rerun time by reason. Rerun time could be defined as the total time required to complete the job less the time used for the last, acceptable run. Another version of this report would identify user-caused downtime, which may be an indication of the need for additional training or an application deficiency. This type of report could help deter, with proper follow-up, systems abuses by on-line terminal users.

• Peripheral performance report

This report should contain the frequency and duration of and reasons for downtime for each peripheral device, This helps to identify failure-prone units requiring service or replacement. This report should cover all terminal devices.

• CPU performance report

A series of reports could be developed that indicate the capacity used versus the capacity available for the CPU.

• Computer utilization summary

This report should indicate available capacity and its use in productive time, downtime, and rerun time. Trends detected in this type of report could aid capacity planning.

• Disk capacity summary

This graphic report should track available capacity versus space allocated. It may be more meaningful if presented by application system with a comparison to prior years.

Other reports that may prove useful include performance tracking of:

• Terminal response time
• Channel utilization
• Communications line failures
• On-line network failures
• Report distribution delays
• Data control errors

USING PROJECT CONTROL PROCEDURES

Although some of the basic tools and reports of project management have been described above, several other factors impact the success of completion and implementation of a major systems project. These factors are grouped in the following major categories:

- Project leadership
- Communications during the project
- Training
- Personnel and staffing
- Testing
- Other factors

Project Leadership

The project and resulting system(s) should provide a number of significant benefits to the organization and its personnel, including the following:

- The project should be a source of pride and accomplishment within the project team and the organization.
- The project should have clearly defined objectives, which are clearly stated and understood by all project and management personnel.
- The project should be completed as close to its original targeted completion date as possible. Otherwise, the time frame for follow-up projects will be extended. Also, one of the most commonly stated problems with MIS projects is that they are not completed on schedule.
- The project team should attempt to follow the strategies common in "joint application development," where users assume ownership of a system and direct or drive the project.
- The system resulting from this work could provide the foundation for a "state-of-the-art" system and become the basis for all future systems.
- Users should be satisfied with the resulting system.

Management and the project team should make every effort to minimize the following potential problem areas:

- Turnover on the project team.
- Roles that are not clearly defined and understood, both within the project team and between the project manager and MIS function.

•   Inexperience at the project manager position.

These factors could contribute to inefficiencies and loss of effectiveness at the management and task level during the project. For example, the learning curve associated with new project team members may create inefficiencies. This may also affect communications with project team members and outside departments.

The project manager should be strong in training skills and personal communications. Strong technical knowledge and skills should also be readily available from the MIS contingent on the team. If additional leadership training is necessary, then this should be obtained prior to beginning the project. More formal training of the project leader can be obtained from a variety of sources, including leadership seminars, audiovisual training courses, or on-site presentations by qualified leadership training instructors. This training does not need to be extensive or time-consuming, but rather at introductory or intermediate levels, depending on the needs of the selected project leaders. Materials provided during these training sessions could be tailored to meet the specific requirements of the systems project.

The involvement of additional qualified personnel at an appropriate level throughout the project will help minimize the impact of staff turnover. This should include attendance at critical meetings, review of correspondence, memoranda, specifications, documentation, and other materials to maintain familiarity with the detailed tasks assigned to various project personnel.

If outside project management personnel are used, the role and responsibilities of the project manager should be documented to the degree necessary to help ensure that responsibilities are clearly understood by all personnel.

Communications During the Project

Throughout the project, various methods of communication can be used, including correspondence, memoranda, status reports (verbal and written), and meetings between project team personnel and with the project leader's functional management. Some of these communications methods may be more successful than others, depending on the individual's communications skills.

Communications can be generally very good if regularly scheduled meetings are held and a conscious effort is made by each party, inside and outside the project team. Unfortunately, communications can suffer due to time pressures or because of a particular person's personality or mode of operation. The net result of this condition could be a feeling of isolation by project team members.

Personnel outside the project team must also be involved in the process or problems could result. If MIS management is uninformed regarding the status of the project, they may not be able to contribute technical and other expertise at the appropriate times during the project. Persons designated as "part-time" project personnel should be included on project-related memoranda and communications if they are expected to contribute at some point in the project.

Likewise, proper communications and coordination with outside departments and committees is important. Hardware, forms, supplies, and outside services may be needed at particular points in the project, and this should be planned for and communicated with the responsible departments.

Communications between organization management and the project team are also important. The project manager should provide regular verbal and written reports to management. Also, management's participation in meetings with the project team may be appropriate when key issues are being discussed or as a morale booster, especially if long hours have been a "norm," rather than the exception.

The need for continuous communications between all parties should be stressed during each major project meeting. Communications should be a standard agenda item. Likewise, the project manager is responsible for continually determining when outside departments and resources should participate in the process.

Because people communicate with others in varying degrees, project management should ensure that team members are comfortable that the proper flow of communications is occurring and that task assignments are understood. A periodic review and assessment by the project manager of team performance will continue to be important. Likewise, organization management should review and assess the project manager's ability to communicate with team members and to meet activity completion dates on a continuing basis.

To ensure the adequacy of communications between functional management and team members who may report directly to these managers, formal status reports should be provided by project management to functional management. The status reports should be prepared weekly, biweekly or semimonthly, and should contain a summarized list of accomplishments or activities during the prior reporting period as well as a list of activities planned during the next two reporting periods. This should assist in identifying part-time project personnel, and other resources, who should be involved in upcoming activities and meetings.

All part-time project personnel should be regularly provided project-related correspondence and memoranda. Part-time project personnel should be included in upcoming activities, following approval of their functional manager, with input from the project manager as appropriate.

Training

Training of user department personnel is as important during the implementation as the design of the system itself. Training sessions should be well-planned and training materials should be designed to meet the desired objectives. Project management should contribute to the planning, review, and implementation of training activities and materials.

Sometimes, training of project personnel prior to beginning the project can save considerable time during the course of the project. Additional training for new programmers on the project team could potentially improve their performance. If new programmers have little or no experience in the development tools to be used, then training is a necessity. The need for technical training for new programmers should be assessed as early in the process as possible so it can be scheduled.

Oftentimes, automated tools may be available, such as an on-line training database, to assist in the ongoing training of new personnel or personnel transferred from one area of responsibility to another. This can represent a significant time savings if employee turnover is particularly high. The on-line training database should contain representative information relating to the functions that can be performed by the system. The training database should be supplemented by a training manual for new employees. Part of the training materials used to train current employees could be adapted for this use.

Personnel and Staffing

Personnel outside the project team need to be accessible throughout the project, especially if they are key sources of information. Project management should keep in mind that the continued pressure to meet project deadlines may ultimately affect employee morale. This could be further intensified by the project schedule which, if not properly estimated, may consider minimal time for sick leave, holidays, and vacations. Project personnel generally work more hours than nonproject personnel, at least for the duration of the project. Hour and staffing estimates should be closely reviewed and approved by the project manager. The project schedule should allow for unidentified tasks and tasks that are concurrent but rely on the same personnel. The interrelationship of tasks should continue to be closely monitored, with sufficient margin for error that the overall project completion schedule can be met.

Staffing levels need to be at an appropriate level, considering the project schedule and related tasks. Underestimating the number of hours required for task completion can significantly impact the project schedule, but it can also impact project team members. Adjustments should be allowed in the project schedule when original estimates are erroneous.

Work load should be spread as equally as possible throughout the project. Some personnel should not be routinely expected to work extra hours to meet or exceed completion dates while others are not. This could apply additional burden and stress on certain project team personnel. Program completion dates should allow for user testing as well as additional programming time because of errors detected during testing. Project management should monitor team activities and individual work loads. They should plan for the involvement of additional full-time or part-time personnel prior to a task becoming "critical" to the successful completion of the project. Project leaders should monitor employee morale to ensure that undue pressure is not concentrated on one or two key individuals.

Project management should delegate tasks rather than attempting to perform these tasks themselves. This should allow adequate time for providing guidance and direction to various team personnel as well as participating in quality-control reviews, project scheduling, and other important administrative matters.

Testing

Testing is an opportunity for project team members to work together. Project team personnel should develop test cases that depict the actual operating environment as closely as possible. Test criteria and data can normally be structured based on detailed design documentation. The combination of test cases, test databases, stress tests, and conversion tests can contribute greatly to the successful implementation of the system.

Management should recognize that some programs or modules may require more testing time than others, due to their complexity. This should be reflected in the test schedule. Following the completion of initial testing activities, time should be allowed in the project schedule for additional program changes and retesting.

Test procedures should be identified early in the development process from the list of functional requirements for each menu and program. The detailed design documents should include a list of functional requirements, which can be tested during the testing phase. Tests could be built as the design is developed if requirements are formally documented. Time spent in building test conditions and in conversion testing could assist the project team in understanding the complexity and time requirements of the conversion process. Stress tests should be designed to provide a measurement of the impact on terminal response time given normal and abnormal production loads. Batch programs should be tested as thoroughly as on-line programs. Otherwise, a number of changes may be required following conversion and implementation.

Other Factors

The design of the system must be frozen during programming. Also, all programming tasks should be concluded prior to user testing. Programs should be frozen during the testing phase. The project manager should ensure that all programs are restricted from programmer access during testing and that changes resulting from the tests are also thoroughly tested.

During the course of the project, MIS standards for systems development, programming, and documentation should be routinely followed. Being behind in a systems implementation project is not sufficient reason for bypassing standard procedures. Technical documentation should be at a sufficient level, especially pertaining to more complicated programs, for an experienced person, other than the original author, to continue to support the system without considerable effort. The project manager should be responsible for ensuring that these standards and guidelines are met prior to approval of program code for unit testing. Deviations from accepted standards should require approval from the project manager and MIS management.

Management should recognize that the ongoing maintenance of the system will require dedicated support staff in the MIS function. The hours required for this support function will increase as additional phases of the project are implemented. Following the conclusion of each phase of implementation, the number of support staff required to maintain the system should be estimated. Support levels should be monitored to help ensure that documentation and design of future applications will minimize ongoing support requirements.

Project Life Cycle Procedures

All MIS projects should follow a phased, step-by-step approach for development of new systems and major enhancement projects. This approach should include the following steps:

- Initiation of a user request
- Initial survey/feasibility analysis
- MIS director review and approval
- MIS steering committee review and approval
- Development of functional specifications
- Systems selection/procurement
- Systems development
- Hardware testing
- Software testing
- Training and installation
- Post-installation review and evaluation

Following is a discussion of each of these areas.

1.   Initiation of a User Request

All projects should begin with a user/project request form being completed by the project initiator. This document should include all of the following information pertinent to the project. Figure 6.1 contains an example of a user/project request form.

2.   Initial Survey/Feasibility Analysis

Following the user request, a feasibility analysis for the proposed application should be performed. This feasibility analysis should address not only the technical feasibility of the project, but also whether the project is consistent with the strategic systems plan. The information used to perform the study should be gathered from user interviews, user documents, vendors, and other specialists. The written results of the feasibility study should be presented to the organization's MIS steering committee.

3.   MIS Director Review and Approval

All pertinent documentation relating to user requests affecting mainframe and departmental systems should be sent to MIS management for review and approval. Major enhancements to central systems and new application systems should be reviewed by the MIS steering committee.

4.   MIS Steering Committee Review and Approval

Once the feasibility study has been completed, its results should be presented to the MIS steering committee for review. If any changes to the proposed feasibility analysis are required, revisions should be prepared for another review and final approval by the committee. A project request does not proceed to the next step of the life cycle until the above steps have been completed.

5.   Development of Functional Specifications

Following the approval of the feasibility study by MIS management and the MIS steering committee, functional specifications for the system should be developed. These specifications are prepared mainly for the mainframe systems users. The specifications help ensure agreement in system design between the system developer and the appropriate departmental function.

Functional specifications should be developed for the user in a format that can be easily understood. For this reason, these general guidelines should be followed in the preparation of functional specifications:

- Users should not be presented with massive reports.
- Documents should be developed in a concise format to improve the reviewer's ability to comprehend and assess the report.
- Reports should be reviewed only by those with knowledge of the topic discussed.

6.   System Selection/Procurement

The actual system selection and procurement process should be performed in accordance with the organization's purchasing procedures.

7.   Systems Development

For packaged software systems requiring custom modification, actual program coding will be necessary. All programming activities for both custom and internal development should follow the existing program development standards.

8.   Hardware Testing

For new additions to the central systems, each component of the hardware should be tested to determine if it satisfies the overall objectives of the system and meets the vendor's technical specifications.

9.   Software Testing

The software should be completely tested. At this step, the programs should be thoroughly tested, using sample data, in order to determine that the software operates in accordance with its detailed design.

10.   Training and Installation

Upon successful testing of the system, actual implementation and training can begin. An implementation plan should be developed to address the following issues:

a.   Site preparation

b.   Ordering of special forms and supplies

c.   Training schedules and personnel planning

d.   Data gathering

e.   Data input

f.   Parallel processing requirements

This implementation plan should include each implementation step, individual responsible, start dates, and completion dates.

11.   Post-Installation Review and Evaluation

Following installation of the system, the system should be reviewed to evaluate whether it meets its cost and performance objectives. All deficiencies of the system should be documented to provide input for necessary modifications and enhancements.

Joint Application Development (JAD)

Joint Application Development (JAD) is a relatively new technique for improving the quality of design and development projects. The JAD technique or process attempts to use consensus building and involvement of user personnel in the design process through a series of workshops. In this way, a partnership is developed between the technical personnel and user personnel involved in the process.

The JAD group or team should consist of approximately 8 to 15 members. The team should have an executive sponsor, which is either a manager or group of managers who empower the JAD team and ensure that they commit sufficient time to the JAD process. The project team should have a team leader who is responsible for the project results. The team leader is the owner of the end product and may be from the business side of the organization. Each workshop should be facilitated by an independent consultant who is primarily responsible for managing the JAD process through completion. One person on the project team should be assigned documentation responsibilities for documenting meeting notes, design criteria and other important discussion items. The business side of the organization should be represented in the team, since these individuals are most familiar with business operation needs. These persons are the end-users of the project deliverable. Systems personnel should also participate in the JAD team, since some of the discussions will revolve around technology issues. Lastly, outside technical experts should be added when internal resources may not have sufficient experience to address certain technical matters.

The JAD process usually consists of several workshops which are used to define the requirements of the project deliverables. The first workshop typically addresses the scope of the project and plans for achieving the end product. The second group of workshops actually define the model and specifications for the end product. The final workshop validates the design and moves the design into the development environment.

Group dynamics and behavior are key to the success of the JAD process. The first workshop should last between 3 and 5 days. After an initial period group dynamics take over and the group will begin working as a team. Later workshops can be shorter in nature. During each successive workshop, it will take at least 3 hours for participants to reestablish the team environment and focus on the project at hand. The objectives of the workshops are to identify and resolve issues, achieve consensus through group discussions and build a solution, which is the end-product or deliverable.

DEVELOPING PROJECTED BUDGETS

As part of the implementation plan, costs associated with each element of the plan should be assembled in budget form. Budgeted costs should include projected expenditures for personnel, equipment, software, supplies, and other MIS costs. Representative costs can be obtained from a variety of sources, including:

- Industry directories
- Current expense budgets
- Hardware and software vendors
- Employment agencies (for salary-related costs)
- Industry surveys

The planning team may decide not to include some expense items in the budget. These may be expenses that are currently incurred but will not significantly change. For example, if the facility costs for a data center will not change due to the implementation of the systems plan, these costs would not have to be identified. Therefore, the costs presented in the projected budget may represent "incremental" cost changes from the previous MIS and organization budget. All costs should be appropriately explained, including the source of the expense and the method used to estimate the expense amount.

Management should recognize when reviewing cost schedules that some potential intangible benefits may result from the plan that are not reflected in the cost schedules. These could include improvements in:

- Timely information
- Better information
- Quality of service
- Reduced necessity in hiring additional staff in the future
- Better cross-selling of services

A cost summary should be prepared that identifies major costs per year by the following cost areas:

- Hardware plan
- Communications plan
- Software plan
- Staffing plan
- Education plan

Detailed costs should be provided for each of the above areas at the
component-cost level, with appropriate disclosure of the source of
expense. There may be one-time and annual recurring costs in both levels
of the cost schedule. These should also be identified.

PLANNING THE IMPLEMENTATION

A good implementation plan will have the following characteristics:

*   Flexibility to allow adjustments in activities and target dates.
*   Milestones so that actual performance can be compared to
    planned performance.
*   Methods for recording and reporting project status, problems,
    achievements, and resource usage.

Figure 6.2 contains a sample format for an implementation plan. It
includes the following information:

*   Activity description
*   Responsible party(s)
*   Status
*   Estimated hours
*   Target start date
*   Target completion date
*   Actual completion date

Project management software can be useful for planning and controlling
the implementation process. Several PC packages are available from
various vendors with this capability. Most packages offer critical-path
analysis, which identifies critical activities that will delay the project if
not completed on schedule.

An estimated timetable for the completion of each task should be
prepared. The number of personnel required in each functional category
should also be identified, including:

*   Management personnel
*   Project management personnel
*   Technical personnel
*   User support personnel
*   Internal audit personnel
*   Vendor personnel
*   Consulting personnel

In addition, it is necessary to consider the additional work load placed on existing staff both during the implementation process and after the system is operational.

Major activities in the implementation process include:

- Organizational issues
- Site preparation activities
- Education and training activities
- Hardware installation activities
- Application software installation activities
- Conversion activities
- Testing activities
- Policy and procedure development activities
- Operation start-up activities
- Post-implementation review activities

1.   Organizational issues

The most effective implementation plans use a team approach including internal personnel, vendor(s), and other outside parties. A systems implementation project committee should be organized that consists of management, technical, and user personnel. This committee should report to an overall information systems steering committee and upper management.

The systems implementation committee should be chaired by an implementation coordinator who is responsible for directing and monitoring the overall implementation effort. The coordinator should have an in-depth understanding of the existing systems, procedures, and operations of the financial institution.

Implementation status meetings should be held on a regular basis and attended by vendor(s) or other outside parties as appropriate, depending on the topics to be discussed. The coordinator should ascertain that each task is successfully completed, problems identified and resolved, and assistance provided when necessary. Many decisions can be determined by the systems implementation committee. However, certain decisions require approval by upper management. Therefore, the committee should keep upper management informed and involved in the implementation process. A useful method to facilitate this objective is to use a project status report.

2.   Site Preparation

Although systems have become smaller and easier to install,
advanced preparation is still required. Prior to the delivery and
installation of the hardware and peripheral equipment, it is
necessary to consider the following issues:

- Work traffic patterns
- Noise
- Maintenance space
- Storage
- Water
- Drainage to reduce the potential damage from internal or
  external flooding
- Electrical power
- Heating and air-conditioning
- Telephone lines
- Access security
- Fire protection
- Humidity controls
- Oversized access door or removable window to facilitate
  transporting equipment in and out of the area

3.   Education and Training

Adequate education and training is an important aspect of the
implementation process. It should include:

- Management training
- Technical training
- User training

Training in the use of the system can be provided by several
methods, including:

- Formal classes directed by professional instructors held
  at the vendor's offices or on-site at the financial
  institution. The advantages of obtaining training at the
  vendor's office are:
  - Special training facilities.
  - Fewer interruptions from daily operations.
- The advantages of training at the financial institution are:
  - More personnel can be involved in the training
    without traveling.

- Existing records, reports, and other materials are readily available.
- On-the-job training using day-to-day situations held at the financial institution.
- Self-teaching materials, generally in the form of audio and video cassettes, supplemented by printed texts and workbooks.
- Self-teaching software, generally in the form of programs capable of interacting directly with the operator in a question-and-answer approach or tutorial.

Regardless of the training method chosen, a system is only as good as the users who work with it. Therefore, it is necessary to develop a detailed training schedule as a part of the overall implementation schedule.

4.   Hardware Installation

Most hardware installation activities are performed by the vendor(s). However, it is the financial institution's responsibility to monitor delivery dates and to ensure that site preparation activities are performed in a timely manner to correlate with the hardware installation activities. In addition, all third-party activities such as installation of communication lines by the telephone company should be coordinated with the other installation activities.

The financial institution should also develop acceptance testing criteria for the hardware and systems software. The benchmarks can be used to determine that the hardware performs as proposed.

Insurance polices should be analyzed to ascertain that adequate coverage is maintained. Major considerations include:

- Hardware
- Software
- Employee fidelity
- Errors and omissions
- Loss of data
- Business interruption
- Extra expense
- Valuable papers

5.   Software Installation

The software vendor(s) are usually responsible for performing the software installation activities. However, the financial institution should monitor these activities and ascertain that they are performed in accordance with contractual agreements.

A critical activity that requires the detailed involvement of the financial institution is setting various parameters in the system. The parameter settings establish the processing and reporting methods to be used. Most software systems are designed with parameters that allow flexibility for the differences between financial institutions.

All program modifications should be closely reviewed to determine if they satisfy the original objectives. In addition, these modifications must be thoroughly tested.

6.   Conversion

The success of the conversion effort is measured by the timeliness and effectiveness of the transition to the new system. Frequently, conversion to a new system also requires major changes in the work flow and organizational structure. Therefore, conversion may impose an abnormally high work load on people, equipment, and facilities.

Advanced planning must be performed for all conversion activities. While delays may be acceptable during some phases of the implementation, they cannot be tolerated during conversion.

Specific conversion dates should be identified and approved by management. These dates are often influenced by business factors such as competitive considerations, nonpeak periods, the date of a move to a new office or facility, or requirements for a calendar or year-end conversion date for new accounting systems. Most conversions contain some element of sequencing whether by systems, by cycle, by branch, or by some other means. Converting in gradual stages helps to ensure that sufficient time is allowed for the conversion process.

The conversion period normally requires the highest level of staffing, so personnel and training requirements are significant during this segment. Estimates should be prepared for all personnel required, and personnel should be identified for each conversion activity.

Adequate supervision over all activities is especially important during conversion. The systems and procedures are new, and more than normal day-to-day supervision should be encouraged. Personnel requirements for the creation and verification of the master files should be identified at this time. Another important consideration is the additional clerical and supervisory effort necessary for the execution and follow-up on conversion procedures.

A final review of the system by internal and external auditors should also be considered. Contingency plans should be developed for each system to be converted. This will allow the financial institution to return to its existing system if significant problems occur during conversion. Public and employee relations may be an important consideration, since the system could have an impact beyond the procedural changes in a single department.

File conversion procedures are used to shift operations to the new system after all testing has been completed and the operating personnel are properly trained. There are two major phases in developing file conversion procedures: (1) determining the sources of the data required for the new master files and the approaches for constructing the new files, and (2) developing the specific procedures.

The sources of data required for the new master files should be identified and documented. Existing manual files may be in the form of lists, reports, index cards, ledger cards, file folders, or charts. The conversion procedures for manual file sources will normally require extensive clerical review, analysis, editing, coding, and transcription of the data to be converted. The process for converting from existing magnetic files will normally require computer conversion programs that have been previously developed and tested.

Procedures must be developed for all manual and automated conversion processing requirements. Special conversion procedures usually need to be developed in one or more of the following areas:

- Input review and analysis and source document preparation.
- Data entry, verification, or other data conversion.
- Special computer program processing.
- Control and balancing.

The control and balancing procedures are particularly important. The scope of this activity must include all procedures required to ensure that records or accounts are properly selected for conversion, that all selected items are accurately and completely entered into the new system, and that all errors identified in the conversion process are corrected and re-entered.

During the conversion process, there may be a lapse of time between the initial transcription of the master file data and the conversion. So procedures must provide for maintenance of master file data until the conversion is complete.

A contingency plan should be developed and appropriate procedures documented so the financial institution is prepared in case something goes wrong. Failure to partially or completely convert to the new system may be due to equipment breakdown, major personnel problems, software problems, or other unforeseen circumstances. Contingency plans are especially important for systems that are an integral part of the mainstream operations--or that represent a significant interface with customers or other external parties.

The conversion process involves the construction of all data files and tables required for the live operation of the new system. Typically, this involves a combination of conversion of data from a predecessor system via specially written de-conversion programs and the creation of specific data that are unique to the new system.

It is especially important that the files to be converted contain current and accurate data. If they are not ready for conversion, a significant effort may be required to clean up the data. If this is the case, this effort should begin at a point that allows sufficient time for the activity to be completed.

The conversion process should contain a number of validation checkpoints and procedures for ensuring the accuracy of the conversion. This may require that the conversion programs have intermediate totals, hash totals, and record counts. Verification may also involve execution of key programs from both the old and new systems, such as trial balance reports. Historical data can further complicate the conversion process, depending on the type, accuracy, and volume of such data. If the accuracy of the historical data is doubtful, it should be reconciled and corrected before it is converted to the new system.

7.   Testing

The principal objective of software testing is to simulate actual operating conditions as closely as possible so that the accuracy and completeness of the programs and the related clerical and control procedures can be verified. Included in this process must be the verification of proper communications between programs, and the testing of all unusual conditions. All systems cycles of the processing must be adequately tested.

Another major objective of software testing is to test the conversion procedures by introducing data in volume. Large volumes of data will test the performance of the system. An acceptance plan that identifies the specific criteria for accepting the system should be developed. The plan should consider acceptance criteria that may be included in the contracts.

Standard software packages from reliable vendors may require less testing than software that has been recently developed or heavily modified. User references may provide a realistic indication of the amount of testing required.

Manual procedures also may require testing. These can sometimes be overlooked as incidental; however, they can impact the success of the system. When major changes in existing manual procedures occur, testing is essential.

Test data should be prepared for all master files and transaction files. The files should be organized so that all interrelationships among them can be tested. The volume of test data should be sufficient to test every condition of the system, but small enough to allow the results to be verified in a reasonable period of time. Results should be predetermined wherever possible for comparison to the test results.

Vendor personnel, internal technical personnel, and user staff should all participate in the testing process. An additional benefit of the testing process is that it provides another method of training.

Testing should be performed as follows:

*   Construct the files required by the system.
*   Process test transactions for the first cycle through the entire system.
*   Verify the results.
*   Correct the programs.
*   Repeat the test for the same cycle until all errors are resolved.

This series of steps should be repeated until the processing of each cycle is performed correctly. The testing of succeeding cycles should not be started until the test for the previous cycle has been completed.

The verification of test results must include:

*   Tracing all transactions through the system to the end of the processing cycle.
*   Verifying all control totals.
*   Footing all reports.
*   Re-computing calculations or comparing them to predetermined results.
*   Verifying master file updates.
*   Verifying the information printed in reports or displayed on the terminal.
*   Verifying that all errors detected in the system during previous tests are corrected.

Processing errors that are identified during the testing process are difficult to control. Therefore, it may be helpful to prepare control forms to ensure that all errors are reported, tested, and corrected.

Several aspects of testing are often overlooked. Testing should include all of the following:

*   Data conversion programs should be tested in the same manner as all other programs.
*   Manual procedures should be tested.

- Documentation should be tested by using it to perform the testing activities.
- Test data should be prepared for invalid and unexpected conditions as well as valid and expected results.
- The system should perform only the processing that is expected, no more than is expected.
- The probability of the existence of additional errors in a particular software module is proportional to the number of errors already identified in it. Therefore, additional testing may be required.

8. Policies and Procedures

New systems often require changes in organizational work flow and other procedures. Although many systems include comprehensive user documentation, they may not address the manual departmental procedures that can be unique to a particular financial institution. Therefore, existing policies and procedures should be revised to correlate to the new system. Changes may include new personnel positions and modifications to position descriptions as a result of changing the duties and responsibilities of various existing personnel.

Specific considerations include:

- Modifying input forms and source documents.
- Revising procedures for preparation and authorization of input.
- Reviewing segregation of duties based on the functionality of the new system.
- Limiting access to restricted areas.
- Analyzing balancing procedures.
- Controlling and maintaining adequate documentation.
- Controlling program changes.
- Revising emergency and evacuation procedures.
- Reviewing the role of internal audit.
- Developing various activity logs such as:
  - Sign-in logs.
  - Sign-out logs.
  - Operator logs.
- Reviewing record retention schedules.

- Developing an EDP policy manual including such items as:
    - MIS steering committee.
    - Systems design standards.
    - Programming standards.
    - Software selection standards.
    - Systems documentation.
    - Program documentation.
    - Operations documentation.
    - User documentation.
    - On-line documentation.
    - Packaged software documentation.
    - Procedures for updating reference library materials.
    - Policies and procedures for password use.
    - Password changes.
    - Security violation reporting.
    - Terminal use.
    - Remote communications.
    - Authorization of program changes.
    - Program change request form.
    - Program testing.
    - Program approval.
    - Procedures for placing programs into production status.
    - Conversion planning considerations and procedures.
    - Access controls for:
        - Program documentation.
        - Database documentation.
        - Reference materials.
        - Data-altering utilities.
        - Hardware/computer room.
        - Data files.
        - Programs.
        - On-site/off-site vault storage.
        - Reports distribution area.
        - Checks and preprinted forms.
    - Console log review procedures.
    - Review procedures for security system account structure.
    - Review procedures for file sizing and retention.
    - Preventive maintenance procedures.
    - Parameter changes.
    - Distribution of output.

- User-defined reports.
- Librarian procedures.
- Emergency procedures.
- Backup procedures.
- Off-site storage procedures.
- Recovery procedures.
- Alternate site agreement(s).
- Disaster recovery plan.

9. Operational Start-up

All steps in this process are critical and must be carefully planned, performed and controlled. It is important to closely monitor and review all initial data and start-up procedures, including the operational tasks, procedures, and system components to ensure that they are working in accordance with user and project specifications and requirements.

The method of cut-over will require careful consideration. The basic cut-over techniques include:

- Parallel operation.
- Limited parallel operation.
- Phased implementation.
- Direct cut-over.

Full-scale parallel operation involves processing all transactions through both the new and the old systems with daily, weekly, and monthly reconciliation of results until all parties are convinced that the new system works. Full-scale parallel operation may require hiring temporary employees to operate the old system while permanent employees are assigned to the new system and the reconciliation of processing results. The primary advantage of parallel operation is that the old system can be used without a loss of time if the new system fails. The major disadvantage is the cost and time associated with this method. In addition, full-scale parallel operation for the purpose of testing the new system can be difficult because generally the existing system and the system to be implemented do not produce comparable results.

Limited parallel operation can facilitate the reconciliation of the old and new systems at a reduced cost. In this operating mode, both the existing and new systems are executed in parallel; however, the new system processes only a selected subset of the total data to be processed. This approach to parallel operation reduces the effort required to input two sets of transactions and to reconcile the results produced. It also significantly reduces the cost of operating in a parallel mode. Limited parallel operation produces the same results as full-scale parallel operation, provided the selected subset of the data to be processed by the new system is representative of all the data to be processed in the production mode.

Phased implementation is the process of installing portions of the system over a period of time rather than installing the entire system at once. The term is also used to describe the process of implementing the entire system at selected locations rather than at all locations at the same time. Phased implementation may or may not be conducted in conjunction with limited parallel operation. Phased implementation is generally recommended when the task of installing the entire system all at once is not practical or when resources are limited.

The fourth technique, direct cut-over to a new system, has some risks but these risks can be minimized through adequate system testing and ensuring that procedures are in place to convert back to the old system if necessary.

The system cut-over technique to be used may vary in each situation. In deciding upon the techniques to be used, consider the following factors:

- Nature of application systems
- Comparability of system outputs
- Resources available (people and hardware)
- Risks
- Costs

If the parallel operation method is chosen, procedures will be required to keep both systems current during the conversion period. For example, two master files as well as other files must be maintained during the operational start-up period.

The direct system cut-over is the most common technique. It is also advisable to have a plan for returning to the old system, if possible, in case of insurmountable problems with the new system. To avoid problems, this technique must be preceded by comprehensive system testing.

10.   Post-Implementation Review

After the system has been operational for three to six months, it should be analyzed to determine if the original objectives for it have been achieved. The post-implementation review process should include an analysis of:

- Software features, functions and capabilities compared to the original requirements
- Costs compared to original cost estimates
- Operating procedures
- Work flow and productivity
- Actual volumes compared to estimated volumes
- Actual performance compared to the performance as proposed by the vendor(s)
- Capacity utilization compared to the capacity as proposed by the vendor(s)
- Internal controls and security
- Balancing procedures
- User satisfaction with the new system

As users become more familiar with the new system, they should strive to refine their use of the system in an effort to increase productivity. The work flow should be streamlined and unnecessary manual procedures should be eliminated. The responsibilities and duties of existing personnel may need to be restructured to increase the effectiveness and efficiency of the system.

Management must be willing to dedicate the time to identify systems refinements and must provide the resources to implement those refinements for the system to remain dynamic and to properly service the informational needs of the financial institution.

Figure 6.1
Sample User/Project Request Form

Project Title:_____   Project Number:_____

Date Submitted:_____   Desired Completion Date:_____

Requested By:_____

Project Type: ☐ New System   ☐ Major Revision   ☐ Maintenance
               ☐ Other_____

Priority: ☐ High   ☐ Medium   ☐ Low

Project Description:_____
_____
_____
_____
_____
_____
_____

BENEFITS

	MIS	USER	TOTAL
Personnel	____	____	____
Equipment	____	____	____
Other:			
_____	____	____	____
_____	____	____	____
_____	____	____	____
Total	____	____	____

Other Benefits:_____
_____
_____
_____

Figure 6.1 (Continued)
Sample User/Project Request Form

PROJECTED REQUIREMENTS AND COST

	NUMBER	TOTAL HOURS	ESTIMATED COSTS
Personnel:			
Supervisory	_____	_____	_____
Systems Analyst	_____	_____	_____
Programming	_____	_____	_____
Technical Support	_____	_____	_____
Operations	_____	_____	_____
User Department	_____	_____	_____
Other	_____	_____	_____
Equipment--MIS	_____	_____	_____
Equipment--User	_____	_____	_____
Other Costs:			
_____	_____	_____	_____
_____	_____	_____	_____
Total	_____	_____	_____

Other Requirements:_____
_____
_____
_____

PROJECT TIMETABLE

	ESTIMATED	ACTUAL
Project Start Date	_____	_____
Project Completion Date	_____	_____

_____   _____   _____
Requested By   Department   Date

_____   _____   _____
Approved By   Department   Date

Figure 6.2
Sample Implementation Plan Format

Activity Description	Responsible Party(s)	Status	Estimated Hours	Target Start Date	Target Completion Date	Actual Completion Date

7 TECHNOLOGY CONSIDERATIONS

Financial institution personnel should attempt to determine the applicability and need for emerging technologies through research and exposure at trade shows and conferences. Emerging technology should be considered during the strategic planning process. This technology may be available today; however, the cost to purchase these systems may be high. The following section describes various new technologies. As their use becomes more common and less costly, these technologies may be extremely useful in the financial industry.

DATABASE MANAGEMENT SYSTEMS

Database management systems (DBMS) were introduced in the early 1960s and have evolved dramatically. A DBMS is a method of classifying and organizing data in a format that can be quickly accessed for query and reporting purposes. One of the original objectives of a DBMS was to reduce redundancy of data, which was often evident in traditional file structures of application systems. Another objective was to allow the user ease of access to the data through query and report-writing functions.

Several types of DBMS structures have evolved, including hierarchical, network, and relational, and each has specific advantages, which are usually measured in terms of responsiveness to user demands and ease of maintainability. Ultimately, the relational concept of data management has emerged as the most desirable, especially if ad hoc query and reporting are key elements in satisfying user needs. Relational DBMSs require greater computing resources, but hardware manufacturers have introduced higher-performance hardware to counteract this disadvantage. Relational "look-alikes" have also been developed that allow organizations that have invested in other forms of DBMS to obtain the similar functionality without a full conversion.

In the early 1980s Ashton-Tate introduced dBASE, which was the first microcomputer-based DBMS that offered the functionality of a true DBMS and that was accompanied by an English-like query language and a programming language for developing custom application software. Several million copies of dBASE were sold, and other software vendors introduced similar products to the booming PC marketplace. Most of these products feature programming languages, query tools, report writers, and screen design aids to assist in the automation of custom application systems at the department and end-user level of the organization. They also typically feature SQL (Structured Query Language) support, which is a nonprocedural language used in accessing data from the DBMS and a de facto standard within the industry.

Two levels of database management systems are clearly distinguishable in the marketplace, primarily separated by the levels of platforms they are designed to operate on: midrange/mainframe DBMSs and microcomputer DBMSs. In the late 1970s, IBM introduced proprietary relational database management systems as part of their hardware and operating software architecture in their midrange systems. This successful product line has led the marketplace because of its power, flexibility, programming tools, and numerous third-party application software offerings. Other vendors followed with similar product offerings in order to maintain their market share.

In the future, it will be important to use database management products that are compatible from the PC and LAN platform to midrange and mainframe systems. Increased emphasis on client/server architecture will influence DBMSs and other development tools in the PC and midrange/mainframe markets. The same processing speed and flexibility will be needed by users of all levels of systems, and this may be a determining factor in the future of DBMS vendors.

CLIENT/SERVER ARCHITECTURE AND DISTRIBUTED DATABASES

With trends in offloading and downsizing, distributed databases are becoming more prevalent in organizational computing. Client/server architecture concepts are described below:

Client: *The user requesting service from the server.*

Server: *The computing device servicing the client request.*

These terms are often used synonymously with "distributed processing," "departmental processing," "distributed databases," etc. Client/server architecture is appealing because it offloads the work on the central system and can provide information more conveniently than a centralized system. Data management is an issue that must be addressed when this architecture is used, since data may reside on many platforms and be accessible through the network to many users.

"Downsizing" and "rightsizing" can be potential methods of reducing total systems costs and significantly reducing development time for new application systems. Financial institutions evaluating downsizing alternatives should be concerned with the cost of re-engineering existing applications, especially if they are custom-developed by an internal programming staff. With trends toward networked workstations and PC-based systems, downsizing may be a very effective method for achieving automation objectives in the shortest period of time.

The term "downsizing" means simply to move an application or multiple applications to a smaller hardware platform. This usually implies a mainframe to midrange migration, but may also include migrating from midrange systems to network-based PCs, such as a local area network (LAN). Downsizing generally implies that an entire application is moved to a smaller hardware platform. The term "rightsizing" implies that only the right part of the application is moved to a smaller configuration of equipment.

For example, platform automation in today's computing environment is generally network-based, using PC workstations connected to a network server, which acts as the control device for communications with the mainframe system--located either internally or in a service center processing environment. Platform automation typically addresses the front-end portion of the loan and deposit application processing. Automated intelligence applied to these front-end processes can help prepare loan documentation or help cross-sell services to a new customer. The data-intensive back end of the processing is still occurring on the mainframe system; however, certain file information is transmitted to the platform application, where it can be worked with by the end user. In this sense, the application has been "rightsized."

Although significant cost savings may be available in automating an application on a PC network versus a mainframe system, the cost savings may not be as pronounced when comparing midrange systems to PC networks. Many midrange systems are priced to compete with larger multi-workstation LANs, and the development tools and the on-line security features available on midrange systems may be more advanced than the PC platform. Similarly, fully featured turnkey application software may be generally available on a midrange system, while PC-based application software may lack the functionality desired by larger financial institutions.

Organization-wide application systems are generally less attractive candidates for downsizing than departmental applications. Departmental applications tend to have a limited number of users and less sophisticated database and integration requirements than organization-wide systems. Consequently, these systems can be moved to client/server architecture with less risk and less potential negative impact on the organization as a whole.

Moving to a client/server architecture may not be a difficult process. Data extraction tools, file transfer tools, query languages, downloading and uploading tools, and PC interface products all contribute to the cultural change necessary to implement client/server technology. The next step is providing graphical user interfaces (GUIs) to end users so data can be represented in a more "user friendly" format--with charts, graphs, and other pictorial representations.

Some productivity gains may be found with client/server technology. Mainframe development time has long been the Achilles' heel of mainframe computing--and the most significant reason for considering platform changes. Lengthy development time equates to high costs, unmet expectations, and dissatisfied end users. Client/server architecture offers the advantage of quickly addressing minimum systems requirements and providing tools that can be implemented by the end user with limited technical support involvement.

Ideally, the use of client/server technology will help an organization better utilize the equipment already in place. Most organizations have significant investments in PC-based systems, which are often primarily used for "resource sharing"--that is, local area networks set up to share hardware resources, such as disk storage devices and laser printers, and software resources, such as spreadsheet software, database management systems, and word processing. These networks, in some cases, may also be using a basic form of electronic mail. Their second purpose is to provide, through terminal emulation, a connection with the mainframe or host system in use by the organization. These intelligent workstations are expensive terminals and may be underutilized, especially in the context of client/server architecture.

Client/server architecture provides the capability for the front-end portion of a major application to be processed on the LAN, while the back-end portion of the application can reside on the mainframe system. Each system should be dependent on the other for the transfer and communication of timely information, and together they should form the entire application system.

The implementation of client/server systems may improve productivity of the organization's nontechnical resources as well as technical resources. Client/server systems should provide tools for the end user for data extraction, reporting, and graphical interfaces. In some cases, both technical and nontechnical personnel will have access to CASE (computer-aided software engineering) tools for developing and enhancing client/server applications.

Although mainframe processing work load can be reduced through client/server technology, this is not the area of greatest benefit to the organization. Data integrity may be improved by providing an environment where information is created and maintained closer to the user department responsible for information ownership. Through good application controls, this information in detailed form can be available to many user departments, but controlled through security practices and procedures. Duplicate information and dispersed information, which may lack consistency and accuracy, could be minimized with proper design of the application.

While client/server architecture offers some significant benefits to the organization, it also can have disadvantages. Application maintenance when dealing with several platforms, data structures, and programming languages, could increase the complexity of change. Consequently, CASE tools that embrace departmental and host processing requirements are important to minimize ongoing support and maintenance of client/server systems. In addition, the lack of standards for client/server technology may reduce the consistency of application systems related to their development or operations. Ultimately, the lack of standards impacts the speed of modification and implementation when application requirements need to change. Some de facto standards already exist in the industry, such as the UNIX or Novell operating systems for server operating software and SQL (Structured Query Language) for interfacing and accessing various database systems. However, more specific standards may be needed for the organization to ensure proper control over the development and implementation process. This can be achieved through a standards committee, which would be responsible for identifying standards for the organization.

OPEN SYSTEMS ARCHITECTURE

Because of the variety of proprietary architectures marketed today, the need for standardization between computer systems has become increasingly important. This implies that the incompatibilities between computer systems must be overcome through an organized, standard approach, which will ultimately assist the organization to interconnect multiple computing resources so that information can be easily accessed across a variety of platforms. Open systems architecture provides the means to accomplish this goal. Open systems typically refers to UNIX-based operating environments, although it can also be associated with interconnectivity of systems through certain technical standards.

A true open systems architecture should allow an organization to use the most current technology available without sacrificing the investment in current application systems. Open systems can provide a number of benefits, such as:

*   Sheltering the current investment in information systems.
*   Eliminating the limitations of a single vendor hardware solution.
*   Improving price/performance of the end-solution, primarily because a number of vendors may offer similar solutions and must compete for the business through lower prices.
*   Standardization at the organization and department levels.

There has been a continuing erosion of the proprietary operating system marketplace. Therefore, each major hardware manufacturer has a product line that offers open architecture, in addition to its proprietary product lines. The transition to the open systems environment has occurred for several reasons:

• The cost of developing and supporting a proprietary operating system has become prohibitive.
• There is an increasing market demand for heterogeneous open systems that permit portability of applications among a variety of computers that support easy connectivity.
• Software vendors are seeking the largest potential market base for their products.
• Hardware vendors are using the open systems architecture to attract application software vendors to their platforms.

The demand for open systems creates two major problems for hardware vendors; first, how to migrate to open systems without exposing their existing customer base to other vendors offering similar products; second, how to cope with smaller profit margins as hardware becomes more of a commodity. From the perspective of the financial institution, the concern is how to take advantage of the trend to open systems without necessarily discarding existing systems. Therefore, it is important to develop a well-planned migration strategy.

CASE TOOLS

Computer-aided software engineering (CASE) is the use of automated tools in performing the various phases of the system's development life cycle. "Upper" CASE refers to design and analysis tools and "Lower" CASE refers to code generation tools. CASE tools assist in the analysis, design, development, testing, implementation, and maintenance of application software and documentation. They also assist in the project management of a software development project in the areas of project estimating, planning, scheduling, tracking, status reporting, and productivity measurement. Typically CASE tools provide a means for "prototyping" an application, that is, quickly building an automated model of an application that simulates the actual application as it may appear to the end user. Prototyping is used to help software designers and end users to agree on the functional design of an application system, prior to actually programming the application. The terms often associated with CASE are "forward software engineering" and "reverse software engineering."

Forward software engineering (FSE) follows the common development cycle steps as described above, that is, analysis, design, development, testing, and implementation. FSE tools use the traditional design elements and generate the data dictionary and documentation for the system.

Reverse software engineering (RSE) can begin at the later stages of the development cycle and actually recreates the design based on the end product. Through the use of screen painters, code generators, and report generators, RSE "begins at the end" of the development cycle and generates the necessary code to produce the data structures and input for the desired result. To be most effective, CASE tools should assist in defining and developing both departmental and host processing requirements as with client/server architecture. This is important to minimize ongoing support and maintenance of client/server systems and helps to ensure that future systems will best utilize the presence of intelligent workstations at the appropriate level.

CASE tools are most beneficial for developing new systems and usually cannot be used for older systems written without CASE tools. Most application software packages were probably not developed with CASE tools.

CASE tools may require major changes in how software development is organized, managed, and controlled. Cultural changes and adaptation may be difficult, because CASE tools require more structured methodologies. Most of the benefit of using CASE tools may occur during the life cycle in the form of reduced maintenance and enhancement costs. Larger financial institutions are more likely to benefit from CASE tools because the size and complexity of their applications are greater. Smaller financial institutions normally have limited technical staff and rely on packaged software.

IMAGING TECHNOLOGY

Imaging systems involve the following components:

- Workstations with high-resolution displays.
- Scanners that can handle the required volume and file formats.
- High-capacity mass storage.
- High-resolution output.
- Specialized software, including image application software, work flow processing software, database software to manage document retrieval, and image compression algorithms.
- Communications.

Technology is advancing rapidly, and industry standards are emerging for operating systems, interfaces, file formats, optical storage, and communications protocols. The processing power of PCs is increasing, and optical storage is decreasing in cost and increasing in capacity. There are new developments in networks, such as the use of fiber optics.

Multiple platforms are used for imaging systems, including:

*   PCs or UNIX workstations
*   Midrange computers
*   Mainframes

The requirements of the application determine the appropriate platform and system architecture. For example, a stand-alone PC may be appropriate for departmental records storage and retrieval, while a high-end midrange or mainframe with centralized processing may be required for larger applications.

Scanners are the primary input devices on imaging systems. Scanners translate the image on a sheet of paper or other surface into a digitized image that a computer can process. Images fall into three categories:

*   Line art--white and black text or illustrations.
*   Continuous tones--shades of gray, as in photographs.
*   Color.

All scanners have four basic components:

*   Document feeder system--usually flatbed or sheet-fed.
*   Sampling device--usually a laser that detects the light reflected from the page and converts it into digital data by dividing the page into a grid of dots. More dots per inch means a higher resolution and a finer image.
*   Controller--converts the voltages emitted by the sampling device into a digital signal comprising binary bits and passes the stream of bits to the computer, along with instructions for where one row ends and the next one begins.
*   Software--scanner software acts as a bridge between the scanner and application programs.

Scanners are often attached to a dedicated scanning workstation, which may have a dedicated server. The scanning station may provide control over such features as threshholding (lightening or darkening an image to compensate for variations in image quality); dithering and filtering (for simulating grayscale); image rotation; scaling; and resolution. After input, image quality must be verified and the images must be indexed for later retrieval. Some systems offer image quality verification and indexing concurrently with scanning. Images are generally compressed after scanning, and usually remain compressed until decompressed for display on a workstation or printout.

Optical disks are typically used as the mass storage devices in imaging systems because of their high storage capacity. Optical storage systems comprise four main parts: the disk drive, the interface between the drive and the computer, the storage medium, and the software that makes it possible to use the system. The optical disk drive contains the optical disk and houses the laser and supporting mechanical and hardware systems. The size, complexity, and price of the drive depend on the format of the optical disk and the type of technology used, such as CD-ROM, WORM, or rewritable disks.

A compact disk with read-only memory (CD-ROM) works much like an audio CD but without converting the digital information to an analog signal. CD-ROM drives are primarily used for volume production and distribution of large databases, and have limited applicability for image processing systems.

Write-once read-many (WORM) disks, unlike CD-ROMs, have the potential for replacing other methods of mass storage, such as microfiche, microfilm, and tape. Like microfiche or microfilm, WORMs record the full document image (text and pictures) but, unlike those media, also allow random-access retrieval instead of time-consuming sequential access. Devices called jukeboxes can be used with WORMs. Jukeboxes, like their audio predecessors, can hold several optical disks, providing the availability of large amounts of on-line random-access information.

Rewritable optical disks are sometimes referred to as magnetic-optical (MO) devices. In rewritable disk technology, lasers record information by heating magnetized areas coated with various metals. The polarity of the magnetized materials can then be read by another laser. Shooting a more powerful laser at the disk erases the data by reversing the established polarity. Rewritable optical disks are appropriate for files that need to be updated regularly. With rewritable disks, files can be moved from one disk to another, and resorted to keep information in a more logical fashion. Both WORM and rewritable optical disks have slower access times and are more expensive than magnetic media.

Imaging systems use optical character recognition (OCR) for text input and indexing. All images must be indexed in a database to allow retrieval. Automatic indexing is extremely beneficial because manual indexing is slow, labor-intensive, and prone to human error. OCR allows prespecified fields to be recognized and transferred to a database.

Employees can spend up to one quarter of every work day searching for documents. By storing all documents in a central database, image processing eliminates this problem. The improved reliability of information storage, the ability to better manage employee work loads, and simultaneous access to the same document by multiple users can increase productivity. Other potential benefits of imaging systems include:

- Lower filing costs.
- Elimination of paper file loss.
- More accurate measurement and reporting systems for clerical productivity.
- Higher productivity.
- Access to files from multiple locations by multiple personnel.
- Faster and more convenient customer service.
- Product differentiation.
- Reduced data entry and retrieval costs.
- Reduction in office storage space.
- Reduction in processing time.
- Decrease in number of transactions and documents.
- Time savings related to:
  - MICR sorting
  - Statement rendering
  - Research
  - Microfilming items
  - Reconciling/settling cash letters
  - Exception item pull (EIP)

-       NSF items
-       Reviewing high-risk items
•   Reduced postage cost.
•   Microfilm savings.

Imaging provides an opportunity to reorganize the process by which tasks, functions, and services are typically performed. The basic work flow, whether in the back office or on the teller line, should be re-evaluated to identify opportunities to simplify procedures, reduce the number of forms needed, and eliminate redundant activities and processing costs. Image processing applications for financial institutions include:

•   Check statements.
•   Proof of deposit processing.
•   Reject repair processing.
•   High-value inclearing signature verification.
•   On-line teller signature verification.
•   Remittance processing.
•   Loan applications, correspondence, and paper files.
•   Merchant sales drafts.
•   Microfilm and microfiche image capture.
•   Wholesale lockbox.
•   Mortgage loan servicing.
•   Credit-card correspondence.

In the future, exchanging check images between financial institutions could reduce float and minimize check handling. Ultimately checks would not have to be moved from the financial institution of original deposit.

There are several potential pitfalls in implementing imaging technology, including:

•   Lack of standards.
•   Lack of integration between image applications. Therefore, applications may not be able to communicate with each other, resulting in duplication of effort.
•   Lack of integration between imaging systems and existing data processing systems. For example, the MICR reader/sorter probably has a different operating system and communication protocol than a loan imaging system. True integration requires a systems architecture that links components and allows independent systems to communicate and share information with each other.

- Lack of telecommunications capacity and compatibility. The existing network may not have the capability to distribute massive amounts of data such as images of checks, signature cards, loan documents, and other data.
- Document redesign. Forms must be uniform and image-ready for character recognition technology to work. Therefore, various customer forms may need to be redesigned, such as checks, deposit tickets, and loan applications.
- Conversion costs. The time and effort involved in converting documents from paper to digital format should not be underestimated. Documents must be scanned, indexed, and checked for quality. Conversion costs could represent at least half of the total system cost.
- Existing technology investment. Most financial institutions have large investments in their current technology, including PCs, LANs, networks, terminals, microfilm, microfiche equipment, and other systems. Replacement costs can be significant.

Image technology has certain security concerns such as password protection, access controls, encryption techniques, physical storage of the media, and backup alternatives. These issues are similar to traditional data processing systems and magnetic media, however the volume of the optical data and their portability increase security concerns.

Imaging requires careful attention to disaster recovery planning. To remain operative despite technical difficulties, institutions should have redundant hardware and storage media or retain manual processing capabilities.

External and internal auditors should understand the impact on internal controls of optical images and paperless-stored transactions. Widespread use of optical scanning can increase the potential for fraud and irregularities. Perpetrators may attempt to alter either the devices that produce the optical information or the devices that read and interpret the optical information (both hardware and software). Auditors should understand the strengths and limitations of imaging systems and continually monitor, test, and evaluate their reliability.

Financial institutions should evaluate the costs and benefits of imaging systems in the context of their overall technology strategy.

EXECUTIVE INFORMATION SYSTEMS

Executive information systems (EIS) are systems that are designed for use by top-level management. They provide the framework to extract available information from various automated systems in a form that can easily be interpreted by management. Most EIS systems provide tools for management to easily define their specific reporting and presentation requirements. The basic components of an EIS system are:

•   Database management system

> The database management system is a composite of extracted data from a variety of organization-wide and distributed or departmental systems. It forms the foundation for the EIS system by organizing the data, controlling the flow of data from various systems, and providing flexibility to add new data elements from additional sources.

•   Query tools and analytical functions

> Query tools are used to view data from a variety of user-defined perspectives. The analytical tools provide the means to compute relevant ratios, summarize categories of data, sort and structure data, and provide general mathematical functionality.

•   Graphics and report writing functions

> The graphical and report writing functions allow the user to define the presentation mode of the information contained within the EIS database. These tools should allow trend presentations, standard graphs and charting, and general report-writing functions.

A number of mainframe and small-system EIS products are available. In some cases, they are quite expensive and may be cost-prohibitive to the average financial institution. However, this technology, similar to most others, will eventually yield to the competitive environment and price declines can be anticipated.

OTHER TECHNOLOGY CONSIDERATIONS

Other technologies that should be considered in the strategic planning process are described below.

- Object-oriented systems development

  To retain the investment in new systems development efforts and to improve programmer productivity, object-oriented systems development strategies are often applied. This strategy calls for the development of programs and systems in entirely self-sufficient modules. Each module contains all the information and data necessary to perform the module's basic function. The module is the *object* which contains the necessary code to perform the needed operations on its data. A number of tools have been developed to assist in working with object-oriented structures, including object-oriented languages and object-oriented databases.

- Expert Systems

  Expert systems are automated systems which imitate the thought process of human experts in solving specific problems. Usually, an expert system is comprised of a number of rules which support the decision-making process when variables are run against the expert model. The expert system can only be as sophisticated as the logic and knowledge base provided by its human originators.

- Lights-out automated operations

  A goal of many data centers is to achieve a total lights-out operation, in which no human intervention is required to operate automated systems. The first step toward achieving this goal is to automate all scheduling, minimizing the number of operator-required tasks for day-to-day operations. A second step is to automate production control activities for job submission and output distribution. The movement from batch-oriented processing to on-line processing has allowed this option to be feasible, since on-line users can now submit their own jobs, and locally attached printers will provide the output. Lights-out automate operations also include automated message handling, tape management, and tape librarian functions.

- Fault tolerant systems

  Fault tolerant processing uses redundant hardware and/or software to prevent the loss or corruption of data in the event of a systems malfunction. Fault tolerance can apply to hardware or software. Hardware fault tolerance deals with redundant hardware, peripherals, and circuitry. If one component fails, processing is automatically shifted to the redundant component. Software fault tolerance uses separate application codes to perform the same function with the results being compared to ensure the accuracy of processing.

- Electronic Data Interchange (EDI)

  Electronic Data Interchange (EDI) is the electronic exchange of data between two parties. The two parties are often trading partners who have a mutual business relationship. Electronic Funds Transfer (EFT) is viewed as a special type of EDI where the two parties are banks, bank customers and/or some financial intermediary. Usually, EDI requires a distinct type of interface, since each participating party may have different computer systems. Consequently, communications protocols and data formats are key factors when implementing EDI communications.

- Frame relay technology

  Frame relay technology is a high-speed data communications technique which allows high-speed transmissions of data between computer systems, often using third-party networks. This technology offers improved speeds over X.25 packet switching, primarily because error correction and flow control are handled at the end-points of the network rather than at each node within the network.

- Multimedia

  Multimedia is commonly defined as the use of audio, text, graphics, and video technologies to present a message. It may involve a single product or combine the technologies from a variety of products. A simple multimedia application may involve the addition of a CD-ROM to a PC. Multimedia helps users "visualize" the message by using the various human senses.

- Microwave LANs

    The facilities of an organization may not be located in areas that are conducive to cabling, such as urban areas where streets would have to be dug up to lay wire or cable. For this situation, technology is now available for interconnecting nodes on a LAN with microwave backbones. Geographically dispersed locations can be interconnected as long as the "line-of-sight" between the facilities or microwave towers is not interrupted or obstructed. Microwave tends to be a more cost-effective solution than fiber-optic cabling for longer distances. By installing a series of microwave bridges and transceivers, an organization can provide a variety of voice, image, and data communications between locations. Some organizations can process network, video, and voice communications in the same microwave dish by dividing the spectrum of bandwidth. This means that an organization can transfer large batch files, exchange E-Mail, and transmit video over the same network.

    Installations of microwave LANs have proven to be extremely reliable in the worst of weather conditions. Microwave communications have been able to withstand sandstorms, windstorms, and hurricanes. Also microwave installation can be an environmentally preferred method of installing a communications network, since it will not interrupt natural ecosystems or endangered species that may be indigenous to the area.

    Another advantage of microwave LANs is that network administration can be simplified. Network administrators can monitor a large multifacility network from their desktops without having to travel to each site. This should assist in standardizing network configurations and network security throughout a multifacility wide-area network.

- Radio LANs

    A number of products are available featuring "wireless" LAN connections. Agreements between telecommunications companies provide for the capability of cellular and radio-based networks. These networks allow users to communicate on a national basis with a broad base of business and technical services.

8 Systems Selection

OVERVIEW

Background

Systems selection should be an integral part of an overall strategic information systems plan. The information systems plan should support and be carefully integrated into the overall strategic plan of the financial institution. Selecting the right system is more critical today than it was 10 years ago because the future survival of a financial institution is absolutely dependent on its technology and information systems. The organization that takes full advantage of automation and technology will ensure that it is better positioned to compete profitably in the future. Therefore, financial institutions should continuously monitor technology and evaluate the need to change or add automated systems.

Financial institution management may directly or indirectly identify the need to change or add automated systems and technology by recognizing one of the following concerns:

- Lack of computing resources.
- Use of older technologies (i.e., hardware, software, communications, etc.).
- Limited management information.
- Lack of operational information.
- Loss of competitive advantage.
- Stagnation in operational and MIS functions.
- Untimely information.
- Turnover of data processing personnel.
- Deteriorating vendor or service center support.
- Lack of software features, functions, and capabilities.
- High data processing costs.

Each of these problem areas may be a symptom of systems obsolescence or indicate the need for systems replacement.

There are three basic automation alternatives available for financial
institutions in today's environment: in-house computers, service centers,
and facilities management organizations. However, each alternative has
several variations that can include distributed processing, microcomputers,
and item capture equipment. The methods and techniques presented in
this chapter apply to all automation and technology alternatives for all
sizes of financial institutions.

While in-house systems and service centers have been available for some
time, facilities management is a relatively new automation alternative for
financial institutions. With facilities management, the financial institution
may or may not own the hardware, but the actual operation of the data
center is managed by an outside company. In other words, the financial
institution provides the facility, and an outside company manages it. The
unique features of this approach include the following:

- The facilities management company typically assumes
  responsibility for an existing in-house computer system.
- The data processing staff (operations and technical personnel) are
  usually hired by the facilities management company.
- The facilities management company usually owns the software.

In today's systems environment, an organization's requirements do not
have to be satisfied by a single source or vendor. Microcomputers and
distributed processing techniques provide several options and alternatives
with service centers, facilities management, and in-house computers.

Equipment and software obsolescence is a continuing concern. In 10
years, the data processing industry has progressed through five
generations of computer hardware, and indications are that changes will
accelerate as technology advances. Software advances have generally been
much slower, but have included many more vendors.

There is no question that hardware must be electronically and mechanically reliable before it can provide you with a valid processing alternative. However, in today's highly competitive technology market, reliable hardware and good maintenance service are available to most financial institutions. Therefore, systems should be selected on the basis of the quality of their programs. Software quality can be elusive. It is difficult to define and even more difficult to measure. But it is an important concept because a program's long-term cost is indirectly proportional to its quality. When it is unreliable, excessively slow, difficult to use, resistant to modifications, or unsuitable to the needs of an organization, problem software can result in additional costs due to the following:

- Excessive overtime for the user departments or technical personnel who have to correct the "bugs" or provide enhancements.
- Lost revenues from poor, inaccurate, or untimely information.
- Additional equipment obtained in an attempt to improve productivity.
- Additional software obtained in an attempt to improve productivity.
- Increased audit activities incurred as a result of poor record keeping.
- Poor productivity, low staff morale and inefficient operations.
- Legal advice required because of erroneous operations.
- Fraud or embezzlement.

So it is important that software be given emphasis and attention equal to, if not greater than, that given to hardware.

The systems selection process consists of a sequence of activities that allow a financial institution to evaluate and choose solutions to meet its information requirements. Systems selection projects are relatively common in financial institutions, though they vary in scope, approach, and formality. Smaller projects may focus on choosing microcomputer software to satisfy a particular need, such as tracking and accounting for fixed assets. Larger selection projects may focus on the complete replacement of the main system and application software as well as peripheral systems, such as the teller equipment, item capture equipment, etc. The financial institution's specific needs should dictate the approach to follow during the systems selection process to ensure that requirements are properly defined and that hardware and/or software are properly evaluated.

Purpose of the Process

The purpose of the systems selection process is to define systems
requirements well enough to be able to evaluate and select hardware
and/or software that will meet the majority of the financial institution's
business needs. These needs are defined as those functions, features, and
capabilities that assist in the operation and management of the financial
institution. It should be assumed that packaged application software is
available to meet the majority of the business needs.

Benefits of the Approach

A number of significant benefits could result from using the structured
project approach presented in this book. Some of these benefits include:

- An orderly, well-planned analysis of systems alternatives.
- A better understanding of probable benefits and costs.
- Selection of systems that satisfy the financial institution's
  automation objectives and requirements.
- Time savings through a standard approach.
- Consistent information provided to each vendor.
- Higher realization of objectives.
- An education process.

Benefits of Using Outside Consultants

Financial institutions may also benefit considerably from using outside
consulting personnel to perform certain activities within the project. Some
potential benefits include:

- Structured approach.
- An independent evaluation of alternatives.
- Industry expertise.
- Hardware expertise.
- Software expertise.
- Vendor knowledge and experience.

Expert Systems

Recently, expert systems have been developed (i.e., SELECT™ and DP/SELECT™) as a logical and economical technique for selecting a system. An expert system automates the selection process and provides the analytical tools needed to make a documented and informed decision. It can significantly reduce the time and effort involved in all aspects of the systems selection process.

SYSTEMS SELECTION PROCESS

Management's involvement in the systems selection process is critical to the successful completion of the project. The assigned individuals within the financial institution should have a clear understanding of the objectives and scope of their assignment and ensure that a proper reporting relationship with management exists before undertaking this responsibility.

Organizations typically fail in their efforts to select the right system because of one or more of the following factors:

* Improper definition of systems objectives and requirements.
* Failure to involve both management and users at adequate levels.
* Underestimating costs and effort required for conversion.
* Failure to adequately plan for expansion.
* Failure to evaluate software properly.

These factors can be minimized through the use of a structured methodology such as the techniques described below. The process and methodology involved in performing a systems selection is illustrated in Figure 8.1. This process can be used as a guide and tailored to fit the specific circumstances at a financial institution.

1.   **Appoint a selection committee**

A selection committee should be appointed to oversee the systems selection project. The selection committee should be responsible for the outcome of the project and should generally direct, monitor, and report on project activities. The group could consist of personnel from the following areas:

- Management
- Operations
- Information systems
- Internal audit

The committee should have five to seven members, with involvement from others as particular topics of interest are discussed. For example, internal audit personnel should be involved in reviewing input, processing, and output controls relating to data entry, processing, and report production as well as audit trails and on-line security. The committee should be structured so its leader has direct responsibility for the success of the entire project.

General responsibilities of the committee should include:

- Establishing the project schedule.
- Assigning responsibilities for major tasks and activities.
- Ensuring adequate resources are committed to the project.
- Resolving differences relating to departmental or application priorities.
- Reviewing requirements lists, the request for proposal, and vendor proposals.
- Comparing RFP responses.
- Preparing a management summary indicating the overall recommendations of the group.
- Coordinating the selection process.
- Providing periodic status reports to management.

The selection committee may also be involved in the implementation process, but the financial institution may determine that an implementation committee could best fulfill the implementation responsibilities.

A single individual should be assigned responsibility for project leadership and for coordinating with management and departmental personnel. This individual should have the following minimal knowledge and skills:

- Data processing expertise.
- A background in similar projects.
- Knowledge of the organization.
- Knowledge of the financial industry.

The project leader should report directly to the selection committee and should have sufficient authority to carry out the assigned responsibilities. This person will likely have operational experience in one or more departments, but it is important that the leader be impartial as data is collected and systems are prioritized, evaluated, and selected. A project of this magnitude requires an adequate amount of time from the project leader and involved departmental personnel. In some cases, this will be a full-time project for several months.

As a preliminary step in the systems selection project, the selection committee should develop a clear understanding of the current situation and management's objectives. To best understand the current situation, the following questions should be answered:

- What does management perceive the problem to be?
- What hardware and software are presently installed in the affected departments?
- What preliminary selection work has been performed (e.g., meetings with vendors, proposals from vendors, etc.)?
- What vendors have been considered thus far?
- What assistance can be obtained from interested third parties (e.g., independent consultants and vendors)?
- What alternatives is management considering (e.g., in-house systems, service centers, software replacement, facilities management, etc.)?
- Does management have reasonable expectations regarding time frame, costs, benefits, etc.?

The selection committee should attempt to develop initial time estimates and a schedule for performing the systems selection project, especially if the project could require several months of effort. The time estimates and schedule will help guide the committee and should help set expectations about the length of time involved in the selection and evaluation process. When reviewed by the management team, the time estimates and schedule may also help identify "missing" activities.

To properly estimate the scope of work to be performed, the selection committee will need to discuss a number of subjects with the board, management, and appropriate department heads. The answers to these questions will help the selection committee estimate hours and prepare the project schedule:

• How much is the financial institution willing to spend for a system?
• Is the financial institution willing to hire outside consulting personnel to assist in the project?
• Will departmental personnel be involved in data collection or other activities?
• How soon does management want the system implemented?
• Is a detailed cost/benefit analysis necessary?
• Does management hope to justify the system based on direct labor savings or some other measurable criteria? How will this information be gathered? How long will it take?
• How many vendors will be considered?

The following questions will provide the selection committee with a general understanding of the level of equipment needed (e.g., PC, LAN, midrange computer, mainframe computer, etc.):

• What applications need to be automated or updated?
• What are the general transaction volumes of these applications?
• How many terminals and printers will be required?
• Where will terminals and printers be located--inside and/or outside the facility?
• How many remote locations will be on-line?

- Is there a need to communicate with computer systems outside the organization?
- Does the financial institution currently have data processing personnel who can assist in the technical evaluation?
- Will management consider the addition of data processing or technical support personnel?

2.   Perform a needs assessment

The needs assessment process involves gaining an understanding of current systems, determining the features required in proposed systems, and identifying current systems costs.

The selection committee needs to understand and document the financial institution's present manual or automated systems so it can define requirements for each application area to be affected by new systems. Documentation of present systems may include one or more of the following items:

- Excerpts from policies/procedures manuals.
- Excerpts from application reference manuals (from presently automated systems).
- Narrative descriptions of each application with input forms and key reports.
- Flowcharts with input forms and key reports.
- Interview notes from departmental interviews.
- Systems understanding checklists and questionnaires.

The selection committee or designated individuals will need to define the features, capabilities, and reports that are desired and required to meet the majority of departmental personnel's needs. These features and requirements may be developed through several techniques:

- The selection committee may develop a questionnaire, similar to Figure 8.2--Systems Selection Department Questionnaire, and ask appropriate personnel to complete it. Questionnaires can then be reviewed and used in developing systems requirements for the application areas.

- The selection committee may furnish examples of requirements to department managers and ask that they develop or modify the requirements to fit their specific needs. The committee can then meet with individual department managers and review the materials. After the meetings, a composite draft can be prepared and submitted to the management team for approval.
- The selection committee may conduct individual interviews or have group meetings with managers and key employees to obtain their ideas regarding features and requirements, and then develop a summary for management's approval.

The list of requirements that the committee develops will be the major component of the RFP and will be used to evaluate and compare various software products.

Occasionally, because of the uniqueness of particular requirements, general software packages that meet such requirements may not be readily available. These applications or requirements need to be identified, as they may have a substantial impact on the cost of implementing automated systems.

The selection committee may need to rate the complexity of unique applications to determine the potential cost of developing or modifying systems or features. The complexity rating can be used to estimate the number of hours and dollars involved in designing, programming, testing, and implementing the systems or systems changes.

In some instances, the organization may decide to eliminate unique requirements from its objectives rather than incur the cost of developing special application programs.

To provide a basis for comparisons with proposed systems, current systems costs should be identified. When possible, departmental personnel should review the prior twelve months' invoices for the following major expense items:

- Hardware lease or rental.
- Hardware maintenance.
- Software license/support fees.

- Outside service center costs.
- Data communications costs.

Other expenses such as the costs of forms, supplies, magnetic media, etc., should also be identified. In some cases, costs may not be significantly different with a new system. If not, this should be noted for discussion and inclusion in the management report.

Current labor costs are easily identified when specific personnel are dedicated to the data processing operation. However, when automating an application area for the first time, management may be interested in the "potential labor savings" through automation. This information can be obtained through a work distribution study or by generally estimating percentages of time spent performing those functions that would be transferred to an automated system.

The selection committee should be cautious in presenting this information as labor "savings." It is more likely to be time made available for other tasks. Automation may not result in a direct reduction in the number of staff hours or in the number of personnel. Personnel savings may only be achieved as attrition occurs.

3.   Determine processing volumes

Selection committee members should also document key volumes for each application area, since this information can subsequently be used to determine specific hardware requirements. Current and future volumes (e.g., five-year) should be used to ensure that the proposed system has adequate capacity for processing today's volume of business with a margin for reasonable growth.

Processing volumes should be included in the RFP and used by the vendors to determine the size, speed, and capacity of the hardware. Future volumes can be estimated by analyzing growth patterns and the future plans of the financial institution.

4.   Develop specifications

The vendors should be provided with the basic information required to prepare a specific proposal. Therefore, the selection committee should develop a request for proposal (RFP) to facilitate this information.

The RFP should be developed in the appropriate level of detail to obtain the desired response from each vendor. A properly designed RFP has many benefits. It can facilitate the comparison and evaluation of vendor responses because each vendor must submit a proposal that matches the financial institution's specifications rather than one in its own format. The RFP process allows the financial institution to obtain meaningful, competitive proposals based on standard criteria. An objectively prepared RFP can also reduce the possibility of favoritism. The RFP should contain the following minimum information:

- Transmittal letter and table of contents.
- Background information.
- Proposal instructions.
- Vendor worksheets.
- Desirable software features, functions, and capabilities.
- Estimated volumes.
- Suggested equipment configuration.
- Security and control considerations.

Transmittal Letter

The purpose of the transmittal letter is to introduce the financial institution and the selection committee to each vendor. It could contain the following information:

- Primary contact person and telephone number.
- Deadline for receiving proposals.
- Specific methods for answering vendor inquiries.
- If vendor visits to the financial institution prior to proposal submission are desired.
- Circumstances for oral presentations of the vendor proposals.
- Anticipated selection date.

The table of contents helps the vendors quickly locate each section of the RFP.

Background Information

The background information should include a description of the financial institution, current systems and processing methods, existing equipment, and the purpose and objectives of the RFP. It should specifically identify all requirements for interface with other systems, equipment, and networks.

The background section of the RFP should also include a description of the prioritized proposal evaluation criteria. This information can help the vendors compare their relative strengths and weaknesses and assess their chances for success.

Proposal Instructions

The specific instructions for completing proposals should include and/or request information pertaining to:

- Specific hardware proposed.
- Expansion capability.
- Systems software.
- Application software.
- Program modifications.
- Hardware service.
- Software support.
- Training.
- Conversion requirements.
- Special facility requirements.
- Implementation schedule.
- Contractual considerations.

Specific instructions could also include stipulations that:

- Proposed hardware be in current production.
- New (versus reconditioned) equipment be proposed.
- Specific interface requirements be met by the proposed system.
- Proposed system be operational at other locations.

Software Features, Functions, and Capabilities

This section of the RFP contains a prioritized listing of all software features, functions, and capabilities required by the financial institution. Figure 8.3 contains a suggested format for documenting these specifications.

Unique or unusual processing requirements may need to be documented in more detail and could include screen designs, file layouts, processing flowcharts, and report formats.

Vendor Worksheets

This section of the RFP should contain the worksheets pertaining to:

- Vendor information.
- Hardware information.
- Costs.
- Vendor references.

These worksheets should be completed by all vendors and included in their proposals. The worksheets help expedite the evaluation process by ensuring that complete information is obtained in a standard format.

Estimated Volumes

The current and projected processing volumes that were gathered during the needs assessment should be included in the RFP. Figure 8.4 contains a suggested format for documenting key volume information. It has specific columns for:

- Current average volumes.
- Current peak volumes.
- Five-year projected average volumes.
- Five-year projected peak volumes.

Vendors need this information to help determine the proper hardware size, speed, and capacity. It is also useful in determining the required expansion capabilities of the system.

Suggested Equipment Configuration

In order to prepare valid proposals, vendors should be provided with guidelines for the equipment configuration. This is especially important for peripheral equipment such as terminals and printers. The combination of volume information and the suggested equipment configuration will help the vendors determine the size, speed, and capacity of the central processing unit (CPU) and disk storage devices.

Security and Control Considerations

The RFP should describe the security and control requirements for the new system. The accuracy and confidentiality of information is essential to the financial institution and must be protected from inadvertent or intentional abuse. Adequate security and controls are necessary to:

- Ensure the integrity and accuracy of management information systems.
- Prevent unauthorized alteration during data creation, transfer, and storage.
- Maintain confidentiality.
- Restrict physical access.
- Authenticate user access.
- Verify accuracy of processing during input and output.
- Maintain backup and recovery capability.
- Provide environmental protection against information damage or destruction.

5.   **Research and preselect vendors**

Published information describing the availability of software packages designed specifically for the financial industry should be used to identify vendors to be considered for evaluation. This information, combined with personal knowledge of the capability of local and nonlocal vendors, will help identify systems that could satisfy a majority of the processing and reporting requirements of the financial institution.

Selecting the right vendors when changing systems can be very difficult. Since the financial institution will live with the decision for a number of years, its importance cannot be overemphasized. Change is difficult for most organizations, so there is a tendency to resist change, which represents the unknown. There may be a tendency to continue with the same vendor or type of system for psychological reasons even if other systems can better serve the needs of the financial institution. To ensure that the best potential vendors are selected, several factors should be considered about each vendor, including its:

- Stability.
- Installation (customer) base.
- Organizational structure and expertise.
- Length of time in business.
- Industry orientation.
- Reputation and references.
- Product offerings.
- Active user group(s).
- Future direction and plans.

Following is a description of these and other key factors.

Vendor Stability

Vendor stability can be defined as the vendor's ability to provide consistently good service and support levels with minimal organizational disruption. Financial strength is the key to a vendor's ability to provide such service and support. For vendors that publish financial information, financial strength is relatively easy to assess. Privately held companies offer more of a challenge. Key information from industry analysts can help develop an understanding of economic strength.

Some vendors attempt to strengthen their balance sheets by claiming excessive asset value for their software products. To determine whether figures are inflated, evaluate the relative age and functionality of a vendor's software compared to others'.

Historic and current performance of gross revenues and profits may provide a key to vendor economic strength. Growth in revenues and profits may indicate new services and customers, while growth in revenues only, with little effect on profits, probably indicates inflationary increases in fees and expenses.

The portion of revenues attributed to hardware sales should be analyzed closely, since margins on hardware sales are often low and tend to inflate revenues while having minimal effect on profitability. Revenues and profits from software sales, training, implementation, and service fees may provide a clearer indication of vendor economic stability.

Installation (Customer) Base

The number of installed customers can provide a measure of the vendor's success in marketing its products. One could assume that the better the system, the more the system will be purchased. This logic is not necessarily correct, since a number of other factors such as level of competition, price, etc., directly affect the installed customer base. However, a large installed user base should generally indicate relative success in marketing their products compared to other vendors. Trend reporting, if available, is a valuable tool in this analysis.

Smaller vendors may offer the following advantages and disadvantages:

Advantages

- Their products may be quite new and, therefore, offer functionality not found in other systems.
- The applications may best use the technical features of the latest generation of hardware.
- They may be eager for new revenue sources and be willing to negotiate prices and service levels.

Disadvantages

- Their products may be unproven. They may not have withstood the "test of time."
- One large customer could consume most of the vendor's available resources.
- Small vendors may be less stable. A small revenue base could be a problem if the vendor becomes overextended.

Larger vendors may offer the following advantages and disadvantages:

Advantages

- Their products may have been proven by many installations.
- Technical resources may be more readily available for trouble-shooting or customer service requests.
- Revenue streams are more constant, potentially indicating economic strength and stability.

Disadvantages

- Negotiations with larger vendors are more difficult.
- Products or services may not be "state-of-the-art."
- Products or services may have been developed for use with older equipment and may not take advantage of some of the technological innovations available today.

Organizational Structure and Expertise

All vendors should have the following organizational functions included in their structure:

- Administration.
- Marketing.
- Customer support.
- Operations (service centers only).
- Technical support (systems development, maintenance, and communications support).

The absence of these functions or high turnover in these areas may indicate that a problem exists. If sales or marketing personnel change frequently, this may indicate that the system is not competitive with other systems. If customer support personnel change frequently, this may indicate that the current customer base is unhappy with the system and is applying pressure for changes and enhancements.

The selection committee should request information relating to structure and makeup of the vendor's organization, including information relating to background, experience, and longevity of key staff. Discussions with current users may assist in this evaluation.

Length of Time in Business

Companies that have been in business for longer periods of time are generally thought to be more stable than relatively new companies. Although the computer industry offers several examples of successful upstart companies, many of these companies are unable to direct financial and other resources into ongoing product maintenance and development at the right time. Usually when a second generation of products is needed to continue competing in the marketplace, revenues fall and the companies are unable to continue without significant loss in posture and market share.

Industry Orientation

Some vendors offer products and services in a broad range of industries. While this diversity appears on the surface to provide for greater economic stability during economic cycles, it could distract the organization's attention from the needs of a specific industry. Vendors that specialize in financial industry products and services must stay tuned to the requirements of the industry to remain competitive. Even within the financial industry, further specialization is common. Some vendors specialize in commercial bank processing while others emphasize processing for financial institutions. Some in-house vendors specialize in asset/liability management, while others emphasize platform automation. The selection committee should attempt to preselect those vendors that can best provide systems in the application areas in need of change.

Reputation and References

Reputation can be communicated by word-of-mouth, through advertising and testimonials, or through more formal reference checks. Reputation can be positive or negative but generally reflects the vendor's historical performance in the areas of service, functionality, training, and support. The selection committee should be concerned with the reputation of the vendor(s) providing both hardware and software support. Surprisingly, a vendor may be exceptionally strong in one region of the country, yet very weak in another due to differences in personnel, operations, communications, etc. All members of the selection committee should network at various conferences and association meetings, gathering input from a variety of sources to identify trends in and status of vendor strengths in the financial institution's region.

Product Offerings

The breadth of product offerings from the various vendors may be a deciding factor in selecting the best alternatives. If a particular vendor can provide only limited application support in certain application areas, it may not provide the best overall solution for the financial institution. For example, platform automation systems are quite common today, but some vendors offer no alternatives for these functions. Consequently, the financial institution may have to coordinate proposals from multiple sources to deliver full functionality to departments requiring automation. This is further complicated if hardware and software interfaces must be developed for applications to communicate with each other. Many vendors offer more than a one-application solution in today's environment.

Active User Group(s)

Some vendors and service centers do not have active user groups to provide input regarding systems enhancements and improvements. Ideally, a user group should consist of representatives from various financial institutions that share common systems (hardware, software, and servicer). The groups should meet regularly and be directed by user, rather than vendor, personnel. Their goals should include the sharing of knowledge and expertise relating to the systems they use and providing feedback to the vendor regarding potential systems improvements and enhancements. Many user associations are involved in detailed testing and approval of new products and in priority-setting activities for future changes.

Future Direction and Plans

The ability to plan for the future is a sign of a strong vendor. Many organizations tend to plan for the short-term rather than three to five years into the future. When this happens, annual sales and profits take precedence over investments in the future. Finding the right mix of short-term and long-term strategies is difficult but necessary for long-term organization stability and success. The selection committee should request copies of formal planning documents to ensure that vendor goals and objectives are consistent with the objectives of the financial institution.

6. **Analyze and evaluate proposals**

The evaluation process can be extremely difficult and complicated because:

- Proposals may meet, exceed, or fall below the specific RFP requirements by varying degrees.
- Technical issues are different for each vendor.
- Terminology varies among vendors.
- It is difficult to compare the relative importance of various selection criteria.

The vendor proposals should be sufficiently detailed and organized to demonstrate an adequate understanding of the financial institution's requirements. The more complete and specific the RFP, the better it serves as a basis for evaluating and comparing alternatives.

The completeness and timeliness of a proposal may be an indication of the general responsiveness of the particular vendor. This may relate to the degree of support that can be expected from the vendor in the future. Each proposal should respond to all RFP requirements or provide a sufficient explanation of any deviations.

Cost Analysis

The first step in analyzing automation alternatives is identifying all one-time and annual operating costs for a system's life cycle so the costs of proposed systems can be compared. The actual length of the various systems' life cycles will vary; however, it can be assumed that a system will be obsolete after five years.

The cost analysis should include only the costs that have an impact on the selection decision. For example, the cost of existing equipment that was purchased in the past may not be relevant when analyzing the cost of a new system. Another example could be the cost associated with space requirements of a system. These costs are probably irrelevant if the financial institution has excess space that could not be rented or used for other purposes.

Even after costs are identified, it can be difficult to compare service centers, facilities management, and in-house alternatives because different costs, variables, and assumptions are used with each approach. In-house systems usually have a higher one-time cost than service centers. Service centers normally have higher annual operating costs than in-house systems. Calculating the net present value of the cash outflows associated with each alternative will facilitate the comparisons.

Figure 8.5 contains a list of typical one-time and annual operating costs that should be considered when performing a comprehensive cost comparison--including both direct and indirect costs. A comprehensive approach is especially useful for comparing a combination of in-house systems, service centers, and facilities management alternatives because it compares the total costs for each alternative.

Hardware Analysis

The selection committee should compare the vendors' hardware configurations and investigate significant variations in speeds or capacities. The central processing unit and disk storage devices are especially difficult to compare because vendors use different hardware and software technology. In addition, the terminology between vendors is different and often confusing.

Because a system's ability to meet the financial institution's future needs is a key selection criterion, it is important to determine the amount of the proposed configuration that will be utilized with the existing volumes, such as:

- Percent of disk storage utilized.
- Number of print hours per day.
- Amount of time required for end-of-day processing, including backup.
- Terminal response time.

Similarly sized financial institutions identified by the vendor as references should also be contacted to discuss their experiences with these issues.

The projected future volumes should be carefully analyzed to ascertain that the proposed hardware configuration can be expanded to accommodate these future needs.

The theoretical limitations of systems can be different than the practical limitations. For example, theoretically it may be possible to connect additional terminals to a system, however the response time may be inadequate because there is a constraint on the internal memory of the central processing unit. In addition, software may not be portable to larger families of hardware from the same vendor. Therefore, it is possible that a complete change of both hardware and software may be required if the system does not have adequate expansion capabilities.

Software

There are several approaches for evaluating the software features, functions, and capabilities. Initially, the selection committee should carefully review the written responses to each desired software feature specified in the RFP.

The committee should assume that reputable vendors will respond honestly. However, an item may be subject to misinterpretation by the vendor, or an item that is only partially supported by vendors' systems might be answered as a standard feature by one (on the basis of that portion that is supported), but might not be answered as a standard feature by another. Further, a vendor may qualify a response or it may be subject to misinterpretation by the evaluator. So it may be necessary for the evaluator to clarify and revise certain responses in order to obtain a more valid comparison.

Other software considerations should include:

• Software flexibility is important in any type of systems alternative. The design should be modular to facilitate adding new applications. In addition, the software should be parameter-driven to allow nontechnical users to change processing routines and procedures (e.g., interest computations, service charge routines, etc.) without modifying the program.

- Software integration is also an important consideration for all alternatives because it allows a financial institution to streamline its overall operations. Duplication of effort in data entry and computer processing should be minimized. Integration can be of particular benefit in the CIF and general ledger applications.
- File transfer capability between a main computer system and a microcomputer can provide end users with a powerful capability.
- It is important to have good documentation that is easy to use and up-to-date. Outdated documentation is a common problem when systems have been modified.
- Many systems provide a report writer software package to allow a nontechnical user to develop special reports. However, as a word of caution, all report writers are not created equal.
- All applications do not have to be acquired from a single source. Microcomputers and distributed processing techniques provide several options and alternatives.
- Attracting, retaining, and managing a qualified EDP technical staff is a common problem that is more acute in nonurban areas. The level of software support provided by the vendor can reduce the need for EDP technical personnel.
- Software support is as important as hardware maintenance. Financial institutions should consider the vendor's ability to provide continuing regulatory changes and other enhancements on a timely basis. Be careful when modifying a standard package, because it could result in an unsupported system. A prerequisite to software modification is the availability of source code; however, many vendors do not provide source code. Source code is in human readable form, whereas object code can only be read by the computer.
- Changing EFT and telecommunications technology requires special analysis because of its severe systems impact. It is important to consider the interface to ATM and POS networks, as well as the processing for microfiche, ACH, and on-line teller terminals.
- Software should be standardized and consistent.
- The software should be easy to use and understand.

- Training and education are important considerations for any software system. Information should be presented in a nontechnical manner. It is helpful if the instructor has previous experience with financial institutions. Tutorials and audiovisual aids can enhance the learning experience.
- A smooth conversion can be a critical concern for a financial institution. It starts with adequate planning and scheduling. Magnetic conversions should be properly tested and reviewed to minimize data conversion errors. Converting after the update on Thursday versus Friday can provide an extra day for contingencies.
- A strong user group can provide the financial institution with a forum to exchange ideas and solve problems. It can also provide the vendor with future direction for software enhancements.

Vendor References

It is important to check several references for each vendor to obtain additional information relating to hardware, software, and support services. The major issues that should be discussed include:

- Installation
- Training
- Software support
- Product enhancements
- Custom programming (if applicable)
- Documentation
- Hardware
- Other issues

Vendor Demonstrations

As part of the evaluation process, the selection committee should schedule and attend in-depth vendor demonstrations.

The agenda for the demonstrations should be developed by the selection committee rather than the vendor. This will allow the committee to focus their time and efforts on issues that are important to the financial institution. The selection committee should also develop specific questions for vendor demonstrations to facilitate subsequent comparison and analysis.

User Site Visits

Visits to user installations of similar systems help verify vendors claims and help obtain additional information from a live processing environment. However, the specific objectives of the user site visit should be carefully planned prior to the visit in order to effectively utilize the time of all parties involved. Specific responsibilities for obtaining particular information should be assigned.

The user visits should be arranged independently by the selection committee rather than the vendor. It is advisable to visit a user with a similar volume profile. It is often assumed that financial institutions in the same peer group have the same type and volume of activity, however this is not necessarily true. During the visit, the selection committee should investigate the capability of the system to adequately process the work load. This information will be useful in determining the proper speed and capacity of the proposed systems.

Benchmarks

The financial institution may desire a benchmark demonstration of the ability of the proposed system to process the existing work load and other requirements outlined in the RFP. Benchmarks can be expensive and time-consuming for both the vendor and the financial institution. For a benchmark to be useful, the financial institution should be directly involved in its planning, development, and execution. Potential benchmarks could include:

- Terminal response time relating to:
    - Single record retrieval.
    - Multiple record retrieval.
    - Interactive update--single record.
    - Interactive update--multiple records.
    - On-line sort--under 1,000 records.

-          On-line sort--over 1,000 records.
-          On-line data entry.
-          On-line data entry with interactive editing.
- End-of-day processing time.
- File backup time.
- Report print time.
- File sort time.
- Data transmission time.

7.   Select hardware, software, and/or related services

The selection committee should develop a list of criteria to be
used in evaluating automation alternatives. These criteria should
assist the selection committee in prioritizing and quantifying
these criteria to best fit the organization's needs. The criteria will
then be used to evaluate the vendor's proposals and assist in
making the systems selection decision.

Based on the above evaluation, each vendor should be ranked
according to management's criteria for selection. A list of
advantages and disadvantages for each alternative should also be
developed. The selection committee should then recommend the
best overall solution, given these findings and conclusions.

A written report containing a summary of the above information
should be presented to management. The report should be
supplemented by descriptions of each alternative and
recommendations relating to contract negotiations and
implementation activities.

8.   Negotiate hardware, software, and service contracts

Once the finalist(s) have been identified through the evaluation
process, contracts for hardware, software, and services should be
negotiated. During the initial phases of contract negotiations, the
institution may choose to work with more than one vendor in an
effort to improve its negotiating position with the best vendor.
Contracts should include provisions that protect both parties and
should be reviewed by legal counsel with experience in the
technical aspects of hardware, software, and related services.

Contracts will vary in complexity and content, depending on the type of products and/or services selected by the financial institution. The reason for developing written agreements for systems-related products and services include:

- Documenting all commitments of the parties involved.
- Defining the responsibilities of all parties for each aspect of the installation and implementation.
- Providing clear technical and legal descriptions.
- Establishing quantitative measures of performance.
- Protecting against potential difficulties and misunderstandings.
- Providing a means of recourse and definition of remedies for potential problems.
- Reducing the risk associated with the acquisition of systems-related products and services.

9.   Implement the system

The implementation process should be a combined effort potentially involving institution personnel, vendor personnel, and outside consulting personnel. The implementation plan should provide specific details regarding the activities, responsibilities, and target dates for the implementation process. A good implementation plan should have the following characteristics:

- Flexibility to allow adjustments in activities and target dates.
- Milestones so that actual performance can be compared to planned performance.
- Methods for recording and reporting project status, problems, achievements, and resource usage.

An implementation plan should include the following information:

- Activity description.
- Responsible party(s).
- Status.
- Estimated hours.
- Target start date.
- Target completion date.

It is important to prepare an estimated timetable for each task and to determine the number of personnel required, including:

- Management personnel.
- Project management personnel.
- Technical personnel.
- User support personnel.
- Internal audit personnel.
- Vendor personnel.
- Consulting personnel.

In addition, it is necessary to consider the additional work load placed on existing staff both during the implementation process and after the system is operational. The following issues and activities should be addressed in the implementation planning process:

- Organizational issues.
- Site preparation activities.
- Education and training activities.
- Hardware installation activities.
- Application software installation activities.
- Conversion activities.
- Testing activities.
- Policy and procedure development activities.
- Operation start-up activities.
- Post-implementation review activities.

10.   Perform a post-implementation review

Once the implementation process has been completed, a post-implementation review should be performed. This typically entails a review of the new system to verify for management that requirements are being satisfied and that the system is functioning satisfactorily. Specific strengths and shortcomings should be identified and a plan developed to address any serious weaknesses.

Figure 8.1
Systems Selection Process

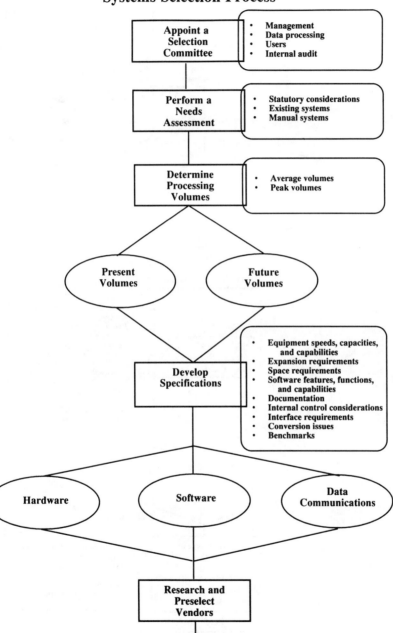

Figure 8.1 (Continued)
Systems Selection Process

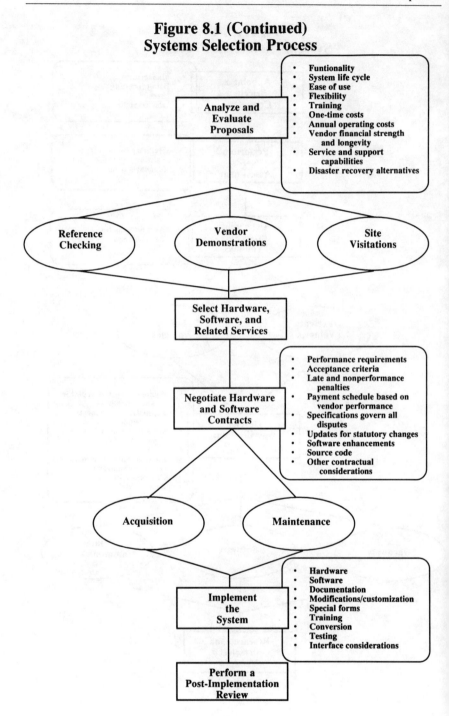

Figure 8.2
Systems Selection Department Questionnaire

A.   Identification Section

Name _____   Date _____

Department _____   Title _____

This questionnaire contains a series of questions regarding the information processing
and reporting needs of your department. Please read each question carefully and
provide answers as indicated. When you are requested to "please explain," keep your
answers brief, but do provide sufficient information. If there is not enough room for
your answer, use the back of the page or additional paper as necessary.

Please complete this questionnaire and return it in the attached envelope to
_____ on or before _____.

An interview may be scheduled with your department following a review of your
answers to this questionnaire. If so, please collect as many of the following materials
as possible prior to the interview:

1.   General documentation of the present method of operation. This may include
      systems narratives, flowcharts, sample copies of the records, forms, reports, and
      other documents.

2.   Current important transaction volume information for applications pertinent to
      the department (such as number of accounts, number of transactions per period,
      etc.).

3.   If your department is automated, a list of the equipment being used and copies
      of the purchase or rental contract(s) and maintenance agreements for hardware
      and/or software.

Figure 8.2 (Continued)
Systems Selection Department Questionnaire

B.   Department Description Section

   1.   Please provide a brief description of your function within the department:

        _____

        _____

        _____

        _____

        _____

        _____

        _____

        _____

        _____

   2.   Please list the names and responsibilities of supervisory personnel in the
        department:

        Name: _____   Responsibility: _____

                      _____   _____

                      _____   _____

                      _____   _____

                      _____   _____

                      _____   _____

                      _____   _____

Figure 8.2 (Continued)
Systems Selection Department Questionnaire

3. Please provide the total number of personnel in the department:

    _____

C. Department Operations Section

    1. What hardware is presently used in the department?

                                                    Quantity

        Terminals   _____
        PCs   _____
        Printers   _____
        LANs   _____
        Other: _____   _____
        _____   _____
        _____   _____

    2. Is there a need for additional equipment in the department? Please explain:

        _____
        _____
        _____

    3. Is there unused equipment in the department? Please explain:

        _____
        _____
        _____

    4. What type of information is received from other departments? Please explain:

        _____
        _____
        _____

Figure 8.2 (Continued)
Systems Selection Department Questionnaire

5.   What type of information is prepared by this department? Please explain:

_____
_____
_____

6.   What information mentioned above is submitted to other departments? (Please name other departments.) Please explain: _____

_____
_____
_____
_____
_____
_____

7.   Are there any improvements that you would suggest in collecting data, processing data, or generating reports?

_____ Yes   _____ No

Please explain: _____

_____
_____
_____
_____
_____
_____

8.   Please list the most important report(s) that you receive (please provide sample copies of these reports):

_____
_____
_____
_____

Figure 8.2 (Continued)
Systems Selection Department Questionnaire

9.   Please list the least important report(s) that you receive (please provide sample copies of these reports):

_____
_____
_____
_____
_____
_____

10. What additional reports (reports you do not now receive) would make your job easier?

Please explain: _____

_____
_____
_____
_____
_____

11. Please list the significant records maintained by your department (please provide sample copies of these records, forms, logs, etc.):

_____
_____
_____
_____
_____

Figure 8.2 (Continued)
Systems Selection Department Questionnaire

12. Can existing programs and systems be improved?

_____ Yes   _____ No

Consider: Could the system be faster or easier to use? Are the displays and reports easy to understand and use? Could the system do more to help you with your job?

Please explain: _____

_____

_____

_____

_____

_____

D. General Questions

1. Should any of the present manual systems and procedures be automated?

_____ Yes   _____ No

Consider: Are some tasks very repetitive and detail-oriented? Are some tasks dependent upon computer-produced records and reports? Are there related areas that are already automated?

Figure 8.2 (Continued)
Systems Selection Department Questionnaire

Potential Systems to Be Automated

Description	Estimated Volume of Activity	Hours Saved Per Month	Other Benefits
_____	_____	_____	_____
_____	_____	_____	_____
_____	_____	_____	_____
_____	_____	_____	_____

2. Please list the areas in your department that you think should **not** be automated (should remain manually prepared).

Description	Estimated Volume of Activity	Hours Saved Per Month	Other Benefits
_____	_____	_____	_____
_____	_____	_____	_____
_____	_____	_____	_____
_____	_____	_____	_____

Figure 8.2 (Continued)
Systems Selection Department Questionnaire

3.   Are you aware of any application programming packages that would be useful in automating your department?

_____ Yes   _____ No

Please explain: _____
_____
_____
_____
_____
_____

4.   Are current systems easy to use?

_____ Yes   _____ No

5.   Is there a need to access information by various methods? (Consider: name, description, date, account number, document number, reference number, etc.).

_____ Yes   _____ No

6.   Are there applications in your department that may require a separate computer?

_____ Yes   _____ No

Please explain: _____
_____
_____
_____
_____
_____

Figure 8.2 (Continued)
Systems Selection Department Questionnaire

7. Please provide any other comments that you would like to make regarding
    automation of your department.

    _____

    _____

    _____

    _____

    _____

    _____

Figure 8.3
Software Features, Functions, and Capabilities
Application Name: _____

Priority (H, M, L)	Feature Description	Type (I,P,O)	Included in Standard Package	Not Included in Standard Package	Comments

H = High   M = Medium   L = Low
I   = Input   P = Processing   O = Output

Figure 8.4
Estimated Processing Volumes

Description	Current Volumes		Five-Year Projected Volumes	
	Average	Peak	Average	Peak

Figure 8.5
One-Time and Annual Operating Costs

Cost Description	One-Time Costs	Annual Operating Costs
Hardware:		
Main computer	X	X
MICR equipment	X	X
Teller terminals	X	X
PCs	X	X
LANs	X	X
Imaging equipment	X	X
Cables	X	
Power isolation transformers	X	
Uninterrupted power supply (UPS)	X	X
Support Equipment:		
Burster	X	X
Decollator	X	X
Tape cleaner	X	
Tape rack	X	
Envelope stuffers	X	
Noise silencers for printers	X	
Jogger	X	
Office Equipment:		
Data media cabinets	X	
Calculators		X
Desks		X
Chairs	X	
Telephones	X	
Outlet strips	X	
Antistatic flooring	X	
Telecommunications:		
Hardware	X	X
Software	X	X
Telephone line installation	X	
Line costs		X

Cost Description	One-Time Costs	Annual Operating Costs
Software:		
Operating system	X	X
Systems software	X	X
Application software	X	X
Custom modifications	X	
MICR software	X	X
Teller terminal software	X	X
ATM software	X	X
ACH software	X	X
PC software	X	X
LAN software	X	X
Imaging software	X	X
Supplies:		
Disks, tapes, and diskettes		X
Stock paper		X
Special forms		X
Printer ribbons		X
Printer bands		X
Output binders		X
Office supplies		X
Site Preparation:		
General construction	X	
Electrical	X	
Fire detection and prevention equipment	X	
Computer room security equipment	X	
Terminal cable installation	X	
Telephone installation	X	
Office furnishings	X	
Air conditioning equipment	X	
Humidity control equipment	X	

Figure 8.5 (Continued)
One-Time and Annual Operating Costs

Cost Description	One-Time Costs	Annual Operating Costs
Transition Costs:		
Personnel	X	
Hardware	X	
Software	X	
Delivery	X	
Installation	X	
Conversion	X	
Personnel:		
Wages		X
Taxes and benefits		X
Training		X
Travel	X	X
Other:		
Electricity		X
Telephone		X
Insurance		X
Rent		X
Microfiche processing		X
Sales tax	X	
Consulting fees	X	
Disaster recovery planning	X	X
Depreciation		X
EDP auditing		X
Income tax effect		X

9 DISASTER RECOVERY PLANNING

OVERVIEW

Background

It is especially important during the strategic information systems planning process to carefully evaluate the disaster recovery capabilities related to the implementation of various technology. Financial institutions depend heavily on technology and automated systems, and their disruption for even a few days could cause severe financial loss and threaten survival. The continued operations of the financial institution depend on management's awareness of potential disasters and ability to develop a plan to minimize disruptions of daily operations.

The possibilities for disasters are numerous. They can happen without warning and when they do, there is no time for planning and organizing, only scrambling to recover. Most disasters and their destruction cannot be prevented, but financial institutions can prepare for the possibility by implementing a plan for expedient and successful recovery.

A disaster recovery plan is a comprehensive statement of consistent actions to be taken before, during, and after a disaster. The plan should be documented and tested to ensure the continuity of operations and availability of critical resources in the event of a disaster.

Many officers and directors may not realize their legal and fiduciary responsibility to protect the financial institution and related assets. If the lack of a disaster recovery plan for operational continuity results in personal injury, physical damage, financial loss, or failure to perform as contracted, the directors and officers could be held liable by individuals, corporations, and shareholders.

Benefits

Benefits derived from developing a comprehensive disaster recovery plan include:

- Reduced legal liability.
- Minimized potential economic loss.
- Decreased potential exposure.
- Reduced probability of occurrence.
- Reduced disruption to normal operations.
- Ensured organizational stability.
- Ensured orderly recovery.
- Minimized insurance premiums.
- Reduced reliance on key personnel.
- Increased asset protection.
- Ensured safety of personnel and customers.
- Minimized decision making during a disaster.
- Compliance with legal and regulatory requirements.

Regulatory Considerations

The Federal Financial Institution Examination Council (FFIEC) issued an interagency regulation regarding disaster recovery planning in July 1989. The regulation pertains to all financial institutions that are regulated by the above agency. The purpose of the regulation is "to alert the board of directors and management of each financial institution to the need for contingency planning for their institution." The regulation applies to institutions that have in-house computer systems and those using service centers.

Information technology has expanded rapidly throughout the operations of financial institutions, including:

- Central computer processing.
- Distributed processing.
- End-user computing (PCs).
- Local area networks.
- On-line teller terminals.
- MICR encoding.
- Item processing.
- ATM units.
- Platform automation systems.

- Branch automation systems.
- Office automation systems.
- Voice and data communications.
- Nationwide networks.

As a result, the new regulation states that "contingency planning now requires an institution-wide emphasis, as opposed to focusing on centralized computer operations."

Specific concerns addressed in the regulation include:

- Many contingency plans do not address all of the critical functions throughout the institution.
- Many serviced institutions have not established or coordinated contingency planning efforts with their service bureaus.
- Many service bureaus have not established contingency plans.
- Many contingency plans have not been adequately tested.

An example of the contingency planning process is outlined in an Appendix to the regulation.

Objectives of Disaster Recovery Planning

The primary objective of disaster recovery planning is to protect the financial institution in the event that all or part of its operations and/or computer services are rendered unusable. Preparedness is the key. The planning process should minimize the disruption of operations and ensure some level of organizational stability and an orderly recovery after a disaster.

Other objectives of disaster recovery planning include:

- Providing a sense of security.
- Minimizing risk of delays.
- Guaranteeing the reliability of standby systems.
- Providing a standard for testing the plan.
- Minimizing decision making during a disaster.

The regulation provides a methodology by which the contingency plan should be developed. The diagram at the end of this chapter illustrates the planning process (Figure 9.1). Based on the various considerations addressed during the planning phase, the process itself and related methodology can be as beneficial as the final written plan.

THE PLANNING PROCESS

Each step of the disaster recovery planning process is described below.

1.   **Obtain top-management commitment**

Top management must support and be involved in the
development of the disaster recovery planning process.
Management should be responsible for coordinating the disaster
recovery plan and ensuring its effectiveness within the
organization. Adequate time and resources must be committed to
the development of an effective plan. Resources could include
both financial considerations and the effort of all personnel
involved.

2.   **Establish a planning committee**

A planning committee should be appointed to oversee the
development and implementation of the plan. The planning
committee should include representatives from all functional
areas of the organization. Key committee members should include
the operations manager and the data processing manager. The
committee also should define the scope of the plan.

3.   **Perform a risk assessment**

The planning committee should prepare a risk analysis and
business impact analysis that includes a range of possible
disasters, including natural, technical, and human threats. Each
functional area of the organization should be analyzed to
determine the potential consequence and impact associated with
several disaster scenarios. The risk assessment process should
also evaluate the safety of critical documents and vital records.

Traditionally, fire has posed the greatest threat to an organization.
Intentional human destruction, however, should also be
considered. The plan should provide for the "worst case"
situation: destruction of the main building.

It is important to assess the impacts and consequences resulting
from loss of information and services. The planning committee
should also analyze the costs related to minimizing the potential
exposures.

4.   Establish priorities for processing and operations

The critical needs of each department within the organization should be carefully evaluated in such areas as:

- Functional operations
- Key personnel
- Information requirements
- Processing systems
- Service
- Documentation
- Vital records
- Policies and procedures

Processing and operations should be analyzed to determine the maximum amount of time that the department and organization can operate without each critical system.

Critical needs are defined as the necessary procedures and equipment required to continue operations should a department, computer center, main facility, or a combination of these be destroyed or become inaccessible.

To determine the critical needs of the organization, each department should document all the functions performed within that department. Management can gather this information by documenting daily activities within each department. An analysis over a period of two weeks to one month can indicate the principal functions performed inside and outside the department, and assist in identifying the necessary data requirements for the department to conduct its daily operations satisfactorily. Some of the diagnostic questions that can be asked include:

- If a disaster occurred, how long could the department function without the existing equipment and departmental organization?
- What are the high-priority tasks, including critical manual functions and processes, in the department? How often are these tasks performed, e.g., daily, weekly, monthly, etc.?
- What staffing, equipment, forms, and supplies would be necessary to perform the high-priority tasks?
- How would the critical equipment, forms, and supplies be replaced in a disaster situation?

- Does any of the above equipment require long lead times for replacement?
- What reference manuals and operating procedure manuals are used in the department? How would these be replaced in the event of a disaster?
- Should any forms, supplies, equipment, procedure manuals, or reference manuals from the department be stored in an off-site location?
- Identify the storage and security of original documents. How would this information be replaced in the event of a disaster? Should any of this information be in a more protected location, e.g., a vault?
- What are the current microcomputer backup procedures? Have the backups been restored? Should any critical backup copies be stored off-site?
- What would the temporary operating procedures be in the event of a disaster?
- How would other departments be affected by an interruption in the department?
- What effect would a disaster at the main computer have on the department?
- What outside services/vendors are relied on for normal operations?
- Would a disaster in the department jeopardize any legal requirements for reporting?
- Are job descriptions available and current for the department?
- Are department personnel cross-trained?
- Who would be responsible for maintaining the department's contingency plan?
- Are there other concerns related to planning for disaster recovery?

The critical needs can be obtained in a consistent manner by a user department questionnaire (see Figure 9.2). As illustrated, the questionnaire focuses on documenting critical activities in each department and identifying related minimum requirements for staff, equipment, forms, supplies, documentation, facilities, and other resources.

Once the critical needs have been documented, management can set priorities within departments for the overall recovery of the organization. Activities of each department could be given priorities in the following manner:

- Essential activities--A disruption in service exceeding one day would jeopardize seriously the operation of the organization.
- Recommended activities--A disruption of service exceeding one week would jeopardize seriously the operation of the organization.
- Nonessential activities--This information would be convenient to have but would not detract seriously from the operating capabilities if it were missing.

5.   Determine recovery strategies

The most practical alternatives for processing in case of a disaster should be researched and evaluated. It is important to consider all aspects of the organization such as:

- Facilities
- Hardware
- Software
- Communications
- Data files
- Customer services
- User operations
- MIS
- End-user systems
- Other processing operations

Alternatives, dependent upon the evaluation of the computer function, may include:

- Hot sites
- Warm sites
- Cold sites
- Reciprocal agreements
- Two data centers
- Multiple computers
- Service centers
- Consortium arrangement
- Vendor-supplied equipment
- Combinations of the above

Written agreements for the specific recovery alternatives selected should be prepared, including the following special considerations:

- Contract duration
- Termination conditions
- Testing
- Costs
- Special security procedures
- Notification of systems changes
- Hours of operation
- Specific hardware and other equipment required for processing
- Personnel requirements
- Circumstances constituting an emergency
- Process to negotiate extension of service
- Guarantee of compatibility
- Availability
- Non-mainframe resource requirements
- Priorities
- Other contractual issues

6.   Organize and document a written plan

A well-organized disaster recovery plan will directly affect the recovery capabilities of the organization. The contents of the plan should follow a logical sequence and be written in a standard and understandable format.

Effective documentation and procedures are extremely important in a disaster recovery plan. Considerable effort and time are necessary to develop a plan. However, most plans are difficult to use and become outdated quickly. Poorly written procedures can be extremely frustrating. Well-written plans reduce the time required to read and understand the procedures and, therefore, result in a better chance of success if the plan has to be used. Well-written plans are also brief and to the point.

An outline of the plan's contents should be prepared to guide the development of the detailed procedures. Top management should review and approve the proposed plan. The outline can ultimately be used for the table of contents after final revision. Other benefits of this approach are that it:

- Helps to organize the detailed procedures.
- Identifies all major steps before the writing begins.
- Identifies redundant procedures that only need to be written once.
- Provides a road map for developing the procedures.

A standard format should be developed to facilitate the writing of detailed procedures and the documentation of other information to be included in the plan. This will help ensure that the disaster plan follows a consistent format and allows for ongoing maintenance of the plan. Standardization is especially important if more than one person is involved in writing the procedures. Two basic formats are used to write the plan: background information and instructional information.

Background information should be written using declarative sentences, while the imperative style should be used for writing instructions. Declarative sentences have a direct subject-verb-predicate structure, while imperative sentences start with a verb (the pronoun "you" is assumed) and issue directions to be followed.

Recommended background information includes:

- Purpose of the procedure.
- Scope of the procedure (e.g., location, equipment, personnel, and time associated with what the procedure encompasses).
- Reference materials (i.e., other manuals, information, or materials that should be consulted).
- Documentation describing the applicable forms that must be used when performing the procedures.
- Authorizations listing the specific approvals required.
- Particular policies applicable to the procedures.

Instructions should be developed on a preprinted form. A suggested format for instructional information is to separate headings common to each page from details of procedures. Headings should include:

- Subject category number and description.
- Subject subcategory number and description.
- Page number.
- Revision number.
- Superseded date.

Figure 9.3 contains an example of a standard format for the disaster recovery plan.

Writing Methods

Procedures should be clearly written. Helpful methods for writing the detailed procedures include:

- Be specific. Write the plan with the assumption it will be implemented by personnel completely unfamiliar with the function and operation.
- Use short, direct sentences, and keep them simple. Long sentences can overwhelm or confuse the reader.
- Use topic sentences to start each paragraph.
- Use short paragraphs. Long paragraphs can be detrimental to reader comprehension.
- Present one idea at a time. Two thoughts normally require two sentences.
- Use active-voice verbs in the present tense. Passive-voice sentences can be lengthy and may be misinterpreted.
- Use descriptive verbs. Nondescriptive verbs such as "make" and "take" can cause procedures to be excessively wordy. Examples of descriptive verbs are:

acquire	count	log	record
activate	create	maintain	replace
advise	declare	monitor	report
answer	deliver	move	request
arrange	determine	notify	restore
assign	discontinue	obtain	retrieve
assist	distribute	operate	review
authorize	document	pay	schedule
back up	enter	perform	select
balance	establish	prepare	store
compare	explain	present	submit
compile	file	print	supervise
complete	inform	process	type
contact	list	receive	verify
coordinate	locate	reconstruct	write

- Avoid jargon.
- Use position titles (rather than personal names of individuals) to reduce maintenance and revision requirements.
- Use front and back sides of pages.

- Avoid gender nouns and pronouns that may cause unnecessary revision requirements.
- Develop uniformity in procedures to simplify the training process and minimize exceptions to conditions and actions.
- Identify events that occur in parallel, and events that must occur sequentially.

The benefits of effective disaster recovery procedures include:

- Eliminating confusion and errors.
- Providing training materials for new employees.
- Reducing reliance on certain key individuals and functions.

Scope

Although most disaster recovery plans address only activities related to data processing, a comprehensive plan will also include areas of operation outside data processing. The plan should have a broad scope if it is to effectively address the many disaster scenarios that could affect the organization. A "worst case scenario" should be the basis for developing the plan. The worst case scenario is the destruction of the main or primary facility. Because the plan is written based on this premise, less-critical situations can be handled by using only the needed portions of the plan, with minor (if any) alterations required.

Planning Assumptions

Every disaster recovery plan has a foundation of assumptions on which the plan is based. The assumptions limit the circumstances that the plan addresses. The limits define the magnitude of the disaster the organization is preparing to address. The assumptions can often be identified by asking the following questions:

- What equipment/facilities have been destroyed?
- What is the timing of the disruption?
- What records, files, and materials were protected from destruction?
- What resources are available following the disaster:
  - Staffing?
  - Equipment?

-        Communications?
-        Transportation?
-        Hot site/alternate site?

Following is a list of typical planning assumptions to be considered in writing the disaster recovery plan:

• The main facility of the organization has been destroyed.
• Staff is available to perform critical functions defined within the plan.
• Staff can be notified and can report to the backup site(s) to perform critical processing, recovery, and reconstruction activities.
• Off-site storage facilities and materials survive.
• The disaster recovery plan is current.
• Subsets of the overall plan can be used to recover from minor interruptions.
• An alternate facility is available.
• An adequate supply of critical forms and supplies are stored off-site, either at an alternate facility or in off-site storage.
• A backup site is available for processing the organization's work.
• The necessary long distance and local communications lines are available to the organization.
• Surface transportation in the local area is possible.
• Vendors will perform according to their general commitments to support the organization in a disaster.

This list of assumptions is not all-inclusive, but is intended as a thought-provoking process in the beginning stage of planning. The assumptions themselves will often dictate the makeup of the plan; therefore, management should carefully review them for appropriateness.

The plan should be thoroughly developed, including all detailed procedures to be used before, during, and after a disaster. It may not be practical to develop detailed procedures until backup alternatives have been defined. The procedures should include methods for maintaining and updating the plan to reflect any significant internal, external, or systems changes. The procedures should allow for a regular review of the plan by key personnel within the organization.

Team Approach

The disaster recovery plan should be structured using a team approach. Specific responsibilities should be assigned to the appropriate team for each functional area of the financial institution. There should be teams responsible for administrative functions, facilities, logistics, user support, computer backup, restoration, and other important areas in the organization.

The structure of the contingency organization may not be the same as the existing organization chart. Figure 9.4 illustrates a sample contingency organization chart. The contingency organization is usually structured with teams responsible for major functional areas, such as:

- Administrative functions
- Facilities
- Logistics
- User support
- Computer backup
- Restoration
- Other important areas

Potential teams include:

- Management team
- Business recovery team
- Departmental recovery team
- Computer recovery team
- Damage assessment team
- Security team
- Facilities support team
- Administrative support team
- Logistics support team
- User support team
- Computer backup team
- Off-site storage team
- Software team
- Communications team
- Applications team
- Computer restoration team
- Human relations team
- Marketing/customer relations team
- Other teams

Various combinations of the above teams are possible, depending on the size and requirements of the organization. The number of members assigned to a specific team can also vary, depending on need.

The management team is especially important because it coordinates the recovery process. The team should assess the disaster, activate the recovery plan, and contact team managers. The management team also oversees, documents, and monitors the recovery process. Management team members should be the final decision makers in setting priorities, policies, and procedures.

Each team has specific responsibilities that must be completed to ensure successful execution of the plan. The teams should have an assigned manager and an alternate in case the team manager is not available. Other team members should also have specific assignments where possible. A conceptual flowchart of the recovery process is illustrated in Figure 9.5.

Data-Gathering Techniques

It is extremely helpful to develop preformatted forms to facilitate the data-gathering process. Information that can be compiled by using preformatted data-gathering forms include:

- Equipment Inventory to document all critical equipment required by the organization. If the recovery lead time is longer than acceptable, a backup alternative should be considered.
- Master Vendor List to identify vendors that provide critical goods and services.
- Office Supply Inventory to record the critical office supply inventory to facilitate replacement. If an item has a longer lead time than is acceptable, a larger quantity should be stored off-site.
- Forms Inventory Listing to document all forms used by the organization to facilitate replacement. This list should include computer forms and noncomputer forms.
- Documentation Inventory Listing to record inventory of critical documentation manuals and materials. It is important to determine whether backup copies of the critical documentation are available. They may be stored on disk, obtained from branch offices, available from outside sources, vendors, and other sources.

- Critical Telephone Numbers to list critical telephone numbers, contact names, and specific services for organizations and vendors important in the recovery process.
- Distribution Register to record and control all copies of the recovery plan issued to various personnel. The distribution register also is used to locate plans when updates are required.
- Notification Checklist to document responsibilities for notifying personnel, vendors, and other parties. Each team should be assigned specific parties to contact.
- Master Call List to document employee telephone numbers.
- Backup Position Listing to identify backup employees for each critical position within the organization. Certain key personnel may not be available in a disaster situation; therefore, backups for each critical position should be identified.
- Specifications for Off-Site Location to document the desired/required specifications of a possible alternative site for each existing location.
- Off-Site Location Inventory to document all materials stored off-site.
- Hardware and Software Inventory Listing to document the inventory of hardware and software.
- Telephone Inventory Listing to document existing telephone systems used by the organization.
- Insurance Policies Listing to document insurance policies in force.
- Communications Inventory Listing to document all components of the communications network.

PC Software

There are several PC-based disaster recovery planning systems that can be used to facilitate the data-gathering process and to develop the plan. Typically, these systems emphasize either a database application or a word processing application. The most comprehensive systems use a combination of integrated applications.

Some PC-based systems include a sample plan that can be tailored to the unique requirements of each organization. Other materials can include instructions that address the issues related to disaster recovery that the organization must consider during the planning process, such as disaster prevention, insurance analysis, record retention, and backup strategies. Specialized consulting may also be available with the system to provide on-site installation, training, and consulting on various disaster recovery planning issues.

The benefits of using a PC-based system for developing a disaster recovery plan include:

- A systematic approach to the planning process.
- Predesigned methodologies.
- An effective method for maintenance.
- A significant reduction in time and effort in the planning and development process.
- A proven technique.

Recently, other PC-based tools have been developed to assist with the process, including disaster recovery planning tutorial systems and software to facilitate the testing process.

7.   Develop testing criteria and procedures

It is essential that the plan be thoroughly tested and evaluated on a regular basis (at least annually). Procedures to test the plan should be documented. The tests will provide the organization with the assurance that all necessary steps are included in the plan. Other reasons for testing include:

- Determining the feasibility and compatibility of backup facilities and procedures.
- Identifying areas in the plan that need modification.
- Providing training to the team managers and team members.
- Demonstrating the ability of the organization to recover.
- Providing motivation for maintaining and updating the disaster recovery plan.

8. Test the plan

After testing procedures have been completed, an initial test of the plan should be performed by conducting a structured walk-through test. The test will provide additional information regarding any further steps that may need to be included, changes in procedures that are not effective, and other appropriate adjustments. The plan should be updated to correct any problems identified during the test. Initially, testing of the plan should be done in sections and after normal business hours to minimize disruptions to the overall operations of the organization.

Types of tests include:

- Checklist tests.
- Simulation tests.
- Parallel tests.
- Full interruption tests.

9. Approve the plan

Once the disaster recovery plan has been written and tested, the plan should be approved by top management. It is top management's ultimate responsibility that the organization has a documented and tested plan.

Management is responsible for:

- Establishing policies, procedures, and responsibilities for comprehensive contingency planning.
- Reviewing and approving the contingency plan annually, documenting such reviews in writing.

If the organization receives information processing from a service bureau, management also must:

- Evaluate the adequacy of contingency plans for its service bureau.
- Ensure that its contingency plan is compatible with its service bureau's plan.

Conclusion

Disaster recovery planning involves more than off-site storage or backup processing. Organizations should also develop written, comprehensive disaster recovery plans that address all the critical operations and functions of the business. The plan should include documented and tested procedures, which, if followed, will ensure the ongoing availability of critical resources and continuity of operations.

The probability of a disaster occurring in an organization is highly uncertain. A disaster plan, however, is similar to liability insurance: it provides a certain level of comfort in knowing that if a major catastrophe occurs, it will not result in financial disaster. Insurance alone is not adequate because it may not compensate for the incalculable loss of business during the interruption or the business that never returns.

Figure 9.1
Disaster Recovery Planning Process

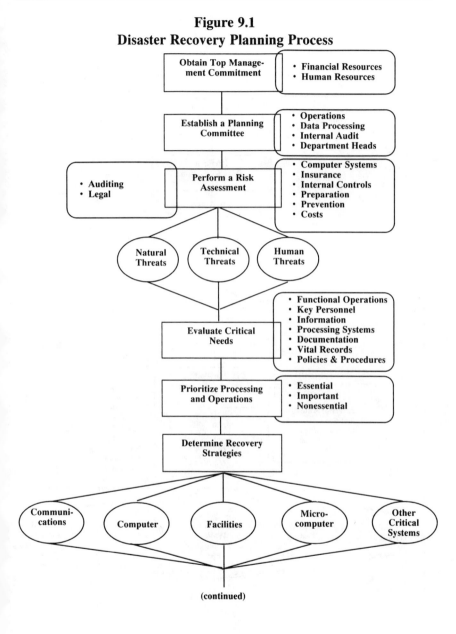

(continued)

Figure 9.1(Continued)
Disaster Recovery Planning Process

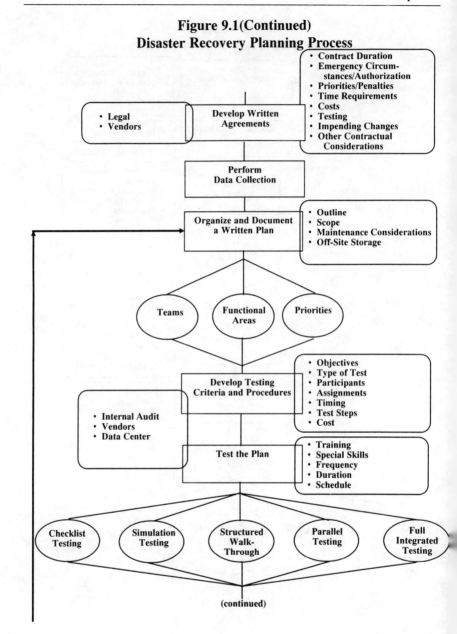

(continued)

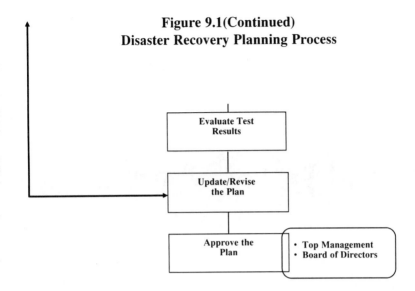

Figure 9.1(Continued)
Disaster Recovery Planning Process

Figure 9.2
User Department Questionnaire

Department: _____

Critical Needs	Fre-quency	Minimum Requirements and Resources				
		Staff	Equipment	Forms/Supplies	Documen-tation	Facilities

Figure 9.3
Standard Format for the Disaster Recovery Plan

SECTION TITLE:	SECTION:
SUBSECTION:	PAGE:
REVISION DATE:	SUPERSEDED DATE:

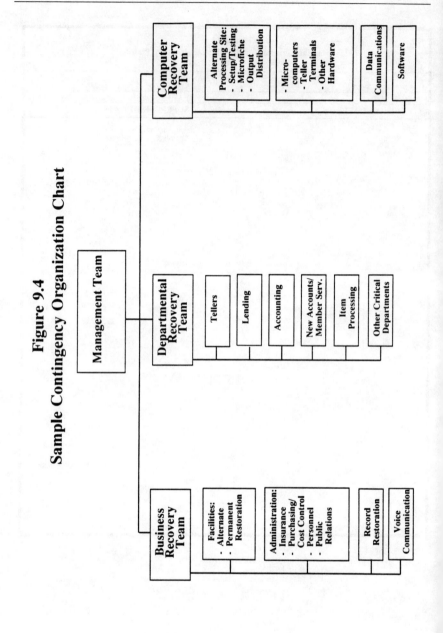

Figure 9.4
Sample Contingency Organization Chart

Figure 9.5
The Recovery Process - Conceptual Flowchart

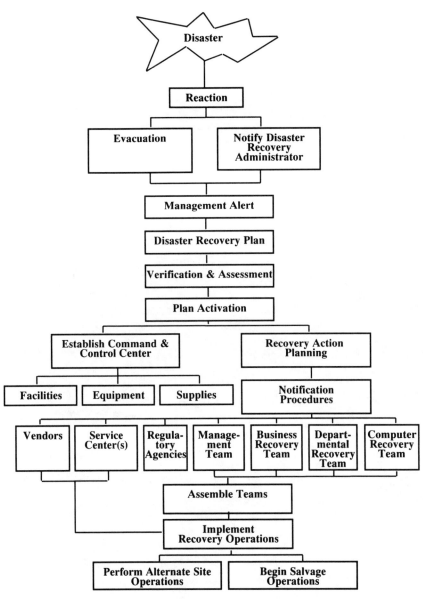

10 SECURITY AND CONTROL REQUIREMENTS

OVERVIEW

Security and controls refer to all the measures adopted within an organization to safeguard assets, ensure the accuracy and reliability of financial records, and encourage operational efficiency and adherence to prescribed procedures. The system of internal controls also includes the measures adopted to safeguard the computer system.

The nature of internal controls is such that certain control procedures are necessary for a proper execution of other control procedures. This interdependence of control procedures may be significant because certain control objectives that appear to have been achieved may, in fact, not have been achieved because of weaknesses in other control procedures upon which they depend.

Concern over this interdependence of control procedures may be greater with a computerized system than with a manual system because computer operations often have a greater concentration of functions, and certain manual control procedures may depend on automated control procedures, even though that dependence is not readily apparent. Adequate EDP internal controls are a vital aspect of a computer system.

Regulatory Concerns

Regulatory agencies are extremely concerned about EDP internal controls because computer processing can circumvent traditional security and control techniques. They have issued a regulation that emphasizes the need for control features. This regulation states that:

"Information, regardless of its source, is a valuable asset to the bank. Its accuracy and confidentiality is essential to the business. Accordingly, it must be protected from abuses such as inadvertent or intentional misuse, disclosure, fraud, and error. Information systems, both the data and the software that creates and stores the data, must be secure."

It recommends designing information security controls to:

- "ensure the integrity and accuracy of management information systems,
- prevent unauthorized alteration during data creating, transfer, and storage,
- maintain confidentiality,
- restrict physical access,
- authenticate user access,
- verify accuracy of processing during input and output,
- maintain backup and recovery capability,
- provide environmental protection against information damage or destruction."

Regulatory examinations normally include an extensive audit of computer procedures and controls. The appendix to this issuance provides additional details on technology controls and various areas of risk.

There are two types of EDP control techniques: (1) general controls that affect all computer systems, and (2) application controls that are unique to specific applications.

GENERAL EDP INTERNAL CONTROLS

Important areas of concern related to general EDP internal controls include:

- Organization controls.
- Systems development and maintenance controls.
- Documentation controls.
- Access controls.
- Data and procedural controls.
- Physical security and contingency planning.

Security is an increasing concern because computer systems are increasingly complex. Particular security concerns result from the proliferation of microcomputers, local area networking, and on-line systems that allow more access to the mainframe computer. Modern technology provides computer thieves with powerful new electronic safe-cracking tools.

Organization controls

A well-planned and properly functioning organization is an important factor in any system of internal control. The organization plan establishes the framework within which the operation functions, and should describe responsibilities for each component of the organization so that no one person has duties that would permit the perpetration and concealment of material errors and irregularities. Usually, the following areas are reviewed and evaluated:

- Segregation of duties between the data processing function and its users.
- Authorization of transactions affecting the system.
- Personnel policies and procedures.
- Planning, budgeting and reporting.
- Segregation of duties within the data processing department.

Systems development and maintenance controls

Standards and procedures for systems development and maintenance provide a cornerstone for the continuity of internal control. They ensure that effective controls are included in all new systems, that the integrity of production programs is maintained, and that the environment in which processing takes place is conducive to proper functioning of application controls. The following areas typically fall under the category of systems development and maintenance controls:

- Written standards and procedures.
- Participation of an administrative steering committee in planning and project completion.
- System and testing techniques.
- System conversion techniques.
- System maintenance procedures.
- Authorization for systems changes.
- Implementation and testing of modified software and new software releases.

Documentation controls

Documentation can provide the means for systems analysts, programmers, operators, and users to understand, maintain, and enhance existing systems. Four levels of documentation should exist:

- Systems documentation.
- Program documentation.
- Operations documentation.
- User documentation.

These levels of documentation will normally provide the foundation for understanding the application systems during the internal controls review.

Access controls

Access to program documentation, source and object programs, production data files, and hardware could affect the results produced by the data processing operation. Improper access controls would defeat the purpose behind adequate segregation of duties. During this part of the review, access limitations placed on employees and other users will be reviewed and evaluated as they relate to data center operations and terminal usage. This includes on-line access as well as physical access to sensitive information and reports.

Data and procedural controls

Many control procedures affecting routine processing of data help ensure that processing results are prompt and accurate. Specifically, the following areas should be reviewed and evaluated:

- Receipt of data, including recording, error correction, and verification.
- Computer operations.
- Internal audit function, if any.
- File backup and reconstruction capability.
- Hardware and software restart/recovery capability.

Physical security and contingency planning

Total destruction of a data center may result in significant loss of business or even business termination. Physical security controls help reduce the risk of accidental or intentional destruction of data, software, and hardware; provide for replacement of records that may be destroyed; and ensure the continuity of operations following a major hardware or software failure.

Password Security Systems

The most widely used computer security and control technique involves the use of confidential character strings known as passwords, user-IDs, and security codes. These terms are used interchangeably by most people. A password can be defined as any character string intended to remain confidential and used to control access by individuals to computer resources including data, equipment, and software. A special type of password is the personal identification number (PIN) that uses a combination of a numeric character string and a magnetically encoded card to control access.

Passwords can be a pervasive aspect of computer security. Although password security may be the best alternative available today, it can be the weakest link in maintaining system integrity. There are several problems with traditional passwords because they can be:

* Misused and mismanaged by individuals.
* Observed in use.
* Tapped from nonsecure lines.
* Simulated by another computer.
* Guessed.
* Traded or loaned.
* Stolen.
* Forgotten.

The effectiveness of using passwords to restrict and control access is based on limiting knowledge of the password to an individual user. Maintaining the confidentiality of a password is dependent on the difficulty involved in decoding it and the ability of the user to remember the password without using a written source. This creates a dichotomy because long, randomly generated passwords are the most difficult to compromise, but are more likely to be written. Conversely, short passwords can be more easily memorized, but are easier to decode or guess.

The number of possible random combinations for various lengths of passwords are listed below. Usually the letters I and O are excluded to avoid confusion with the numbers 1 and 0. This leaves 24 available letters and 10 numbers.

Password Length	Number of Combinations
1	34
2	1,156
3	39,304
4	1,336,336
5	45,435,424
6	1,544,804,416
7	52,523,350,144
8	1,785,793,904,890

Sources of Passwords

Passwords can be selected, issued, and maintained by the following sources:

- User.
- Central administrative function.
- Computer.

User-Selected Passwords

The advantage of user-selected passwords is that only the user and the computer know the proper control string. If the user never discloses the password, its confidentiality will be maintained. The disadvantages of user-selected passwords are:

- Potential lack of randomness.
- Possible infrequency of change.
- Permanent loss of the password if the user forgets.

It is a human tendency to choose a password that is meaningful to the individual. Therefore, user-selected passwords may be closely associated with the individual such as name, spouse, dog, child, address, telephone number, birth date, car license, and other easily remembered possibilities. However, this increases the chance of discovery of such passwords by someone who knows the individual versus a stranger. The resulting lack of randomness can undermine password security.

The frequency of password change impacts confidentiality. The chance of disclosure increases over time. Passwords can become common knowledge in the workplace if not frequently changed.

Forgotten passwords create special problems, especially for occasional users. Reestablishing access security can be a lengthy procedure during which needed information may not be available to the user.

Central Administrative Security Function

A central administrative security function can generate passwords on a random basis, ensure frequency of change, and retrieve forgotten passwords. The disadvantage inherent in this approach is the lack of confidentiality because both the administrator and the user know the password. An additional concern is that the password must be communicated between them.

Computer-Generated Passwords

The computer can generate random passwords and enforce change procedures. An administrative function is required for adding new passwords and reestablishing access when passwords are forgotten.

No system of password generation can provide absolute security and password systems, in themselves, do not provide complete security. They are only one aspect of overall security and control.

Password Distribution

Password security is especially vulnerable during password distribution. Users must be informed that they are authorized to use the system and must have a means of obtaining their password. It can be difficult to ensure that the recipient of the password is the same person who is authorized for access. Techniques for securing password distribution include:

- Direct contact--this method can be effective, but it may be extremely time-intensive in large organizations for face-to-face contact with each user. Geographically disbursed locations create additional difficulties.
- Telephone contact--this method is widely used and relatively inexpensive. However, there are several opportunities for disclosure in using the telephone.

- Manager distribution--many organizations use known and trusted managers in the distribution process. This method eliminates the need to contact users directly and establishes management accountability. Sealed envelopes containing individual passwords are sent to the appropriate manager. The disadvantage with this approach is it relies on trust and increases the number of people involved in the security process.

- Self-mailing envelopes--this method sends the password, receipt, and return envelope to the appropriate individual. The signed returned receipt is the confirmation that the user received the password. The major disadvantage with this approach is that disclosure is possible if the mail is not strictly controlled.

Password Security and Control Techniques

The level and degree of protection provided by a password security system varies significantly between organizations and computer systems. If a password is compromised, a perpetrator can "impersonate" the user--another computer crime technique--and perform specific functions that have originally been intended only for the authorized user. A good password security system should:

- Allow the organization to specify whether password changes will be controlled by the security administrator or the user at the time of installation.

- Provide password security by:
  - User
  - Application
  - Function within the application
  - Transaction within the application

- Store and report the date of last password change for each user.
- Automatically generate passwords upon user request.
- Prevent the user or security officer from changing the present password to a prior password.
- Mask (hide) passwords during entry.
- Direct the user to a default menu after proper sign-on if no menu is specified.
- Restrict the ability to enter certain transactions by terminal (i.e., allow only certain terminals to input financial transactions).
- Monitor unused or inactive passwords.
- Monitor passwords with excessive usage.
- Produce a terminal activity report, indicating the sign-on/off times, system accessed, and functions performed for each terminal user.

- Produce a security violations report, showing all unauthorized attempts to access the system.
- Randomly generate passwords.
- Encrypt passwords.
- Establish password levels based on:
  - File
  - Program
  - Menu
  - Library
- Automatically log-off terminals after a predetermined number of invalid access attempts.
- Automatically log-off users when their terminals remain inactive for a specified time. This control method reduces the risk associated with unattended terminals.
- Inform the user after each log-on of the last successful access by the user and any unsuccessful intervening access attempts. Users can then report any suspicious events.
- Arrange the terminal to inhibit an observer from viewing the keystrokes of the operator during the log-on process.
- Limit the number of terminals that a user can concurrently be logged-on a system. Usually a user should only be logged-on one terminal at a given time.
- Limit the amount of time allowed for log-on by user.
- Require a minimum of six-character passwords. Passwords must be long enough to resist exhaustive searches of all combinations.
- Automatically notify and require users to change passwords after a predetermined period of time.
- Maintain an audit trail of all password changes.
- Restrict access to specific functions by:
  - Terminal
  - Time of day
  - Day of week
- Prohibit printing of passwords.
- Establish a maximum number of attempts for successful log-on. Errors can occur, so users should be allowed more than one attempt to correctly enter a password. However, a maximum number of attempts should be established to prevent automated attacks on the system and random guessing. Terminals or communication ports should be disabled after the maximum allowed attempts have been exceeded.
- Provide alarm system for users under duress.
- Provide a time-and-date stamp for all access attempts.
- Generate an audit trail of all access attempts.

- Require multiple levels of passwords to access extremely sensitive information. Multiple levels of software security can provide greater protection than a single level that an unauthorized user might be able to circumvent. Multilevel password schemes normally do not delay a legitimate user, however they can significantly improve protection from intrusion.
- Restrict the use of programmable function keys (PF keys) or terminal function keys (F keys) in log-on procedures. The use of programmable keys to automatically perform log-on procedures can violate password protection and system integrity.

APPLICATION EDP INTERNAL CONTROLS

Application controls are security techniques that are unique to a specific computer application system, such as demand deposit accounting, savings, certificates of deposit, payroll, and various loan systems. Application controls are classified as:

- Input controls,
- Processing controls, and
- Output controls.

Input Controls

Input controls typically address the origination and authorization of transactions, the recording and error handling associated with transactions, and the filing or retention of source documents. Input controls are usually found at the user department level, because users are most often responsible for source document control and data entry for the application.

Input controls should be designed to provide reasonable assurance that data received for computer processing have been properly authorized, converted into machine-sensible form, and verified, and that data (including data transmitted over communication lines) have not been lost, suppressed, added, duplicated, or otherwise improperly changed. Input controls include controls that relate to rejection, correction, and resubmission of data that were initially incorrect.

There are four basic categories of input that must be controlled:

- Transaction entry: Because transaction entry normally represents the largest volume of activity, it usually accounts for the greatest number of errors.
- File maintenance transactions: File maintenance (updating) often involves a limited volume of data, originates from restricted sources, and has a relatively long-term impact on the file or files that are updated. Errors in the maintenance of master files can have a continuing impact on accounting transactions.
- Inquiry transactions: These transactions do not change the file that is referenced, but may cause decisions that may result in other transactions or inputs.
- Error correction transactions: Error correction can be a very complex procedure. It could involve reversal, adjustment of the original transactions, re-entry of the original transaction, or some combination of these entries. Error correction is usually more complex than the original transaction entry and offers a greater opportunity to create additional errors.

Input control methods include:

- Structured data entry, allowing transactions to be entered in a defined sequence and also providing the same edit checks and field verifications on each transaction.
- Structured error correction, ensuring that each transaction entered during error correction is subject to the same input controls as the original transaction.
- Control totals for a group of transactions, sometimes dollar totals, hash totals, or record counts.
- Review and change capability, with the ability to review and edit original data before releasing the data for processing.

Edit routines should be used to detect and print listings of input errors or exceptions. Examples include:

- Transaction limit tests.
- Cross checks between record fields to verify acceptable relationships or completeness of records.
- Sequence checks of prenumbered documents.
- Completeness tests.
- Logic tests.
- Verify all code values used on input documents.
- Check digits to verify customer account numbers.
- Anticipation controls.

- Comparison to a range of values for reasonableness tests.
- Cross-footing of related fields.
- Test for invalid numerics.
- Test for proper mathematical sign.
- Date checks.

Processing Controls

Processing controls are automated controls built within the application programs and the processing flow that reduce the likelihood of erroneous conditions being caused by:

- Program errors and omissions, which relate to the accidental or intentional creation of an error during processing.
- Hardware errors, where equipment malfunction may cause erroneous data, lost transactions, etc.
- Error handling, which ensures that errors identified during processing are corrected and subject to the same level of controls as the original transaction.

Computer-generated transactions are of special interest to users and internal/external auditors. These transactions are generated based on the entry of another transaction or based on specific conditions met by the transaction. They are the result of the execution of specific programming routines and, therefore, must be tested since the transaction has no source document indicating specific value and authorization. Computer-generated transactions are one of the more vulnerable areas in computer processing, and an area where computer crime has been detected in a number of instances.

Processing controls also consider the ability of restart/recovery procedures to ensure that the same data is not processed twice, that data is not lost, and that data is not erroneously processed.

Processing controls should be designed to provide reasonable assurance that computer processing has been performed as intended for the particular application; i.e., that all transactions are processed as authorized, that no authorized transactions are omitted, and that no unauthorized transactions are added. Such controls should be designed to prevent or detect the following types of errors:

- Failure to process all input transactions, or erroneously processing the same input more than once.
- Processing and updating of the wrong file or files.
- Processing of illogical or unreasonable input.
- Loss or distortion of data during processing.

Output Controls

Output controls refer to the control over balancing and reconciling an application, control over output distribution, and the controls relating to negotiable items and records retention.

Output controls should be designed to assure the accuracy of the processing result (such as account listings, terminal displays, reports, magnetic files, or disbursement checks) and to assure that only authorized personnel receive the output. Output controls should be designed to ensure that all input is processed, processing is accurate, and output is distributed to authorized personnel or groups.

Some potential exposures and concerns relating to this area are:

- Output balancing and reconciliation, ensuring that transactions have been accurately and completely processed.
- Output distribution, ensuring that the transportation and delivery of output, including printed copy, magnetic media, and microfiche, is controlled and limited to authorized recipients.
- Confidentiality, ensuring that information about the organization or an individual is not accidentally or intentionally released.
- Negotiable items, ensuring that negotiable items (i.e., checks, bonds, etc.) are accounted for and assets are protected.
- Records retention and disposal, ensuring that the necessary records of business operation are retained according to regulatory requirements and that storage and waste disposal methods protect the confidentiality of information.

Both general and application internal controls are important protection techniques. However, the cost of a particular internal control procedure should not be significantly higher than the potential benefit received. Compensating manual controls can usually be established when a specific EDP control is not cost-justified. In addition, it is important to establish and maintain an adequate mix of preventive, detective, and corrective control techniques.

Communications Security

Communications security is an increasing concern to financial institutions. One method for improving control is to use security modems.

The purpose of security modems is to control access and to protect information.   A modem is a <u>mo</u>dulation/<u>dem</u>odulation device that transforms data from the computer in digital form to analog form for transmission over a communications facility such as a telephone line. A modem at the other end of the communications line is used to restore the analog signal to the original digital form for another computer.

The speed at which data modems operate is defined as the baud rate, or bits per second (bps). Low-speed modems transmit at 1200 baud, and high-speed modems can operate at 9600 baud or faster.

Modems may have several security features and capabilities, such as callback, password protection, and encryption. One of the methods of protecting networks is the callback approach. A system with callback capabilities can call a user back at a predetermined location listed in the security directory to confirm user authorization. Callback devices usually operate in the following manner:

1.   A remote user dials into the computer using a keyboard or touch-tone telephone.

2.   The callback unit intercepts the access attempt.

3.   The callback device requests a user identification number and a password.

4.   The remote user enters the requested information.

5.   The callback device disconnects the remote user and scans its directory for the user identification to locate a corresponding telephone number.

6.   If the user identification information matches that of an authorized user, the callback device will dial the corresponding telephone number for the particular user. If the information does not match, the callback device should warn the system of an unauthorized access attempt.

The major security advantage of the callback approach is that the callback device links the caller to both the correct identification information and a specific location. Therefore, security cannot be circumvented simply by attempting an endless number of password combinations.

AUDITING CONSIDERATIONS

The proliferation of computers necessitates that the internal audit process be more involved in preventing and detecting computer crime. The *FFIEC EDP Examination Handbook* defines the role of the internal auditor as follows:

> "Internal audit includes an independent appraisal of operations for the board of directors. Auditors evaluate the effectiveness of day-to-day controls to ascertain whether transactions are recorded and processed in compliance with standards set forth by the board of directors and senior management.
>
> Auditors should furnish management with analyses, appraisals, recommendations and other pertinent comments concerning the activities reviewed. These comments will assist management in delegating their responsibilities more effectively. The internal auditor is legitimately concerned with any phase of business activity where audit can be of service to management, and must look beyond accounting financial records to obtain a full understanding of the operations under review."

> "The internal auditor's activities should include:
>
> - Reviewing, appraising, and reporting on the soundness, adequacy, and application of accounting, financial and other operating controls.
> - Assisting in the promotion of effective control at reasonable cost.
> - Ascertaining the extent of compliance with established policies, plans, procedures and law.
> - Ascertaining the extent to which assets are accounted for and safeguarded from loss.
> - Ascertaining the reliability of management data developed within the organization.
> - Appraising the quality of performance by others in carrying out their assigned responsibilities.
> - Recommending alternatives for the correction of control deficiencies.

The responsibilities of internal auditors in a financial institution should be clearly established in a written policy statement or charter adopted by the institution's board of directors.

This charter should clearly state the auditor's right of access to all records, policies, plans, procedures, properties, and personnel relevant to the matters under review. Failure to do so may denote a lack of commitment and direction to audit by the directors."

It also states:

"The internal audit staff of the financial institution must have sufficient EDP expertise to perform data processing audits. This expertise should be commensurate with the degree and sophistication of the data processing function, regardless of the institution's size. However, if the internal expertise is inadequate, other sources such as management consultants, CPA firms, qualified EDP professionals, or possibly correspondent banks should be solicited to aid or replace the EDP audit function."

BC-226 specifically addresses the involvement of the internal audit function in auditing microcomputer systems (i.e., end-user computing). It states:

"The audit area should serve as an independent control reviewing microcomputer use throughout the bank. Audit involvement in microcomputer systems may begin at a general level with a review for compliance with the internal policies and procedures discussed above and may extend to detailed testing in particular areas such as the use of logical access controls. Audit procedures and work programs should be expanded to provide for adequate coverage of microcomputer systems. Responsibility for microcomputer auditing should be clearly assigned and plans for microcomputer audits should be built into the audit schedule."

Recently, expert systems have been developed (i.e., I/A Xpert™) that provide an automated technique for conducting internal audits and documenting the results. These systems normally use a risk-based audit planning approach to assist internal auditors and management to understand the levels of risk in their financial institutions. Some systems also have the capability to compare the audit risks in each module to the estimated audit hours. These systems also can include comprehensive internal audit procedures, workplans and internal control questionnaires pertaining to all areas of the financial institution.

Computer-Assisted Audit Techniques

Auditors can use a variety of computer-assisted audit techniques. Computer-assisted audit techniques are basically audit procedures that are performed with the aid of computer systems. Several techniques are described below.

•   Generalized Audit Software

There are several audit software packages available that allow an auditor to develop specific programs for auditing various data files. Most packages can perform varied audit functions, including:

-       Reading data from computer files.
-       Selecting all or only certain records for processing.
-       Performing specified computations.
-       Sampling, sorting, and summarizing data.
-       Printing audit reports.

•   PC Software

Auditors can use PCs for administrative and planning functions, audit reports, presentations, electronic workpapers, and audit programs. PCs also can improve the efficiency of the audit function in areas such as analytics, sampling, and risk analysis.

•   Comparison Programs

Comparison programs are used to compare the source or executable versions of operational programs with authorized copies that have been investigated and secured by the auditor. This technique is used to verify that unauthorized program changes have not been entered in a particular program.

•   Program Tracing and Mapping

Software is available that monitors the execution of a program and prints a report of unexecuted program code. The auditor should determine if the unexecuted program code is legitimate, or is a potential computer crime concern, such as a trap door or a Trojan Horse.

•   Flowcharting Programs

Flowcharting programs create diagrams that document and analyze the processing and program logic flow. This information can assist the auditor to better understand complex programs.

•   Report Writers and Query Utilities

The rapid increase in data stored on computer systems and the awareness of its availability has resulted in the development of several relatively easy-to-use report writer and query utilities. These packages are usually already installed on many systems and generally require minimal training to use.

•   Test Data

Test data can be used to test processing and controls in operational programs, and then compared to predetermined results. Test data can be used to verify:

-   Input validation routines, error detection, and transaction data control procedures within programs.
-   Processing logic and controls regarding data files.
-   Specific calculations.
-   Program modifications.

•   Integrated Test Facility

An integrated test facility allows test data to be included with all other data for routine processing. It uses the same programs and files as normal transactions except the test data is processed to separate accounts that do not impact the normal processing results.

REFERENCES

Corban, Douglas M., and Robert F. Shriver. "EDP Engagement: Software Package Evaluation and Selection." *American Institute of Certified Public Accountants (AICPA)* Technical Consulting Practice Aid. New York, NY: AICPA, 1989.

Federal Financial Institutions Examination Council (FFIEC). *EDP Examination Handbook.* Washington, DC: FFIEC, 1988.

Shriver, Robert F., and Geoffrey H. Wold. *Information Systems Management and Technology: The Selection Process for Financial Institutions.* Rolling Meadows, IL: Bank Administration Institute, 1990.

Wold, Geoffrey H. "A Revisit of Data Processing Alternatives." *Financial Managers' Statement.* Vol. 10, No. 2, March 1988, pp. 76-78.

------. "An Examination of the Systems Selection Process." *Independent Banker,* Vol. 40, No. 12, December 1990, pp. 26-48.

------. "Are You Ready for ATMs?" *Independent Banker,* Vol. 36, No. 4, April 1986.

------. "Before Purchasing a Microcomputer." *Independent Banker,* Vol. 36, No. 7, July 1986, pp. 27-29.

------. "Biometrics: Fingerprints, Signatures and Keystrokes." *Financial Operations,* Winter 1988, Vol. 3, No. 4, pp. 16-18.

------. "Blocking Computer Crime." *Independent Banker,* Vol. 37, No. 2, February 1987, pp. 42-44.

------. "Computer Crime: The Undetected Disaster Part I of III." *Disaster Recovery Journal*, Vol. 4, No. 1, January, February, March 1991.

------. "Computer Crime: The Undetected Disaster Part II of III." *Disaster Recovery Journal*, Vol. 4, No. 2, April, May, June 1991.

------. "Computer Crime: The Undetected Disaster Part III of III." *Disaster Recovery Journal*, Vol. 4, No. 3, July, August, September 1991.

------. "How to Prepare a Disaster Recovery Plan." *Financial Managers' Statement,* Vol. 9, No. 4, July 1987, pp. 31-32.

------. "Planning for EDP Needs." *Independent Banker,* Vol. 3, No. 7, July 1985, pp. 18-19.

------. "Platformation." *Financial Operations,* Vol. 4, No. 3, Fall 1989, pp. 11-13.

------. "Preparing for Disaster and Planning for Recovery." *Independent Banker,* Vol. 36, No. 10, October 1986, pp. 42-44.

------. "Say the Secret Word." *Financial Operations,* Vol. 2, No. 4, Winter 1987-88, pp. 14-16.

------. "Selecting the Right DP System." *Credit Union Technology,* Vol. 2, No. 6, November/December 1992, pp. 22-25.

------. "Step by Step." *Credit Union Management,* Vol. 14, No. 7, July 1991, pp. 45-47.

------. "Strategic Information Systems Planning." *Financial Managers Society, Inc.,* Technical Publication, 1990.

------. "The Disaster Recovery Planning Process Part I of III." *Disaster Recovery Journal,* Vol. 5, No. 1, January, February, March 1992.

------. "The Disaster Recovery Planning Process Part II of III." *Disaster Recovery Journal,* Vol. 5, No. 2, April, May, June 1992.

------. "The Disaster Recovery Planning Process Part III of III." *Disaster Recovery Journal,* Vol. 5, No. 3, July, August, September 1992.

------. "The New Disaster Recovery Planning Regulation." *Independent Banker,* Vol. 40, No. 2, February 1990, pp. 45-48.

------. "When Disaster Strikes." *Credit Union Management,* Vol. 11, No. 4, April 1988, pp. 22-24.

------. "Words of Caution on Electronic Spreadsheets." *Independent Banker,* Vol. 36, No. 1, January 1986, pp. 16-18.

Wold, Geoffrey H., and Joseph C. Rocheleau. "Selecting PC-based Disaster Recovery Planning Software." *Disaster Recovery Journal,* Vol. 5, No. 4, October, November, December 1992, pp. 24-32.

------. "Selecting PC-based Disaster Recovery Planning Software." *Disaster Recovery Journal,* Vol. 5, No. 6, January, February, March 1993, pp. 24-32.

Wold, Geoffrey H., and Robert F. Shriver. *Disaster Proof Your Business: A Planning Manual for Protecting a Company's Computer, Communications & Records Systems and Facilities.* Chicago, IL: Probus Publishing Company, 1991.

------. *Disaster Recovery Compliance Made Easy: Step-by-Step Guide for Preparing, Evaluating and Testing a Savings Institution's Emergency Plan.* Chicago, IL: U.S. League of Savings Institutions, 1988.

------. *Disaster Recovery for Banks: A Comprehensive Program for Today's Regulatory Climate.* Rolling Meadows, IL: Bank Administration Institute, 1988.

------. *Disaster Recovery Planning Manual for Financial Institutions.* Rolling Meadows, IL: Bank Administration Institute, 1990.

------. *Systems Selection Workbook for Credit Unions.* Madison, WI: Credit Union Executives Society, 1991.

------. *Techniques for Preventing and Detecting Crime in Financial Institutions: Computer Crime.* Rolling Meadows, IL: Bank Administration Institute, 1989.

GLOSSARY OF TERMS

Acceptance testing: The formal testing conducted to determine whether a software system satisfies its acceptance criteria, enabling the customer to determine whether to accept the system.

Access: The ability and the means necessary to read, write, modify, or communicate data or otherwise make use of any systems resource.

Access category: One of the classes to which a terminal, transaction, user, program, or process in a computer-based system may be assigned, based on the resources or groups of resources that each is authorized to access.

Access control: A means of limiting access to system resources.

Access control mechanisms: Hardware, software, or firmware features and operating and management procedures in various combinations designed to detect and prevent unauthorized access as well as permit authorized access to a computer system.

Access list: A catalog of users, programs, terminals, and transactions, including the specifications of the access categories to which each is assigned.

Access method: A technique for moving data between a computer and its peripheral devices: for example, serial access, random access, virtual sequential access method (VSAM), etc.

Access period: A segment of time during which access rights prevail.

Access time: The time that elapses between an instruction being given to access some data and those data becoming available for use.

Access type: The nature of access granted to a particular device, program, or file (e.g., read, write, execute, append, modify, delete, create).

Active wiretapping: The attaching of an unauthorized communications device, such as a terminal, to a communications circuit to obtain access to data by generating false messages or control signals or by altering the communications of legitimate users.

Add-on security: The retrofitting of protection mechanisms, implemented by hardware, firmware, or software, on an operational computer system.

Address: An identification (number, name, label) for a location in which data are stored.

Addressing: The means of assigning data to storage locations and subsequently retrieving them on the basis of the key of the data.

Administrative security: The management constraints, operational and accountability procedures, and supplemental controls established to provide adequate protection of sensitive data.

Algorithm: A computational procedure.

Alphabetic test: The checking of whether an element of data contains only alphabetic or blank characters.

Alphanumeric: A character set that includes numeric digits, alphabetic characters, and other special symbols.

Analog signal: An electrical signal that is represented as continuous wavelike signals. Each complete wave is called a cycle. The number of cycles completed in a second is the signals frequency and is expressed as Hertz (Hz).

Application controls: Methods of ensuring (1) that only complete, accurate, and valid data is entered and updated in a computer system; (2) that processing accomplishes the correct task; (3) that processing results meet expectations; and (4) that data is maintained.

Application program: A specific, task-oriented program, such as a payroll-processing program, supplied or designed to suit individual user needs.

ASCII: American Standard Code for Information Interchange.

Assemble: To convert a routine coded in nonmachine language into actual machine language instructions.

Assertion: A logical expression specifying a program state that must exist or a set of conditions that program variables must satisfy at a particular point during program execution.

Asynchronous transmission: Transmission in which each information character is individually synchronized, usually by means of start and stop elements. Also called start-stop transmission.

Audio response system: A system whose output consists of audible signals and transmitters that simulate spoken language.

Audit: The performance of an independent review and examination of system records, operational procedures, and system activities to test for the adequacy of system controls, to ensure compliance with established policy and procedures, and to recommend any necessary changes in controls, policy, or procedures.

Audit trail: In computer systems, a step-by-step history of a transaction, especially a transaction with security sensitivity. Includes source documents, electronic logs, and records of accesses to restricted files.

Authentication: The act of verifying the identify of a station, originator, or individual and the right to access specific categories of information. Typically, a measure designed to protect against fraudulent transmission by verifying the validity of a transmission, message, station, or originator.

Authorization: The granting of the right of access to a user, terminal, transaction, program, or process.

Automated security monitoring: The use of automated facilities (e.g., software) to ensure that the security controls of a computer system or network are neither circumvented nor violated.

Backup: Any duplicate of a primary resource function, such as a copy of a computer program or a data file. This standby is used in case of loss or failure of the primary resource.

Backup operation: A method of operation implemented to complete essential tasks (as identified by risk analysis) following the disruption of the information processing facility and continuing until the facility is either restored or permanently relocated.

Backup procedures: Provisions made for the recovery of data files and program libraries and for the restarting or replacement of computer equipment following a system failure or disaster.

Bandwidth: The range of frequencies that can pass over a given circuit. Generally, the greater the bandwidth, the more information that can be sent through the circuit in a given amount of time.

Batch: In computer operations, the processing of a group of related transactions or other items at planned intervals. Large cyclic processing needs such as deposits and loans benefit from this individual processing of application programs. In many systems, batches are processed overnight or during periods of off-peak usage.

Batch control: An information processing technique in which numeric fields are totaled and records are tabulated to provide a comparison check for subsequent processing results.

Baud: Unit of signaling speed for data transmission. If each signal event represents only one bit condition, baud rate is the same as bits per second. When each signal event represents an amount other than one bit, then baud rate does not equal bits per second.

Between-the-lines entry: Access gained by an unauthorized user through active wiretapping to momentarily inactivate the terminal of a user legitimately assigned to a communications channel.

Binary: Relating to the numbering system that has a base of two values, 0 and 1.

Binary search: A method of searching a sequenced table or file. The procedure involves selecting the upper or lower half based on an examination of its midpoint value. The selected portion is then similarly halved, and so on until the required item is found.

Binary synchronous communication (BSC/BISYNC): A half-duplex, character-oriented synchronous data communications protocol originated by IBM in 1964.

Bit: A binary unit of information that can have either of two states, 0 or 1.

Bounds checking: The testing of computer program results to ascertain whether the program has access to storage outside its authorized limits.

Bounds register: A hardware or firmware register that holds an address specifying a storage boundary.

bps: Bits per second. Relates to the speed of data transfer.

Brevity lists: A coding system that reduces the time required to transmit information by representing long, stereotyped sentences with only a few characters.

Browsing: The searching of computer storage to locate or acquire information without necessarily knowing whether the information exists or its format.

Buffer: A storage area that holds data temporarily while it is being received, transmitted, read, or written. It is often used to compensate for differences in the speed or timing of devices. Buffers are used in terminals, peripheral devices, storage units, and CPUs.

Bug: A logic error in a computer program. "Bug" refers to unintentional errors.

bus: A network topology that functions like a single line, which is shared by a number of nodes.

Byte: A group of bits or binary digits processed as a unit. Bytes can represent alphabetic character(s) or number digits.

Callback: A procedure that verifies the identity of a terminal dialing into a computer system or network by disconnecting the terminal, verifying the caller's ID against an automated control table, and then re-establishing the connection, if authorized, by having the computer system dial the telephone number of the caller.

Catalog: A directory of all files available to the computer.

CD-ROM (compact disk with read-only memory): A computer peripheral that employs compact disk technology to store large amounts of data.

Certification: The acceptance of software by an authorized agent, usually after the software has been validated by the agent or its validity has been demonstrated to the agent.

Certified public accountant (CPA): An independent professional accountant registered and licensed by a state to offer auditing and accounting services to clients.

Channel: A magnetic track running along a length of tape that can be magnetized in bit patterns to represent data.

Check digit: 1. A bit used to verify the accuracy of a byte or word of memory. 2. A digit used to verify the accuracy of a number. One common use is in credit-card account numbers, where the check digit is calculated from the other numbers in the account number. If one enters an account number and the number in the check digit position is not equal to the number calculated, the computer assumes that the number entered is an incorrect account number.

Cipher system: A system in which cryptography is applied to plaintext elements of equal length.

Ciphertext: When information is encoded, the coded result is unreadable without knowing the encryption key (see Encryption). The unreadable text is called ciphertext. See also Plaintext.

Coaxial cable: A physical network medium that offers large bandwidth and the ability to support high data rates with high immunity to electrical interference and a low incidence of errors.

Code system: Any system of communication in which groups of symbols represent plaintext elements of varying length.

Communications security: Protection that ensures the integrity and authenticity of telecommunications by applying measures that deny unauthorized persons access to information of value in a telecommunications system.

Compact disk (CD): A technology for storing large amounts of digital data on a plastic disk. A low-power laser is used to read the information stored on the disk. The CD is best known as a recording medium for ultra-high-fidelity music.

Compartmentalization: The isolation of the operating system, user programs, and data files from one another in main storage to protect them against unauthorized access or concurrent access by other users or programs; in addition, the breaking down of sensitive data into small, isolated blocks in order to reduce the risk to the data.

Compile: To translate a high-level language source program into an object module or program written in machine language. A compiler is a program that translates a source program into an object module after checking its syntax and produces a listing of the source program with diagnostics that may affect the source program's execution.

Compiler: A computer program which in addition to performing the functions of an assembler has the following characteristics: (1) it makes use of information on the over-all logical structure of the program to improve the efficiency of the resulting machine program; (2) it usually generates more than one machine instruction for each symbolic instruction.

Completeness: The condition in which all necessary parts of an entity are included. Completeness of a product often means that all its requirements have been met.

Compromise: Unauthorized disclosure or loss of sensitive information.

Compromising emanations: Electromagnetic emanations from a computer system that may convey data and that, if intercepted and analyzed, could allow disclosure of sensitive information being processed by that system.

Computer program: A series of operations that perform a task when executed in logical sequence.

Computer security: The practice of protecting a computer system against internal failure, human error, attack, and natural catastrophe that might cause the improper disclosure, modification, or destruction of information or the denial of service.

Computer system: An interdependent assembly of elements that includes computer hardware at a minimum and also usually entails software, data, procedures, and people.

Computer system security: The technological safeguards and managerial procedures applied to computers and networks--including related hardware, firmware, software, and data--in order to protect organizational assets and individual privacy.

Concealment systems: A method of keeping sensitive information confidential by embedding it in irrelevant data.

Condition test: In a program, a comparison of two data items to determine whether one value is equal to, less than, or greater than the second value.

Conditional branch: The alteration of the usual sequence of program execution following the test of the contents of a memory area.

Confidentiality: The degree to which sensitive data about both individuals and organizations must be protected.

Configuration: A term that refers to equipment that will be assembled to work as a unit. It includes the options chosen as well as peripheral devices.

Configuration management: Control of changes to a system's hardware, software, and firmware by means of procedures to ensure that such changes will not create a security exposure or capacity problems.

Consistency: Logical coherency among integrated parts; also, adherence to a given set of instructions or rules.

Contingency plans: Emergency response, backup operation, and post-disaster recovery plans maintained by an information processing facility.

Control: A protective action, device, procedure, technique, or other measure that reduces exposure.

Control break: A point in program processing at which some special processing event takes place; for example, a change in the value of a control field in a data record.

Control field: A field of data in a record that identifies and classifies the record.

Control logic: The specific order in which the computer is to carry out processing functions.

Control signals: Computer-generated signals for the automatic control of machines and processes.

Control statement: A command in a computer program that establishes the logical sequence of processing operations.

Control structure: A program that contains a logical construct of sequences, repetitions, and selections.

Control totals: Accumulations of numeric data fields that are used to check the accuracy of the input data, data being processed, or output data.

Control unit: A component of the central processing unit that evaluates and executes program processing.

Control zone: An area around a computer system that is subject to physical and technical controls to protect against unauthorized entry or compromise of sensitive information.

Controllable isolation: Controlled sharing in which the scope or domain of authorization can be reduced to an arbitrarily small set or sphere of activity.

Controlled sharing: The application of access control to all users and components of a resource-sharing computer system.

Controller: This responds to requests from the operating system or application by instructing the device to position the drive heads over the appropriate drive track.

Conversational program: A program that allows interaction between a computer and its user.

Conversion: The process of replacing a computer system.

Correctness: The extent to which software is free from design and coding defects; also, the extent to which software meets its requirements and user objectives.

Cost-risk analysis: The assessment of the cost of potential loss or compromise of data in a computer system without data security safeguards versus the cost of providing data protection.

Cost/benefit analysis: The determination of the financial advantages of developing a system based on a comparison of its projected costs and its expected benefits.

CPU (central processing unit): The part of the computer that houses the electronic circuits that control the hardware, arithmetic logic unit, and main memory. Functions include decoding the instructions that control the electronic circuits, performing arithmetic and logic operations, and monitoring machine performance.

Cryptanalysis: The process of converting encrypted messages into plaintext without initial knowledge of the key employed in the encryption algorithm.

Cryptographic system: The documents, devices, equipment, and associated techniques that together provide a means of encryption.

Cryptography: The process of creating unintelligible plaintext and converting encrypted messages into intelligible form.

Cryptology: The field of study that encompasses both cryptography and cryptanalysis.

Cylinder: A collection of hard drive tracks on the same vertical coordinate of the drive platters.

DASD: Direct-access storage device.

Data capture: The process of collecting and encoding data for entry into a computer system.

Data communications: The movement of data between geographically separate locations via public and/or private electronic transmission systems.

Data contamination: The deliberate or accidental compromising of data integrity.

Data dictionary: A catalog of all data types, giving their names and structures, plus information about data usage.

Data encryption standard (DES): The cryptographic standard most commonly used in EDP. It is specified in the U.S. National Bureau of Standards Federal Information Processing Standards Publications (FIPS PUB) Nos. 46, 74, and 81.

Data flow analysis: A graphic analysis technique designed to trace the behavior of program variables as they are initialized, modified, or referenced during program execution.

Data integrity: The assurance that computerized data is the same as its source document form: that is, it has not been exposed to accidental or malicious modification, alteration, or destruction.

Data management system: System software that supervises the handling of data required by programs during execution.

Data protection engineering: The methodology and tools used to design and implement data protection mechanisms.

Data representation: The manner in which data in a computer system and its peripheral devices is characterized.

Data security: The practice of protecting data from accidental or malicious modification, destruction, or disclosure.

Data-dependent protection: The safeguarding of data at a level commensurate with the sensitivity of the individual data elements rather than the entire file.

Database: A collection of interrelated data stored together with controlled redundancy to serve one or more applications; the data are stored so that they are independent of programs which use them; a common and controlled approach is used in adding new data and in modifying and retrieving existing data within a database.

Database management system: The collection of software required for using a database, and presenting multiple different views of the data to the users and programmers.

Debugging: The process of correcting static and logical errors detected during coding or testing, with the primary goal of obtaining an executable piece of code.

Decryption: The process of transforming ciphertext back into plaintext.

Dedicated line: A communication line (link between a terminal and a computer) that is dedicated to a single terminal. See also Dial-up line.

Dedicated mode: The operation of a computer system in such a way that the central processing unit, peripheral devices, communications facilities, and remote terminals are used and controlled exclusively by a group of users in order to process specific types and categories of information.

Degauss: To erase, or demagnetize, magnetic recording media (usually tapes) by applying a variable, alternating current.

Degradation: Slowdown in the response time of a computer system.

Diagnostics: Electronic circuitry or programs that test various computer functions to help diagnose the cause of a problem.

Dial-up line: A communication line that is given to the first terminal that dials in to a computer. See also Dedicated line.

Dial-up terminal: A remote terminal that is connected to a telecommunications line where the connection between the terminal and the computer is initiated at the remote terminal. Several remote terminals may share a single telecommunications line that is connected to the computer.

Disaster recovery plan: Management policies and procedures designed to maintain or restore operations, possibly at an alternate location, in the event of emergencies, system failure, or disaster.

Disk subsystem: Term referring to the hard disk assembly of the computer and its controller electronics.

Distributed processing: The use of computers at various locations, each of which is connected to a central computer. This allows preliminary processing to be handled by the "distributed" computers and eases the load on the central computer.

Documentation: The written narrative detailing the development and operation of a program or system.

Downloading: Connecting to another computer and copying a program or file from that system.

Dump: The contents of a file or memory output as listings that may be formatted.

Dynamic analysis: The execution of program code to detect errors by analyzing the code's response to input.

Dynamic processing: The technique of swapping jobs in and out of computer memory. This technique can be controlled by the assignment priority and the number of time slices allocated to each job.

Eavesdropping: The unauthorized interception of computer emanations that contain data through methods other than wiretapping.

Echo: To display characters on a terminal as they are entered into the system.

Edit: To inspect a line of text, a field, or a data element to verify its accuracy.

EDP (electronic data processing): Processing data by computer.

Electromagnetic emanations: Signals transmitted as radiation through the air or through conductors.

Electronic document file: A magnetic storage area housing electronic images of papers and other documents.

Electronic journal: A computerized log file, usually stored on magnetic media, that summarizes in sequence system processing activities and events.

Electronic mail: Messages passed via computer from one user of a network to another. Some mail systems can link to other networks and mail systems. They may have mailboxes, name and address lists, and other features.

Emanation security: The practice of denying unauthorized interception and analysis of sensitive data contained in computer system emanations.

Encryption: The process of changing information (plaintext) so that it becomes unreadable. There are many ways to do this; one involves using the data encryption standard (DES). The resulting ciphertext cannot be read without the key used to encrypt it. Most enciphering methods also include something similar to a checksum, adding a level of protection and other benefits such as error-correcting codes.

Encryption algorithm: A set of mathematically expressed rules for encoding information by application of a key to its usual representation.

End-to-end encryption: The practice of encrypting information at its point of origin in a communications network and decrypting it at its destination.

Entrapment: The deliberate planting of apparent flaws in a system to detect attempted penetrations; also, confusing an intruder about which flaws to exploit.

Ethernet: The Ethernet system is a standard established by three companies: Xerox, Intel, and DEC. The system utilizes baseband transmission on a special coaxial cable, at ten million bits per second. (10Mb/s) The total cable length can be 2.5 kilometers, each node (CS/1xx) is placed 2.5 meters apart on the cable. The system can have as many as 1,024 nodes. The encoding method is Manchester Code, the data is Packet Switch, the access method is CSMA/CD.

Evolution checking: Testing to ensure the completeness and consistency of a software product at different levels of specification when that product is a refinement or elaboration of another.

Exception report: A management report that highlights abnormal business conditions. Usually, such reports prompt management action or inquiry.

Expert system: The application of computer-based artificial intelligence in areas of specialized knowledge.

Exposure: A form of potential loss or harm, such as erroneous recordkeeping, unmaintainable applications or business interruptions, that could affect an organization's profitability.

Fail safe: The automatic termination and protection of programs or other processing operations when a hardware, software, or firmware failure is detected in a computer system.

Fail soft: The selective termination of nonessential processing affected by hardware, software, or firmware failure in a computer system.

Failure access: Unauthorized and usually inadvertent access to data resulting from hardware, software, or firmware failure in a computer system.

Failure control: The methodology used to detect and provide fail-safe or fail-soft recovery from hardware, software, or firmware failure in a computer system.

Fair Credit Reporting Act: A federal law that allows individuals the right of access to credit information pertaining to them and the right to challenge the accuracy of such information.

Fault: A weakness in a computer system that allows circumvention of its controls.

Feasibility study: An investigation of the legal, political, social, operational, technical, economic and psychological effects of developing and implementing a computerized system.

Federal Computer Fraud Act: The Counterfeit Access Device and Computer Fraud and Abuse Act of 1986 outlaws unauthorized access to the federal government's computers and to certain financial databases protected under the Right to Financial Privacy Act of 1978 and the Fair Credit Reporting Act of 1971.

Federal Privacy Act: A federal law that allows individuals to discover what information pertaining to them is on file and how it is being used by government agencies and their contractors.

Fetch protection: A system-provided restriction that prevents a program from accessing data in another user's segment of storage.

Fiber-optics: A technology that uses light as an information carrier. Fiber-optic cables (light guides) are a direct replacement for conventional coaxial cable and wire pairs. The glass-based transmission facility occupies far less physical volume for an equivalent transmission capacity; the fibers are immune to electrical interference.

Field: A basic unit of data, usually part of a record that is located on an input, storage, or output medium.

File: An aggregation of data records organized on a storage medium for convenient location, access, and updating.

File allocation tables (FAT): Located at the beginning of the disk drive, this area tells the computer where files are located on the disk.

File creation: The building of master or transaction files.

File inquiry: The selection of records from files and immediate display of their contents on a terminal output device.

File maintenance: The alteration of a master file by either changing the contents of existing records, adding new records, or deleting old records.

File protection: The processes and procedures established to inhibit unauthorized access to and contamination or elimination of a file.

File updating: The posting of transaction data to master files or the maintenance of master files through record additions, changes, or deletions.

Foreign Corrupt Practices Act: A federal law that requires public companies to maintain books, records, and accounts in sufficient detail to accurately reflect the transactions and dispositions of their assets and to maintain a system of reasonably strong internal accounting controls.

Formal analysis: The application of rigorous mathematical techniques to the analysis of a system solution. The algorithms employed may be analyzed for numerical properties, efficiency, and correctness.

Format: The physical layout of data characters, fields, records, and files.

Formulary: A technique for allowing the decision to grant or deny access to be made dynamically at the access attempt, rather than at the time the access list is created.

Front-end processor: A computer to which input and output activities are off-loaded from a central computer so that the latter can operate primarily in a processing mode.

Function: In computer programming terminology, a processing activity that performs a single, identifiable task.

Functional specification: The chief product of systems analysis: the detailed logical description of a new system. The specification contains input, processing, storage, and output requirements that detail the functions of the system.

Functional testing: The application of test data derived from the functional requirements.

General controls: Controls over the EDP system operations as a whole, including the design, security, and use of computer programs; the security of data files and controls over access. Consists of system software and related manual procedures.

Generally accepted accounting principles (GAAP): Standards or guidelines for the preparation of financial statements to achieve the objectives of understandability, reliability, and comparability. Also used as criteria for judging the acceptability of accounting methods. Those accounting principles that have received substantial authoritative support, such as the approval of the Financial Accounting Standards Board, the American Institute of Certified Public Accountants, or the Securities and Exchange Commission are considered generally accepted accounting principles.

Generally accepted auditing standards (GAAS): Quality guidelines issued by the American Institute of Certified Public Accountants regarding the conduct and report of the field work and audit of a public accountant.

Hacking: An unauthorized attempt at accessing a computer system. The term is most often used in relation to a person who attempts to enter a system from a remote location by circumventing network access controls. Typically, hackers are individuals who spend an inordinate amount of time working on computers for other than professional purposes.

Handshaking procedures: A dialogue between a user and a computer or between computers or programs whose purpose is to identify and authenticate the identity of a user. Identification and authentication are accomplished through a sequence of questions and answers that are based on information either stored in the computer or supplied to it by the initiator of the dialogue.

Hardware: The physical equipment and devices that make up a computer system.

Head: The hard disk component that reads and writes data to the hard disk media.

HEX: Short for hexadecimal. A numbering system based on 16 rather than 10. Most computers operate using hexadecimal numbers.

Identification: The process of recognizing users or resources as those previously described to a computer system, generally through the use of unique, machine-readable names.

Impersonation: An attempt to gain access to a system by posing as an authorized user.

Incomplete parameter checking: Inadequate checking of system parameters by the operating system for correctness and consistency, resulting in system exposure to unauthorized access.

Information: Data that, as a result of processing by computer or other means, is meaningful.

Indexed-sequential storage: A file structure in which records are stored in ascending sequence by key. Indices showing the highest key on a cylinder, track, bucket, and so on, are used for the selected retrieval of records.

Input/output or I/O: Writing to or reading data from a computer's memory or the computer writing to or reading from one of its peripheral devices.

Input controls: Techniques and methods for verifying, validating, and editing data to ensure its accurate entry into a computer system.

Inquiry processing: The process of selecting a record from a file and immediately displaying its contents.

Inspection: A formal analysis technique that involves manual review of program requirements, design, or code for errors.

Instrumental input: The process by which machines capture data and store it in a computer.

Integration testing: The progressive testing of software and hardware in a system until all intermodule links have been integrated.

Integrity checking: The testing of programs to verify the soundness of a software product at each phase of its development.

Interdiction: The act of impeding or denying access to system resources.

Interface analysis: The process of checking and verifying the performance of intermodule communications links.

Interleaving: The alternating execution, in a multiprogramming environment, of programs residing in memory.

Internal auditing: The investigation and evaluation of an organization's system of internal controls on a year-round basis by an in-house professional staff. Also, evaluating the efficiency of individual departments within the organization.

Internal control: All measures used by a business to guard against errors, waste, or fraud and to ensure the reliability of accounting data. Designed to aid in the efficient operation of a business and to encourage compliance with company policies.

Investigation: The phase of the systems development life cycle in which the business problem or need is identified and a decision on whether to proceed with a full-scale study is made.

Isolation: The separation of users, processes, and resources in a computer system from one another as well as from the controls of the operating system.

Job accounting system: Systems software that tracks the services and resources used by computer system account holders.

Jukebox: A device containing one or more CD-ROM drives and capable of housing multiple CD-ROM disks. Its operation is analogous to the musical jukebox popular in the 1940s and 1950s.

Kbyte (K, KB, kilobyte): 1,024 bytes.

Key generation: The creation of a key or a distinct set of keys.

LAN (local area network): Computers can be linked into networks with various kinds of wires, cables, or electronic linkages. A LAN may connect many different computers, or even different kinds of computers, as well as printers, large disk drives called file servers, and other devices. A local area network is one that is geographically close together, usually in one building or a small group of buildings. A LAN does not make use of public carriers in linking together its components (although it may have a "gateway" outside the LAN that uses a public carrier). See also WAN.

Language translator: Systems software that converts programs written in assembly or a higher-level language into machine code.

Laser (light amplification by stimulated emission of radiation): A device that produces a narrow, coherent beam of light. In a CD-ROM drive, a tiny laser provides the light source for reading data from CD-ROM disks.

Latency: The time it takes to find the first bit of data for a specified record. Latency plus the time it takes to read the record are called access time.

Leased line: Usually synonymous with dedicated line.

Limit check: An input control test that assesses the value of a data field to determine whether it falls within a set limit or given range.

Link encryption: The application of online cryptography to a communications link so that all data passing through the link is encrypted.

Linkage: The combination of data from two systems in order to derive additional information.

Lock/key protection system: A system that safeguards data and resources by matching a supplied key or password with that specified in the access requirements.

Logical database: A database as perceived by its users; it may be structured differently from the physical database structure. In IBM's Data Language/1, a logical database is a tree-structured collection of segments derived from one or more physical databases by means of pointer linkages.

Logical drive: The portion of the device that was subdivided by the controller or operating system.

Logical error: A programming error in an otherwise syntactically valid program that causes processing to take place incorrectly.

Logical operation: A comparison of data values in the arithmetic logic unit to determine whether a value is greater than, equal to, or less than another value.

Logical operator: A programming symbol that indicates a comparison operation between two or more data values.

Logical organization: The structuring of data elements in such a way that they meet processing needs.

Loophole: An error of omission or oversight in software, hardware, or firmware that allows circumvention of the access control process.

Master file: A file containing control information that is used by multiple programs and is updated by transactions during file maintenance processing.

Mature system: A fully operational system that is performing all functions as intended.

Mbyte (M, MB, megabyte): 1 million bytes.

Media: The physical surface of a hard disk, optical drive, or floppy diskette used to store information written and read by the device heads.

Memory bounds: The limits in a range of storage addresses assigned to a protected region in memory.

Microprocessor: A chip that contains the necessary circuitry and components to conduct arithmetic, logical, and control operations.

Modem (*modulator/demodulator* unit): A device that converts data from a form compatible with data processing equipment to a form compatible with transmission facilities and vice versa.

Msec (millisecond): A unit of time equal to 1/1,000 of one second.

Multiaccess rights terminal: A terminal able to be used by more than one class of user (e.g., users with different access rights to data or files).

Multiplex: The use of a common physical channel in order to make two or more logical channels, either by splitting of the frequency band transmitted by the common channel into narrower bands, each of which is used to constitute a distinct channel (frequency-division-division multiplex), or by allotting this common channel in turn, to constitute different intermittent channels (time-division multiplex).

Multiplexer: Equipment that permits simultaneous transmission of multiple signals over one physical circuit.

Mutually suspicious: Pertaining to interactive processes in systems or programs containing sensitive data that are designed to extract data from one another while protecting their own data.

Nak (negative acknowledgement character attack): A technique that seeks to gain access to those systems whose operating system leaves them unprotected during asynchronous interrupts.

Network: An integrated aggregation of computers and peripherals linked by communications facilities.

Networking: A method of linking distributed data processing activity by means of communications facilities.

Numeric test: An input control method designed to verify that a data field contains numeric digits only.

Object program: The binary form of a source program produced by an assembler or a compiler. The object program (the final translation) is composed of machine-word or machine-coded instructions that the specific computer can execute after link editing.

On-line: A processing term that categorizes operations that are under the direct, immediate control of the CPU. Interactive and real-time systems are among those classified as on-line systems.

Operating systems: Software that controls the execution of computer programs and that may provide scheduling, debugging, input/output control, accounting, compilation, storage assignment, data management, and related services.

Output controls: Techniques and methods for verifying that processing results meet expectations and that they are communicated to authorized users only.

Overlapped processing: The simultaneous execution of input, processing, and output functions by a computer system.

Overwriting: The destruction of magnetically stored data by recording different data on the same surface.

Packet: A collection of bits that contain both control information and data. The basic unit of transmission in a packet-switched network. Control information is carried in the packet, along with the data, to provide for such functions as addressing, sequencing, flow control, and error control at each of several protocol levels. A packet can be of fixed or variable length, but generally has a specified maximum length.

Packet switching: A data communications technique in which data is transmitted by means of addressed packets and a transmission channel is occupied for the duration of transmission of the packet only. The channel is then available for use by packets being transferred between different data terminal equipment.

Parallel interface: An interface that permits parallel transmission, or simultaneous transmission of the bits making up a character or byte, either over separate channels or on different carrier frequencies of the same channel.

Partition: A memory area assigned to a computer program during its execution.

Passive wiretapping: The unauthorized monitoring or recording of data while it is being transmitted over a communications link.

Password: A string of characters that authenticates the ID of a user, a specific resource or an access type.

Penetration: Successful unauthorized access to a computer system.

Penetration profile: A list of the activities required to penetrate a computer system.

Penetration signature: A description of a set of conditions in which system penetration might occur.

Penetration testing: An attempt by special programmer/analyst teams to penetrate a system to identify security weaknesses.

Performance monitor: Systems software that tracks the service levels of a computer system.

Phased conversion: A procedure for installing new systems that involves incremental implementation of the modules of the system.

Piggyback entry: Unauthorized access to a computer system by means of another user's legitimate connection.

Plaintext (also cleartext): Original form (usually readable) of information or data. When plaintext is encrypted, the result is ciphertext.

Polling: A method of controlling the sequence of transmission by devices on a multipoint line by requiring each device to wait until the controlling processor requests it to transmit.

Port: The entrance or physical access point to a computer, multiplexor, device, or network where signals may be supplied, extracted, or observed.

Post-implementation review: An evaluation of a system after it has been in operation from three to six months.

Preprocessors: Software tools that perform preliminary work on a draft computer program before it is fully tested on a computer.

Principle of least privilege: A security technique in which only the minimum access authorization necessary to perform a task is granted.

Print suppress: The elimination of the printing of characters in order to preserve their secrecy (e.g., the characters of a password as it is entered by a user).

Privacy: The act of releasing data to legally authorized personnel only.

Privacy protection: The establishment of administrative, technical, and physical safeguards to ensure the security and confidentiality of data records by protecting against anticipated threats or hazards that could result in substantial harm, embarrassment, inconvenience, or unfairness to an individual about whom information is maintained and that puts the organization at legal risk.

Privileged instructions: A set of instructions generally executable only when the computer system is operating in the executive state (e.g., while handling interrupts) and hence not executable from an applications module. These instructions typically are designed to control the protection features of a computer system.

Procedural language: A computer programming language that requires the programmer to determine the logical sequence of program execution in addition to the processing itself.

Process control: The monitoring and control of production and manufacturing processes.

Process description: A formal narrative that describes in sequence the processing activities and procedures of a computer system.

Processing controls: Techniques and methods to ensure that processing produces accurate results.

Processor: Hardware that contains memory functions and the central processing unit.

Program: A set of related instructions that, when followed and executed by a computer, perform operations or tasks. Applications programs, user programs, system programs, source programs, and object programs are all software programs.

Program analyzer: A software tool that modifies or monitors an application program to allow the automatic collection of information on the program's operating characteristics.

Program development process: The activities involved in the development of a computer program, including problem analysis, program design, process design, and program coding, debugging, and testing.

Program maintenance: The process of altering program code or instructions in order to meet new requirements.

Programmable read-only memory (PROM): Computer memory chips that can be permanently programmed to carry out a predefined process.

Programming specifications language: A complete description of the input, processing, output, and storage requirements necessary to code a computer program.

Proof of correctness: The inference, based on mathematical logic techniques, that a relation assumed true at program entry implies that another relation between program variables holds true at program exit.

Protection ring: One of a hierarchy of privileged modes in a computer system. Certain access rights are granted to users, programs, and processes according to the mode in which they are authorized to operate.

Protocol: A set of rules and conventions that govern the orderly and meaningful exchange of information between or among communicating parties. Both hardware protocols and software protocols can be defined.

Protocol convertor: A device for translating the data transmission code and/or protocol of one network or device to the corresponding code or protocol of another network or device, enabling equipment with different conventions to communicate with one another.

Pseudoflaw: A false loophole embedded in an operating system to snare unsuspecting intruders.

Pseudocode: Program processing specifications written as structured, English-like statements that can readily be converted into source code.

Purging: The orderly review and removal of inactive or obsolete data files.

Query: A message that, when sent to a computer system, requests a programmed search of available data for a specific item. Query may also be the facility in a database that allows a user to view data but not to manipulate and therefore change it.

RAM (random access memory): Computer main memory.

Random access: To obtain data directly from any storage location regardless of its position with respect to the previously referenced information. Also called direct access.

Real-time processing: On-line processing that enables inquiries to reflect the actual status of records, which are updated in place.

Real-time reaction: The detection, diagnosis, and reporting of a penetration attempt as it occurs.

Record: A group of related data items treated as a unit by an application program.

Recovery: Restoration of an information processing facility and related resources following physical destruction or damage.

Recovery procedures: Those actions required to restore a system's computational capability and data files following system failure or penetration.

Regression testing: The running of test cases that have previously executed correctly in order to detect errors that may have been created during software correction and modification.

Remanence: The residual magnetism that remains on magnetic storage media after degaussing.

Residue: Data left in memory after processing operations but before erasing or rewriting.

Resource: Any function, device, or collection of data in a computer system that can be allocated for use by users or programs.

Resource sharing: The concurrent use of a computer system resource by more than one user, job, or program.

RFP (request for proposal): A document that describes the systems and technology needs of a financial institution in the format of specifications that can be submitted to vendors to obtain their written proposal responses.

Ring: A network topology in which stations are connected to one another in a closed logical circle. Typically, access to the media passes sequentially from one station to the next by means of polling from a master station, or by passing an access token from one station to another.

Risk analysis: A formal examination of an organization's information resources, controls, and vulnerabilities in both manual and automated systems. Risk analysis assesses the loss potential for each resource or combination thereof, together with its rate of occurrence to establish a potential level of damage in dollars or other assets.

ROM (read-only memory): Computer memory chips with preprogrammed circuits for storing permanent, nonmodifiable instructions or programs.

Sanitizing: The degaussing or overwriting of sensitive information stored on magnetic or other electronic media.

SAS (statements on auditing standards): Released by the American Institute of Certified Public Accountants to guide external audits conducted by public accountants.

Scavenging: The unauthorized searching of residue for data.

Scheduling program: Systems software that schedules and monitors the processing of production jobs by the computer system.

SCSI (small computer system interface): For interconnecting computer systems and peripherals.

Sector: The smallest single physical unit of data storage on the hard disk.

Secure operating system: An operating system that effectively controls hardware, software, and firmware functions in order to provide a level of protection commensurate with the value of the data resources it manages.

Security administrator: The person who is responsible for managing security procedures.

Security audit: An evaluation of the adequacy of data security procedures and measures and of their compliance with policy.

Security controls: Techniques and methods to ensure that only authorized users can access the computer system and its resources.

Security filter: A set of software or firmware routines and techniques that prevent the automatic forwarding of specified data across unprotected communications links or to unauthorized persons.

Security kernel: The core of a computer system--implemented in hardware, software, or firmware--that implements the fundamental security procedures that control access to system resources.

Security software: Systems software that controls access to data in files and allows only authorized use of terminals and related equipment. Control usually is exercised through various levels of safeguards, which are applied according to user need.

Seepage: The accidental disclosure to unauthorized individuals of data, access to which should be controlled by security safeguards.

Selection: A program control structure, created in response to a condition test, in which one of two or more processing paths may be taken.

Sensitive information: Any information that requires a degree of protection and that therefore should not be made generally available.

Sequential processing: Accessing records in ascending sequence by key; the next record accessed will have the next higher key, irrespective of its physical position in the file.

Serial interface: An interface that requires serial transmission, or the transfer of information in which the bits composing a character are sent sequentially. Implies only a single transmission channel.

Serial processing: Accessing records in their physical sequence. The next record accessed will be the record in the next physical position/location in the field.

Simulation: The use of an executable model to represent the behavior of an object. During testing, the computational hardware, the external environment, and even the coding segments may be simulated.

Simultaneous processing: The simultaneous execution in a multiprocessing environment of two or more program instructions.

Slave computer: A front-end processor that handles input and output functions for a host computer.

SNA (systems network architecture): The network architecture developed by IBM.

Software: Computer programs that direct computer processing and that can be stored and manipulated by a computer system.

Software life cycle: The period from the conception of a software product to the end of its usability. The software life cycle typically is segregated into phases, including requirements, design, programming, testing, conversion, operation, and maintenance.

Sort: To arrange a file in sequence by a specified key.

Source document: The form in which data is recorded before its entry into a computer system.

Source program: A version of a computer program written in human-readable statements. In this state, a program can be reviewed, analyzed, updated, and read by a compiler. It must be compiled before it can be executed by a computer.

Spoofing: The deliberate inducement of incorrect action on the part of a user or resource.

Spooling: A technique that maximizes processing speed through the temporary use of high-speed storage devices. Input files are transferred from slower, permanent storage and queued in the high-speed devices to await processing, or output files are queued in high-speed devices to await transfer to slower storage devices.

Standards audit: A review undertaken to ensure that the organization is adhering to applicable standards.

Statement testing: A method of satisfying the criterion that each statement in a program be executed at least once during program testing.

Static analysis: The analysis of the form and structure of a software product that does not require its execution. Static analysis can be applied to the requirements, design, or code.

Swapping: A method of computer processing in which programs not actively being processed are held in special storage devices and alternated in and out of memory with other programs by priority.

Symbolic evaluation: The process of analyzing a program execution path through the use of symbolic expressions.

Symbolic execution: The analytical technique of dissecting each program path.

Synchronous transmission: Transmission in which there is a constant time between successive bits, characters, or events. The timing is achieved by sharing or clocking.

System: An integrated set of elements designed to work together to direct the control and management of computer processing functions.

System development life cycle (SDLC): The organizational arrangements and procedures involved in developing new computer applications or modifying existing systems or programs.

System integrity: The state of a computer system when there is complete assurance that, under all conditions, the system is based on the logical correctness and reliability of the operating system and the logical completeness of the hardware, software, and firmware that implement the protection mechanisms and data integrity.

System integrity procedures: Procedures established to ensure that hardware, software, firmware, and data in a computer system maintain their integrity and are not tampered with by unauthorized personnel.

System software: Computer programs and related routines that control non-user-related functions and the processing done by computer hardware.

System test: The process of testing an integrated hardware/software system to verify that the system meets its specified requirements.

Table driven: An indexed file in which tables containing record keys are associated with related data for the purposes of record retrieval or processing action.

Tbyte (T, TB, terabyte): 1 trillion bytes.

Technological attack: An attack perpetrated by circumventing or nullifying hardware, software, or firmware access control mechanisms rather than by subverting system personnel or users.

Telecommunications: With respect to data communications, a general term applied to data that is transmitted by electrical, optical, or acoustical means between separate computing facilities.

Teleprocessing: A form of information handling in which a data processing system utilizes communications facilities (originally, but no longer, an IBM trademark).

Teleprocessing security: The practice of protecting a teleprocessing system from deliberate, inadvertent, and unauthorized disclosure, acquisition, manipulation, or modification of information.

Terminal identification: The means used to establish the unique identification of a terminal by a computer system or network.

Test data: Data that simulates operational data in form and content and is used to evaluate a system or program before it begins operation.

Test data generators: Software tools that help generate data files that are used to test the execution and logic of application programs.

Testing: The execution of a program or system, fully exercising its processing capability on sample data sets to determine whether it meets processing specifications.

Threat monitoring: The analysis, assessment, and review of audit trails and other data collected to identify system events that may constitute violations or precipitate incidents involving data privacy.

Throughput: The amount of work a computer system can handle within a specified time.

Time-dependent password: A password that is valid only at a certain time of the day or during a specified period.

Token passing: A mechanism whereby each device receives and passes the right to use the channel. Tokens are special bit patterns or packets, usually several bits in length, that circulate from node to node when there is no message traffic. Possession of the token gives a node exclusive access to the network for transmitting its message, thus avoiding conflict with other nodes that wish to transmit.

Token ring: The token access procedure used on a network with a sequential or ring topology.

Topology: 1.   Physical topology: The configuration of network nodes and links. Description of the physical geometric arrangement of the links and nodes that make up a network, as determined by their physical connections.

2.   Logical topology: Description of the possible logical connections between network nodes, indicating which pairs of nodes are able to communicate, whether or not they have a direct physical connection.

Examples of network topologies are:

- Bus
- Ring
- Star
- Tree

Traffic flow security: The protection that results from those features in some cryptography equipment that conceal the presence of valid messages on a communications circuit, usually by causing the circuit to appear busy at all times or by encrypting the source and destination address of those messages.

Transaction: An input record applied to an established file. The input record describes some "event" that will cause a new file record to be generated or cause an existing record to be changed or deleted.

Transactional processing: The processing of transactions as they occur rather than in batches.

Transfer rate: A measure of the speed with which data are moved between a direct-access device and the central processor (usually expressed as thousands of characters per second or thousands of bytes per second).

Trap door: A breach intentionally created in a computer system to collect, alter, or destroy data.

Trojan horse: A computer program that is apparently or actually useful and that contains a trap door.

Unit testing: The testing of a module for typographic, syntactic, and logical errors as well as for correct implementation of its design and the meeting of its requirements.

UNIX™: A real-time, multitasking, multiuser operating system. A registered trademark of AT&T Information Systems.

Update: The altering of master records to reflect the current business activity contained in transactional files.

Uploading: Connecting to another computer and transferring a program or file to that system. See also Downloading.

Utility: A program that performs a standard function such as sorting, copying, compressing, spooling, cataloging, etc.

Utility program: A standard routine used to assist in the operation of the computer (e.g., a conversion, sorting, printout, or tracing routine).

Vaccine: A program or group of programs that provides some kind of protection against computer viruses.

Validation: The determination of the correctness, with respect to user needs and requirements, of the final product of a development project.

Validation, verification, and testing: A procedure of review, analysis, and testing applied throughout the software life cycle to uncover errors, determine that functions operate as specified, and ensure the production of quality software.

Verification: The demonstration of software consistency, completeness, and correctness between each stage of the development life cycle.

Verifying: The process of ensuring that transcribed data has been accurately entered by keyboard.

Virtual: Conceptual, or appearing as, rather than actually being. An adjective that implies that data, structures, or hardware appear to the application programmer or user to be different from what they are in reality, the conversion being performed by software.

Virtual memory: Memory that can appear to the programs to be larger than it really is because blocks of data or programs are rapidly moved to or from secondary storage when needed.

Virus: A program intended to do something in your system that you did not ask to have done. The key characteristic that makes a program a virus is that it attaches itself to another program and it reproduces. Computer viruses are so named because they come along with other programs, in much the same way a disease virus infects a cell and is reproduced as the cell reproduces.

Walkthrough: A manual analysis technique in which the developer of a software module describes its structure and logic to colleagues.

WAN (wide area network): Similar to a LAN, except that parts of a WAN are geographically dispersed, possibly in different cities or even on different continents. Public carriers like telephone companies are included in most WANs; a very large WAN might have its own satellite stations or microwave towers.

Word: A group of characters that the computer operates on as a unit.

Working storage: A portion of storage, usually computer main memory, reserved for the temporary results of operations.

WORM (write-once, read-many): An optical disk technology in which the user may write to the disk as well as read from it. Once written, however, the data on the disk cannot be erased.

Write: To record information on a storage device.

INDEX

FOR ADDITIONAL INFORMATION

McGladrey & Pullen is a national certified public accounting and consulting firm. Founded in 1908, the firm now provides a full range of financial and management advisory services for clients in all facets of governmental, financial and industrial activity.

McGladrey & Pullen specializes in information technology consulting and has assisted numerous organizations in developing strategic information systems plans. Based on the specific needs of an organization, experienced McGladrey & Pullen consultants can perform various information technology related consulting services, such as:

- Developing strategic information systems plans.
- Evaluating outsourcing alternatives.
- Performing needs assessment studies.
- Evaluating current systems capacities and capabilities.
- Developing requests for proposal documents.
- Evaluating vendor proposals and preparing a management report.
- Reviewing and negotiating vendor contracts.
- Developing the implementation plan.
- Performing project management.
- Preparing disaster recovery plans.
- Presenting seminars and special training on information technology.

McGladrey & Pullen has developed a PC-based expert system that provides an automated technique for performing the needs assessment, developing a Request for Proposal (RFP) and evaluating vendor responses. The straight-forward, easy-to-follow menu selections are designed to provide a systematic method of selecting and implementing new and improved information technology. McGladrey & Pullen also has PC software to facilitate the disaster recovery planning process.

For information regarding these services, please call or write:

Geoffrey H. Wold
McGladrey & Pullen
1800 Town Square
445 Minnesota Street
St. Paul, MN 55101
(612) 293-8440

Robert F. Shriver
McGladrey & Pullen
900 Davenport Bank Building
Davenport, IA 52801-1992
(319) 326-5111

About the Publisher

PROBUS PUBLISHING COMPANY

Probus Publishing Company fills the informational needs of today's business professional by publishing authoritative, quality books on timely and relevant topics, including:

- Investing
- Futures/Options Trading
- Banking
- Finance
- Marketing and Sales
- Manufacturing and Project Management
- Personal Finance, Real Estate, Insurance and Estate Planning
- Entrepreneurship
- Management

Probus books are available at quantity discounts when purchased for business, educational or sales promotional use. For more information, please call the Director, Corporate/Institutional Sales at 1-800-998-4644, or write:

Director, Corporate/Institutional Sales
Probus Publishing Company
1925 N. Clybourn Avenue
Chicago, Illinois 60614
FAX (312) 868-6250